Celebrating the
Family

Celebrating the
Family

The MyFamily.com Guide to
Understanding
Your Family History

From the editors of MyFamily.com/Ancestry Publishing

FRIEDMAN/FAIRFAX

A FRIEDMAN/FAIRFAX BOOK

© 2002 by Michael Friedman Publishing Group, Inc.

This edition published by the Michael Friedman Publishing Group, Inc.,
by arrangement with Ancestry® Publishing, an imprint of MyFamily.com, Inc.

Library of Congress Cataloging-in-Publication Data available upon request.

ISBN 1-58663-592-1

Printed in the United States of America

1 3 5 7 9 10 8 6 4 2

Distributed by Sterling Publishing Company, Inc.
387 Park Avenue South
New York, NY 10016
Distributed in Canada by Sterling Publishing
Canadian Manda Group
One Atlantic Avenue, Suite 105
Toronto, Ontario, Canada M6K 3E7
Distributed in Australia by
Capricorn Link (Australia) Pty, Ltd.
P.O. Box 704, Windsor, NSW 2756 Australia

Acknowledgments

The editors would like to thank the following individuals for their support and contributions to this book:

Loretto Dennis Szucs, David Farnsworth, Dave McGinn, Andre Brummer, Alyssa Hickman Grove, Paul Rawlins, Darla Isackson, Barbara Krasner-Khait, Kellene Ricks Adams, Jeannette Bennett, Karen Frisch Dennen, George G. Morgan, Heather Stratford, Megan Vandre, Janet Haniak, Janet Bernice, Christine Burnett, Maryruth Farnsworth, Laryn Brown, Ann Irwin, Pamela Nielsen, Sandra Browning, Kathy Ling Chu Yu, Francine Shumway Sumner, Rosalind Sandack, Nathaniel Marunas, Kevin Ullrich, Christopher Bain, Jennifer Browning, Esther Yu, Robert Davis, Jennifer Utley, and Matthew Wright.

Table of Contents

Preface

Discussions about families in the United States these days have grown as popular and commonplace as apple pie and baseball. Presidential inaugural addresses tout the importance of stable families to ensure a secure nation; ecclesiastical leaders espouse the virtues of family life; even popular magazines feature the hopes and dreams of national icons and stars who have innumerable stories to relate about their famed families' successes and failures. To be sure, family is on the minds of everyone. And it isn't likely to change in the near future.

Undoubtedly, the discussion originates to some degree from the growing national concern for the stability of families. While news reports dishearten us and statistics stagger us, at the same time, studies indicate that the second most popular hobby in the United States is none other than researching the history of families. "Where did I come from?" "Who am I?" "How can I learn more about my family's past?" are only a few of the questions posed by millions of Americans who are turning to the past—through records, photographs, the Internet, genetic research, and more—to better understand their present and their future.

The editors of MyFamily.com, Inc. created this book with your family in mind. It is designed to help you get started in your search for your family history—using a variety of accessible and popular resources. Its nine chapters focus on the characteristics of families as they relate to discovering your personal family history. It is the guide to finding the perfect portal for your entry into one of the nation's most valued subjects and popular pastimes. This book offers practical ways for families to get connected, to reach out to each other, and to foster the familial relationships they are seeking to maintain.

Within these pages, you'll find that family history is much more than just names and dates of faceless deceased family members. It is a photo of a loved one. It is a phone call or holiday newsletter from a distant cousin or brother across town. It is a colorful scrapbook prepared after the birth of a new grandchild. It is a wartime story told by your veteran uncle at a family reunion. It is the moment your six-year-old asks Daddy why he calls Grandma "Mom." It is all of this and more.

While the scope of this book may seem daunting at first, you'll find the text approachable and easy to read. Practical tips, personal stories, and fun and interesting family photos of the past and present fill the book and make it a captivating visual and intellectual treasure. Once you have browsed the subjects introduced here, you are sure to find a starting point that fits your interests so you can join the millions of other Americans who are connecting to their families.

Traditions are glue, the common ground around which family evolves.
—Steven J. Zeitlin

CHAPTER ONE

Creating the Ties That Bind

Your Family Traditions

Every year for Thanksgiving, each member of Debbie and Stas Mintowt's family writes a short speech about what he or she has been thankful for during the past twelve months. They tie the speeches with ribbons, put them next to their place settings, and read them aloud at Thanksgiving dinner. The entire family participates—even the children. The youngest child, Alex, was five years old when he wrote his first "thankful" speech.

"It's a nice way to not just breeze through the day without a thought to what it's all about," says Debbie. "Plus, we keep the speeches for memories. And, if we have any family or friends join us, they have to join in the tradition, too. No one escapes!"

Debbie and Stas have created a simple family tradition that works as an important family ritual on two levels: First, their thoughtful custom brings the family together in an activity that affirms their common values and their love for one another—the primary goal of family traditions. Second, because the family keeps all the speeches after the holiday is over, they're creating an archive of family events, thoughts, and feelings throughout the years that future generations of the Mintowt clan will be able to enjoy while learning more about their family.

Ritual and tradition are important elements of human life, not just in the context of families, but also in the spheres of religion, education, culture, social interaction, and more. Traditions connect the participants in a common endeavor (such as being a family) with a common goal, and they're ideal for transmitting values to children. Ritual can be educational, therapeutic, and even have a soul-healing aspect.

For several years, intensive research and teen surveys have consistently revealed that the more often children eat dinner with their parents, the less likely they are to smoke, drink or use illegal drugs. . . . Our goal is to create a symbolic day to highlight the importance of parental involvement and encourage Americans to make family dinners a regular feature of their lives.

—Joseph A. Califano

"Family traditions are about what a family likes about itself and wants to continue," says folklorist Steven J. Zeitlin. "Traditions become a focal point that all members have in common, activities that are bonding. They can be as simple as playing board games together, or as elaborate as religious rituals. Traditions are glue, the common ground around which a family revolves."

A recent survey of ninety thousand teenagers examined why some teens are less likely to indulge in risky behavior such as drinking, drugs, and sex. The one predictor: The kids who stayed on the straight and narrow felt emotionally connected to their families. Strong family traditions are one way of building a powerful family bond. Joseph A. Califano Jr., president of the National Center on Addiction and Substance Abuse at Columbia University in New York City, knows this; recently he announced the launch of an annual event his center calls "Family Day—A Day to Eat Dinner with Your Children." Writing to newspaper columnist Ann Landers to publicize the event, Califano said, "For several years, intensive research and teen surveys have consistently revealed that the more often children eat dinner with their parents, the less likely they are to smoke, drink or use illegal drugs. . . . Our goal is to create a symbolic day to highlight the importance of parental involvement and encourage Americans to make family dinners a regular feature of their lives."

Family rituals—even one as simple as taking the time to eat dinner together—can help a family feel like a family, rather than a collection of housemates. "The power of ritual to comfort and heal and teach is enormous, and all parents have this power," says Meg Cox, author of *The Heart of a Family: Searching America for New Traditions That Fulfill Us*.

In the 1970s and '80s, psychiatrists studied families with histories of alcoholism. They found that in families who practiced rituals consistently and seriously, there was a much lower chance the alcoholism would be passed on to the next generation. And a psychologist's 1992 survey revealed that college students who came from homes where strong traditions were a part of family life had an easier time adjusting to college life. The rituals gave them a firm grounding and contributed to their self-esteem.

A United Nations study of orphaned children in Bosnia whose villages had been bombed found that "talking therapies" were of little practical value in aiding the healing process, but an attempt to recreate the traditions and rituals of their childhoods gave the children a continuity which made it possible for them to look to the future. On a similar note, with the terrorist attacks in America, the ensuing war on terrorism, and the sense of unease many feel as a result, folklorist Annie Hatch says, "I think it is the strength of family traditions that will help us feel ordinary and secure again. We will even take more time to participate in family prayer, customs, and rituals to help become centered again. We will need to persevere through this upheaval to our world view by returning to the small things and activities that remind us we have a safe place in this world. Family traditions will be a huge part of this."

Amid the rapid pace, constant flux, and uncertainty of contemporary life, it's reassuring to have traditions and rituals that a family can depend on to always remain the same. If those traditions have been passed down from earlier generations, so much the better; a family's sense of connection to its forebears, of being part of a history larger than itself, is enhanced even more. But it's never too late to create new family traditions that your children can pass on.

Remembering the Family's Past

Just as many cultural and religious traditions symbolize historical events, family traditions can evoke a family's roots. The Smithsonian's folklore collection includes the story of the Dreschlers, whose family patriarch settled on a barren patch of land in Kansas, where he planted a large grove of maple trees. He considered the trees sacred and never cut one down. At Christmas time, since there was no tree, gifts were always laid at each family member's place at the dining table. Now, subsequent generations of the clan buy small Christmas trees, but they continue the family custom of placing presents on the table rather than under a tree.

The Smithsonian collection also includes Kathy Kundla Crosby's story of how her family stayed connected to its Russian Slovak heritage. She talks of going with her family to her grandparents' house for Christmas Eve dinner as a child. Before they could eat, the entire group would kneel for an hour to pray. The grandparents prayed in Slovak while the children thought about how hungry they were. Then the youngest child in the family would sit in a basket filled with straw, to represent the infant Jesus. Kathy, who was the youngest until her cousin was born, recalls

13

how uncomfortable the straw felt as it pricked her legs. The family would then eat garlic before starting the meal, to ensure their good health throughout the coming year. Although it was raw garlic, Kathy says she loved it.

In the Box household, a Christmas tree–trimming tradition has grown out of a custom the parents began when they were first married years ago. They couldn't afford expensive holiday ornaments, so they bought penny candy and used it to decorate their first tree. The family still decorates their tree with candy today, but they buy chocolate-covered cherries to enjoy while they're decorating so that no one will eat the ornaments.

Traditions that continue customs started by your forebears are priceless. They link you to your relatives in a real and palpable way, creating an appreciation of their lives and an awareness of their legacies to you and your kin. If you don't already have handed-down traditions in your family, use the information in chapter four on researching family history to help you get started. Interviewing older family members can unlock a treasure trove of details about family customs.

If you don't uncover any specific family traditions in your research, use what you do know about your ancestors to create new rituals. Do you have Swedish or Finnish ancestry somewhere in your lineage? Start a Saint Lucia ceremony in your family. Before sunrise on the morning of December 13, the youngest daughter in the family puts on a white robe and a red sash and wears a crown of tall, lighted (or electric) candles resting on evergreens. She wakes her parents and serves them coffee and special pastries. Her siblings accompany her, with the boys dressed as "star boys" in long white shirts and pointed hats, carrying "star wands." The custom dates back to the legend of Lucia, a fourth-century Christian virgin martyred for her beliefs. The Saint Lucia ceremony also represents the traditional thanksgiving for the return of the sun.

Many American families have begun celebrating the holiday Kwanzaa over the past twenty years. Started in 1966 by Dr. Maulana Ron Karenga, the holiday promotes the celebration of African culture as a means for unifying the African-American community in the United States. This holiday has evolved into a marvelous way for African-Americans to connect with the lands and traditions of their ancestors.

The name *Kwanzaa* is derived from the Swahili word for "first," and many suggested customs for the celebration are based on harvest, or "first fruit," rituals that are found all over the African continent. The holiday runs for a week, the day after Christmas through New Year's Day, and a different principle—self-determination, creativity, cooperative economics, and unity are a few—is the focus of each day. The celebration each day begins with the lighting of a candle, and the week ends in a huge feast. Gift-giving is a common but optional feature. African music, food, costumes, and crafts play a large role in the festivities. The holiday leaves plenty of room for innovation and imagination on the part of the participants, and it's a great way to teach children important values and give them a sense of identity.

One family that has celebrated Kwanzaa for twenty years starts each night with a candle-lighting ceremony; then one of the children describes that night's principle. Each family member takes a turn talking about how he or she plans to incorporate that principle into daily living in the year ahead. Another family invites friends and neighbors to their Kwanzaa celebrations, where inexpensive gifts are exchanged and the seven principles are discussed at each night's gathering. Then, in June or July, the family holds a barbecue and invites the same families who joined them for Kwanzaa. Everyone gets a chance to talk about how well they've managed to make the principles a part of their lives during the preceding months.

There's no reason to limit yourself to rituals from your own ethnic background, however. If you're of Polish descent but find something about holiday traditions from Mexico that you really like, try some out on your family. The main thing is to have traditions everyone will enjoy participating in year after year. (See the sidebar on the following pages about Christmas traditions from various countries for ideas you might want to try with your own family.)

Christmas Around the World

Christmas in Germany

As in many other European countries, yuletide celebrating in Germany begins on December 6, St. Nicholas Day, when children place shoes by the fireplace in the evening. During the night, St. Nicholas travels to each house carrying a book of sins in which all the bad things the children have done are written. If they've been good, St. Nick fills the shoes with treats. If they've been bad, they find their shoes filled with twigs.

The fir tree's Christian roots began in Germany almost one thousand years ago, when St. Boniface, who converted the German people to Christianity, is said to have seen a band of pagans about to sacrifice a young boy while worshipping an oak tree. Supposedly St. Boniface angrily cut down the oak tree, and a young fir tree sprang up from its roots. In the sixteenth century, fir trees were brought indoors at Christmas.

In Germany, the tree is unveiled just prior to the Christmas Eve feast. While Dad distracts the kids in another room, Mom brings out the tree and festoons it with candy, nuts, cookies, fruit, toys, angels, tinsel, and candles or lights. Gifts are placed under the tree. Colorfully decorated plates for each family member, piled with fruit, nuts, and sweets, are set out nearby. Then the children are allowed to enter, and the family sings carols and opens presents.

Christmas Eve is sometimes called *Dickbauch*, which means "fat stomach," because legend has it that people who don't eat well on Christmas Eve will be haunted by demons during the night. To prevent this frightening possibility, dishes such as suckling pig, white sausage, *Reisbrei* (a sweet rice pudding spiced with cinnamon), and macaroni salad are served. Christmas Day means a meal of roast goose, *Christstollen* (long loaves of bread filled with nuts, raisins, and dried fruit), *Lebkuchen* (spice cookies), marzipan, and Dresden *Stollen* (a moist, rich fruit bread).

Christmas in Mexico

Las Posadas is the Mexican people's delightful build-up to Christmas Eve. It begins December 16 and commemorates Mary and Joseph's travels from Nazareth to Bethlehem. Each night of the celebration, two children lead a procession. They carry a small platform bearing figures of Joseph and Mary riding a burro. The rest of the procession hold candles and sing the "Litany of the Virgin" as they near the door of the home assigned as the first "posada" ("inn"). The group chants a traditional song and wakens the master of the house to ask lodging for Mary and Joseph. The household threatens to beat the visitors unless they move on, until the owner of the house realizes who his guests are. Then he throws open his doors and welcomes them in. They all kneel around the *crèche*, or *nacimiento*, and offer Ave Marias and a prayer.

Then it's time for a *piñata*, food, and dancing. The piñata, a clay or papier-mâché container that's often shaped like a bull or donkey, is brightly colored, filled with candy and toys, and hung from the ceiling or a tree. One by one, the children are blindfolded, spun around, and told to hit the piñata with a stick. When a child finally breaks the piñata, there is an explosion of treats, and the children scramble to gather the goodies.

On Christmas Eve an extra verse is added to the Ave Maria that tells the Virgin Mary the divine night has come. Children dressed as shepherds stand by the *crèche* while the group kneels and sings a litany, then a lullaby to the Christ Child.

At midnight the birth of baby Jesus is celebrated with fireworks, bells, and whistles. Worshippers flock to church to attend the *misa de gallo*, or mass of the rooster. After mass, families go home to a feast, often consisting of tamales, rice, chile rellenos, *champurrado* (a sweet drink made with chocolate), *arroz dulce* (a rice dessert), and *menudo*, which is said to wake you up faster than strong coffee.

A Russian Slovak Christmas

In the days leading up to Christmas, a traditional Slovak greeting is, "I wish happiness and peace to this house, to you, your wife, your children, and the whole family." On December 6, St. Nicholas Day, children who promise to be good all year receive candy, chocolate, nuts, and fruits in the shoes they've left on the window sill before going to bed. Bad children find their shoes filled with coal.

Christmas Eve dinner starts with the appearance of the first star in the sky. The legs of the dinner table are tied with an iron chain to symbolize family togetherness. After lighting candles and singing carols, the family prays over the meal. The mother then makes a cross with honey on the forehead of each member of the family to protect against evil. Special waffles are eaten after being dipped in honey (bringing the goodness and health of the bees) and garlic (to frighten away the evils of illness). Also on the menu are *bobalky*, rolls garnished with sugar and ground poppy seeds. These are followed by sauerkraut soup, breaded fish, and potato salad. Fish scales placed under each plate represent wealth and abundance. *Hriatuo*, a hot drink made from honey or sugar, butter, and clear alcohol, is often served, along with *slivovica*, plum brandy.

After dinner, friends and relatives visit each other, and *kolednici* and *vinsovnici* (carolers and well-wishers) arrive. The visitors are always given food and drink to keep them warm. Later, everyone attends Midnight Mass.

Christmas in Italy

One delightful Italian ritual is the heralding of the impending festivities by *piferari*, or pipers. They descend from the mountains of the countryside playing tunes on their bagpipes, filling the air with anticipation of the celebration to come. Another custom is the burning of the Yule log, which must stay lighted until New Year's Day. Like so many yuletide traditions, this blends pagan and Christian worship. The pagans believed in fire as a purifying and revitalizing force and thought the old year and its evils were destroyed as the log burned; Christian legend says Mary enters the homes of the poor at midnight while people are at Mass and warms baby Jesus before the glowing log.

On Christmas Eve, people go from church to church to see the magnificent nativity displays. Artisans create intricate landscapes around the manger scene, complete with grottoes, trees, lakes, rivers, the lights of Bethlehem in the background, and angels hung from wires.

In some regions, the Italian Christmas Eve banquet consists largely of fish—as many as ten or twenty fish dishes. In Rome, the traditional Christmas Eve dish is *capitone*, a large female eel that is roasted, baked, or fried. North of Rome, the menu may include pork, sausage packed in a pig's leg and smothered in lentils, or turkey stuffed with chestnuts. Christmas sweets include *panettone* (cake filled with candied fruit), *torrone* (nougat), and *panforte* (gingerbread), made with hazelnuts, honey, and almonds. Peasant folklore holds that nuts symbolize the fertility of the earth and aid in the increase of flocks and family. In ancient Rome, honey was eaten in December so the New Year would be sweet.

On Christmas Eve, Italian children put out their shoes for the female Santa Claus, La Befana, to fill with toys, candy, and fruit. Children who have misbehaved find their shoes filled with coal.

Christmas in Australia

Christmas takes place on December 25th, during summertime in Australia.  People often spend part of Christmas day with their families at the beach. Christmas dinner is just as likely to be salads, cold meat, and seafood as the traditional meal, which is roast turkey and plum pudding. Children believe that Santa Claus leaves presents for them under the Christmas tree on Christmas Eve. One popular Australian song states that six white boomers, or large kangaroos, pull Santa's sleigh.

Keeping the Faith: Personalizing Religious Traditions

Religious rituals are another source of family traditions. These powerful connections to a historical and spiritual heritage can be adapted to meet the needs of your family. Pam Silberman, who is descended from Ashkenazi (eastern European) Jews, and her husband, Bryan Gibson, chose to follow a Jewish custom when they had their first baby. In this tradition, parents name the child in honor of a deceased relative. Pam and Bryan had been close to Bryan's grandmother, Winifred, before she died. But since they weren't fond of the name Winifred, they used just the "W" of her name and named their baby girl Willa. "Since the Jewish faith doesn't really include the concept of an afterlife, this is a way of

memorializing dead loved ones," Pam explains. "And Ashkenazi Jewish tradition says you steal the soul of a living relative if you name a child after him or her. That's why you don't find any Juniors in the Jewish tradition." To honor Pam's late father, Willa's middle name is James.

Another example is the Jewish family that celebrates the Seder, the ritual dinner that begins the eight-day holiday of Passover, by starting not with the story of the Jews leaving Egypt, as is traditional, but with the tale of the exodus of the father's kin from Russia and of the mother's from Germany. The family incorporates the religious message of the traditional text—the liberation of the ancient Israelites from slavery—into a retelling of their own family history, augmenting the meaning for the family.

A number of religions, such as Judaism and Mormonism, counsel their followers to put aside a portion of their income—often ten percent—which will then go into church coffers or be donated to charity. One Jewish family has taken this religious ritual and made it part of their regular family Monopoly game: when a player passes "Go" and collects two hundred dollars, he or she is expected to set aside twenty dollars to this purpose.

Another family's holiday tradition is based on Christian church ritual. On Christmas Eve, all the family members act out the nativity scene after dinner, with everyone getting to play a different role—Mary, Joseph, angel, shepherd, or baby Jesus—each year.

Religious customs are ideal springboards for creating family traditions. Incorporating church rituals into the fabric of family life lends a spiritual dimension to daily living and serves as a thread to a divine element that many find vital. Think about which rituals from your religious tradition speak to you the most (or, if you don't belong to an organized religion yourself, from a spiritual tradition that you find appealing), and then consider ways to "secularize" these customs, weaving them into family activities.

Aunt Gertrude's Goulash: Traditions and Food

Many family rituals and traditions involve special foods, especially those prepared for holidays. Having a distinctive menu for family occasions—whether it's a holiday or just a family event—strengthens the family bond and fosters an important sense of continuity if those menus are reproduced by subsequent generations of the clan.

Gail Hickman and her family always have the same menu for dinner on Christmas Eve: shrimp and crab claws with spicy cocktail sauce, crusty French bread, and a green salad. "When my sister and I were little girls, often that was what our family ate on New Year's Eve," Gail explains. "Then, when my sister and I had both married and would take our own families to visit Mama and Dad on Christmas Eve, Mama started serving the shrimp and crab on that night instead."

Dessert on Christmas Day in the Hickman family is always an old-fashioned English plum pudding with a sweet, creamy sauce, a tradition carried over from the family's English and Scottish forebears. "My grandmother had made plum pudding for years. Then my mother took that recipe and used it to develop her own recipe," Gail says. "But the sauce has never changed since my grandmother's time."

Sugarplum Pudding Recipe

2 cups pitted dried prunes, cut up	2 tsp. ground allspice
4 eggs, well-beaten	2 tsp. cinnamon
2 cups brown sugar, firmly packed	2 tsp. nutmeg
2 cups flour	½ tsp. cloves
1 tsp. baking soda	2 cups buttermilk
1 tsp. baking powder	1 to 1½ cups finely ground suet
2 tsp. salt	1 cup seedless raisins

In separate bowls soak prunes and raisins in hot water. In large bowl of electric mixer, combine beaten eggs and sugar. Beat well until light and well-blended. Sift together flour, soda, baking powder, salt, and spices. Add to egg mixture alternately with buttermilk. Drain prunes and raisins. Stir in suet, prunes, and raisins. Place in greased tins. (Coffee cans work well.) Cover tightly with foil. Place a rack or inverted saucer in bottom of large, heavy saucepan or Dutch oven. Add water to a depth of 2 inches. Bring water to a boil. Then place tightly covered puddings on the rack. Boil gently. (Or use a steamer.) Steam for 2½ to 3 hours or until cake tester inserted in pudding comes out clean. Let puddings stand a few minutes after removing, or they can be refrigerated for up to 2 weeks, then reheated before serving. Run knife around edge of mold. Pudding should come out easily onto serving platter. Makes 3 12-ounce containers filled two-thirds full.

Pudding Sauce

¼ cup butter	1 to ½ cups boiling water
1 cup sugar	½ pint whipping cream
2 Tbsp. flour, rounded	

Mix butter, sugar, and flour well in a heavy saucepan. Add boiling water. Cook over medium heat, stirring often until sauce becomes thick and transparent. Turn to simmer. Cover and simmer about 10 minutes. Stir twice. Whip cream until stiff. Fold into hot sauce. Keep covered until ready to serve. Makes 2½ cups.

From LaRue Carr Longden, mother of Gail Hickman

Gail's family tradition for the Fourth of July was to visit her husband's parents in a nearby town to see a parade travel down a street near her in-laws' home. Afterward, the family would gather at the house for a big meal, always capped by a particular dessert. "Grandma and Grandpa Hickman would hand-crank this wonderful lemon ice cream,"

Gail says. When her in-laws passed away, Gail and her husband adopted the homemade lemon ice cream tradition for Fourth of July celebrations with their own children.

Jane Reilly's memories of Easter revolve around the special pecan tarts her mother always made to celebrate the holiday. "In my forty-two years of life, I have never known her to bake

that dessert except on Easter morning," Jane says, adding that when she and her husband lived in a different state than her mother, "it was not unusual for her to send us pecan tarts in the mail for Easter." When Jane visited Toronto, Ontario, on vacation, she was surprised to see pecan tarts for sale in nearly every bakery she went into. "I haven't told Mom that in other places of the world I could eat them every day if I wanted to," Jane says. "But I did not buy any while I was in Toronto."

Annie Hatch remembers the "money cakes" she and her brothers enjoyed on their birthdays while they were growing up. "Mom would add coins to the batter before baking," Annie explains. Sometimes her mother was able to make sure the birthday child got the piece of cake with the best coin—a quarter—in it. "She experimented with wrapping coins in Saran wrap and tin foil a few times, but plain [well-washed] coins are the best," Annie notes. She hasn't started the tradition with her young children yet but plans to when they get older.

Another family has a simple yet meaningful Christmas Eve dinner tradition. Before the meal, the grandfather of the clan divides an apple into as many sections as there are members of the family. Each person eats his or her apple slice; this is meant to ensure that the family will remain together throughout the coming year.

Although it may seem like a minor part of family ritual, eating the same foods on special occasions can create a welcome sense of familiarity and tradition in a family. There are a number of ways to create this ritual in your own family.

If certain holiday and special-event foods already exist in your clan, you're ahead of the game. Make sure you record the recipes and learn how to make the dishes, if someone else in the family has been the keeper of the recipes (and the chef). And don't be afraid to adapt or replace foods that have lost their popularity in the family over the years. If Aunt Sally's lemon bars on Halloween are no longer a favorite, bake chocolate chip cookies (or whatever the whole family enjoys) next year, and make that your new tradition.

If your family doesn't have a tradition of customary foods to eat on holidays, this is your chance to be creative and come up with menu traditions that will work in your family. Is cherry pie a favorite dessert? Why not use it to replace cake at family birthday celebrations? If everyone loves those hard-to-make raspberry tarts, serve them only on Valentine's Day or the first day of summer.

Tips for Building New Family Traditions

If you've decided to create some new traditions for your family, here are some tips from family ritual expert Meg Cox.

- Rituals need to have structure—a beginning, a middle, and an end. The beginning is the preparation, the middle is the action, and the end is the moment of "integration and celebration." To use a dinner prayer as an example, there is the request that someone say grace, then the prayer itself, then the "amen" at the end. Creating a suitable environment for the ritual—through the lighting of candles, for example—is a necessary part of the first step, so that the participants will feel something important is about to begin.

- Two things give a ritual its power and meaning: a focus of concentration that screens out everyday distractions, and the calling up of a deep-seated "emotional or psychological truth" on the part of the participants. This truth that is celebrated may be a spiritual faith, a conviction of the importance of the family union, or a belief in a principle that conveys social or environmental benefit.

- One way to approach the creation of a tradition is to organize it around one of the four elements: earth, air, fire, or water. Planting something—a tree, some flowers—in the earth can be a wonderful way to symbolize a new venture, from a baby on the way, to a change in careers. A ritual that makes use of the air connotes lightness and letting go of something heavy; balloons, kites, pinwheels, confetti, and soap bubbles all make great use of air and wind. Fire can represent many ideas: the sun, hearth and home, warmth, destruction that makes way for rebirth. Candles and bonfires play crucial roles in any number of traditions. Finally, water means cleansing, baptism, and purification, and can be used in a variety of ways in rituals, both playful and solemn.

- Rituals often call for words. The main thing is to use language that comes from the heart and expresses the event's emotional or psychological truth. Unless you're a person who is spontaneously eloquent, you'll want to take time to think about what is going to be said beforehand. Great works of poetry and literature can be valuable resources for poignant or insightful nuggets that articulate what you want to say. And don't forget to include your sense of humor.

- Although it makes sense for a ritual to have a leader, that person should be willing to "share the microphone." Giving everyone a chance to say something contributes to the necessary give-and-take of a tradition.

- A finishing touch, or an appropriate closing event for a ritual often includes celebrating with food. This can be as simple as passing around the traditional homemade honey candy, or gathering around the dinner table for a special feast. Sharing egg nog or having Thanksgiving dinner are just two examples of how food plays a memorable role in family rituals.

Don't feel like you have to stick only to conventional holidays, either. Eating pumpkin pie on the first day of autumn, cherry cobbler on May Day, and peach melba on Arbor Day can be fun ways to mark transitions in the calendar and commemorate highlights in the year that would otherwise go unnoticed.

Knowing where your ancestors came from opens the door to many wonderful foods traditionally served in various countries during the holidays.

One on One: Bonding with Your Children

In the hustle and bustle of daily life in large families, it's easy for some kids to feel lost in the shuffle, and even an only child can feel that he or she doesn't get enough time alone

with Mom or Dad. Activities that include all the members of the family are important for uniting the entire clan, but it's also important to create traditions that allow each parent to bond individually with each child in the family.

Alicia Harrison and her father developed a tradition of having breakfast together on (or as near as possible to) the first day of spring each year. The ritual began one year when Alicia was seven or eight years old. She and her father awoke before the rest of the household and, feeling hungry, decided to go downtown to the coffee shop at a hotel in their city and have breakfast together. "It was so nice to have some time alone with my dad," Alicia remembers. "We were able to really talk about things, and we grew closer as a result." The tradition continued through her college years and when her father passed away it became a cherished memory for her.

There are many ways to make a tradition that creates and preserves a bond between a parent and child. Many fathers will take a son hunting or fishing as a "male bonding" ritual, but if these activities don't suit you, consider a hike in the mountains or a bike trip through the woods as a regular outing for just you and your son. One woman has fond memories of making pancakes with her father on Sunday mornings. Another mother has begun a traditional "movie night" alone with her teenage daughter once a month. Other ideas include a ritual shopping trip each autumn to buy school clothes, with lunch at a favorite restaurant as a special treat; a regular game of tennis, golf, basketball, bowling, or any sport both you and your child enjoy where you can go head-to-head (an effort should be made to keep this ritual fun and not too competitive); having a corner of the garden that you and your child plant together each spring; and taking a music or pottery class with your child. The possibilities are endless. The goal is to find something you both enjoy doing together, and then keep doing it.

The Gang's All Here: Community Traditions

Many people practice rituals and traditions with groups of friends and relatives they consider their communities—sort of extended families. These traditions work in the same ways as those created by biological families: to bind members of the group with a common purpose and a sense of fellowship and love. These customs can easily be adapted for biological families (and vice-versa).

Julie Willis takes part in a special tradition each year with her female friends. The group gathers for a cookie exchange party on the Saturday before Christmas (unless Christmas Eve falls on that day, in which case they reschedule it). Each woman brings three dozen cookies; they must be made from a recipe that has been passed down from mother to daughter in the woman's family. The hostess hands out a festive tin to each woman as she arrives at the party. They have a light brunch; then each woman goes through the line and takes three of each "family heirloom" cookie. Prizes of upscale kitchen utensils are given for the best-looking cookies, the best-tasting cookies, and the most labor-intensive cookies. Colorful holiday attire is *de rigueur* (one woman is renowned for wearing pink earrings shaped like Christmas bulb ornaments each year). The group has been having these parties for close to ten years. "The women who have young children bring them along," Julie says. "It's nice to have an event where the single women and the moms in our circle of friends can get together."

The Lindsay family's New Year's Eve party includes an unusual ritual. All friends and relatives of the family are invited to the party. A little before midnight, everyone goes into the basement playroom, where Dr. Lindsay plays a recording of Tchaikovsky's *1812 Overture*. The lights are turned out and everyone holds hands in the dark to listen to the stirring music. "It sounds like kind of a weird thing to do, but it's a really great experience," says longtime partygoer Carolyn Carr. "You feel an almost electric connection to all the other people in the room, and the quiet parts of the music give you time for introspection—thinking over the past year and planning for the next." At midnight, the guests rush outside, banging pots and pans. Afterward, they return to the living room and join hands in a circle to sing "Auld Lang Syne."

One group of women friends gathers once a week for an event they call "Craft Night." Each woman takes turns hosting the potluck dinner, and they all bring a portable craft or project they have underway (knitting, crocheting, scrapbooks, arranging photos in an album, and so on) but don't usually get time to work on. They talk and laugh as they work. A group of men has a tradition of going on an all-day outdoor excursion once a month—mountain biking in the summer, skiing in the winter—then going to eat at a restaurant afterward.

As with any tradition, the idea is to find something the entire gang enjoys doing together, then make the effort to get organized so it happens on a regular basis. Be sure to rotate the responsibility of organizing and/or hosting the ritual so that no one in the group feels unduly burdened.

Just as family traditions help your family stay in tune with one another, creating traditions with your friends can help cement friendships and build a network that supports the whole group, spreading joy in times of success and offering encouragement in times of challenge.

Druid for a Day: Winter Solstice Rituals

An ancient holiday that has seen a resurgence in popularity in recent years is December 20 or 21, the winter solstice. This is the shortest day of the year, the day that marks the return

of the sun, with days getting longer and nights shorter. Because of its emphasis on sun cycles and the natural world, it acts as a welcome earth-oriented balance to the commercialism that can pervade the Christmas holiday.

Ideas for family celebrations of the solstice abound. As with so many ceremonies, the lighting of candles can play a large role. One family arranges candles on a table like the spokes of a wheel, symbolizing the circle of life, with a larger candle in the center. They say a family prayer about the returning of the light; then each member takes a candle, lights it at the center flame, and says an individual prayer or announces an intention for the coming year.

Some families celebrate by eating foods the sun has helped to nurture, such as nuts, fruits, sweet potatoes, and winter squash. Others set up a "solstice tree" with ornaments that pay homage to the sun. Another idea is to set off fireworks and sparklers against a backdrop of snow in the front yard. A rural family decorates trees in the woods behind their house with ears of corn and pine cones spread with peanut butter, creating a feast for their feathered neighbors. Some families follow an old Celtic tradition that says you should turn on all the lights in your house and open all the doors, to persuade the sun to return the next day.

Since it's a holiday not yet influenced by years of cultural conditioning and advertising hype, the winter solstice offers a remarkable opportunity to invent your own imaginative traditions, celebrating the earth's cycles and fostering in your family a feeling of being connected to nature.

'Tis a Gift to Be Simple: Everyday Rituals

Traditions and rituals aren't only for holidays and special occasions, and they don't have to be elaborate. Incorporating small rituals into the daily functioning of a family draws everyone closer and makes them feel like they're part of a well-run team.

DAILY

Dinnertime. Most American families eat dinner together less than fifty percent of the time. Researchers have found that the average home dinner in the U.S. lasts fifteen to twenty minutes, but children spend an average of twenty-five hours a week watching television. These are compelling arguments for turning off the television during dinner and creating a time for the family to share their thoughts and feelings about the day's events.

Starting supper with a prayer or moment of silence can set a warm and respectful tone for the meal, allowing everyone to leave the day's aggravations behind and focus on good food and conversation. Annie Hatch's family is one that has a regular dinner prayer. When the extended clan is together—a recent occasion was Annie's mother's seventieth birthday—the

Saying Grace

If you don't already have a custom of saying grace over your evening meal but want to begin, here are three simple and lovely prayers from three major religious traditions as an example:

A Catholic grace: *"Bless us, O Lord, and these Your gifts, which we are about to receive from Your bounty. Through Christ, our Lord, Amen."*

Martin Luther, founder of Protestantism, is credited with, *"Come, Lord Jesus, be our guest. Let these gifts to us be blessed. In the name of the Father, Son, and Holy Spirit. Amen."*

A Jewish blessing: *"Lift up your hands toward the sanctuary and bless the Lord. Blessed are You, O Lord our God, King of the universe, who brings forth bread from the earth. Amen."*

family recites a German prayer that Annie's parents learned while living in Germany in the 1950s. Annie and her siblings said it daily while growing up, so now they can repeat it verbatim "without knowing what it means," says Annie. "We also clasp hands, encircling the table when we say 'Amen.'" Annie says the ritual reminds her of family dinners when she was growing up and "makes the event now more important. And Mom always says it's nice to say a prayer so we all start eating at the same time." Even a simple moment of silence can serve as a break from the toil of the day and an opportunity for quiet reflection and perspective.

Some families let dinner talk chart its own course. Others organize supper conversations around certain topics. One idea is to assign each family member the job of choosing and researching a current-events topic he or she finds interesting; then, when it's that person's night to preside over the dinnertime dialogue, the "expert" tells a little about the topic, and the rest of the family asks him or her questions about the subject. Although it may seem like a chore at first, it can grow into an awareness of the world around you and a healthy desire to learn.

One family sets aside some dinners for talking and other dinners at which they're allowed to read at the table. Another has a custom in which the mother or father reads to the family during dinner, with the choice of book rotating among the children; this creates a world of stories and characters that everyone in the family knows and loves. Also, making dinner together a daily event, during which values, ideas, and happenings of importance to the family are discussed, is invaluable for creating a rich home life and a sense of togetherness.

Bedtime. Parents of young children know that bedtime is rarely a child's favorite event. But going to bed can be a time for soothing rituals that let your children let go of the day, prepare their minds for a night without nightmares, and give you the opportunity to let them know they are loved and protected.

There's the woman who opens the front door at night with her toddler daughter to say good night to the trees, the stars, and the moon; or the father who, on summer nights, concentrates with his son on the sound of crickets as a quiet meditation and release of the day's worries. One woman uses her finger to draw a circle on her second-grader's forehead as a place for the good dreams to enter.

Reading a favorite story to a child at bedtime is a wonderful and time-honored tradition in many families. A delightful variation on this is when the parent or child invents the story, extending and embellishing it night after night. One woman who makes up tales for her children is writing down the stories and plans to have them bound as keepsakes for her kids.

Bedtime can be the perfect opportunity to find out what's really on a child's mind. Rubbing your children's feet or scratching their backs helps relax them for bed and may also loosen their tongues, giving you a chance to talk about their fears and desires. One idea is to give your child the chance to tell you one thing that made him or her angry or sad that day and one thing that was a happy event. You, in turn, can tell about something he or she did that day that made you proud. Even just repeating certain phrases every night—"I love you," "Sleep tight, don't let the bedbugs bite," and so on—can be a soothing balm that helps coax your child to sleep.

WEEKLY

Scheduling one night a week to spend with just the family is an easy tradition to begin—and one that pays great dividends in terms of family closeness. Whether it's a night of faith-based activity, a family meeting, an evening of fun, or a mixture of all three, "family night" is a terrific way to unite the clan.

One family sets aside Saturday night as pizza night. The whole family pitches in to make homemade pizza from scratch, with all their favorite toppings. Then they watch a video or go to the local dollar-a-movie theater. Another family has weekly video nights where they only watch films that have won Academy Awards for best picture. Yet another family plans weekly game nights, when charades, puzzles, or board games are the order of the day. Even watching a favorite weekly television program together can be instructive if you take the time to talk about what you've seen afterward, turning your children into critical consumers of television.

MONTHLY

Building a ritual around the phases of the moon may have a somewhat pagan ring to it, but celebrating the full moon can be an entertaining way to acknowledge the moon's cycles and may even spark an interest in astronomy or the other sciences in your children. One father takes a monthly walk with his children on the night of the full moon. They discuss what wildlife they see or make observations about the constellations, but they also talk about their dreams and memories. On the night of the full moon, another family makes a small fire in a fire pit they have in their backyard (weather permitting) and roasts marshmallows over it.

A family book group is another way to bring the family together once a month. You may want to include the entire family, or you may want to have a mother-daughter book club and a father-son book group. These groups can be a marvelous family tradition for preteens and teenagers, since this is an age when many children begin struggling with issues of identity, self-image, and peer pressure. A book group is a perfect forum for talking about many concepts, a place where kids can begin to feel confident expressing their

opinions and being valued for their contributions to a discussion. Letting each child choose the month's book (with some parental guidance) is the way to begin.

Another educational yet fun monthly activity could be called "around the world in thirty days." At the beginning of the month, have a child close his or her eyes and point to a spot on the map to pick a country. Spend the rest of the month learning about that country, using encyclopedias, library books, and materials on the Internet. What does the countryside look like? What are the clothing and food like? What is daily life like for the people there? Try making some of the dishes that the country is known for. Some Internet sources may even have sound clips featuring language pronunciation.

Your Family Traditions

When you're getting ready to create new traditions, focus on what's important to your family. If sports are a family passion, build some rituals around athletic events. If everyone loves to read, think about a family book group. If enjoying good food draws the clan together, consider taking cooking classes as a family and assigning certain dishes to each family member when the next holiday rolls around.

Do you feel strongly about doing charity work? Organize some traditions that involve thinking of others, such as serving meals in a soup kitchen on Thanksgiving or caroling in nursing homes and hospitals at Christmastime.

Look at the calendar and see if there are times of the year that are lacking in ritual celebrations in your household. Perhaps you need to think about inventing rites to commemorate the change of each season, or spend more time planning a really great family vacation each summer. Learn about your family's ethnic background and find ways to celebrate any ethnic holidays that apply. If your larger family group—aunts, uncles, cousins, grandparents, and so on—doesn't already have a family reunion each year, think about starting one. It's easy if each branch of the family takes a turn organizing it each year.

Robert C. and Doris Alder Sumner began giving their grandchildren one $2 bill each for both Halloween and Valentine's Day, nearly twenty years ago when the bills were relatively rare. The bills always came in small white envelopes with one festive sticker, and three words, "Happy Valentine's John," or "Happy Halloween Kristian." The tradition as expanded to include the grandchildren's spouses, and ten great-great grandchildren. The children do not spend their $2 bills, but keep them as a cherished remembrance of just one of hundreds of family traditions.

Remember, too, that there are times when traditions need to change. Children will outgrow some of them; a matriarch or patriarch of the clan who was a keeper of the ritual flame may die. It has become increasingly common for married parents to divorce. After a remarriage, it's crucial that stepparents take the time to forge relationships with their new stepchildren, and making a tradition that you perform alone with the stepchild is an excellent way of doing this. One stepfather makes waffles for his stepdaughter on Saturday mornings and then watches cartoons with her. A stepmother takes her teenage step-daughter out to lunch once a month.

The Smithsonian folklore collection includes the story of one family who, after the father left the family right before the holidays, agreed to change their Christmas traditions. They had always gotten a tall, thin tree, and they decided to get a short, fat one instead. They bought new decorations. And they didn't put up the train set around the bottom of the Christmas tree, as was their custom, because the father had been the only one who played with the trains. One son said it was a surprisingly good holiday, one where the mother and children just enjoyed being together, and they've maintained their changed traditions ever since.

Folklorist Steve Zeitlin notes, "Rituals are an interesting combination of tradition and innovation—bringing the past to bear on the present—having the past be very present now. People can use tradition to change as well as to stay the same. Traditions need constant upkeep. It's never easy; a family needs to create its own world. It's easy to get hooked on television and movies and other cultural distractions."

Keep in mind that spontaneity is an important element in any tradition, and rigid adherence to a practice that has lost its luster and become hollow will only alienate family members. Be flexible in your rituals, and know that you can adapt or drop those that have lost their meaning. And remember that building tradition into your daily family routines can be good practice for the bigger traditions that come with holidays and special events.

Cultivate your traditions carefully, and they will nourish your family for years and, hopefully, generations to come. As Steve Zeitlin says, "Traditions are where you live, where you're born and where you die. Tradition is where the meaning of our lives is found."

What you have caught on film is captured forever…
it remembers little things long after you have forgotten everything.
—Aaron Siskind

CHAPTER TWO

Capturing Images
of the Past
Your Family Photographs

Shortly after their children began to leave home, Grace and Dean Pearce started holding family reunions every five years or so. As many members of the family as possible would return home for several days, and these occasions were always ideal for taking pictures. The most recent of these reunions, however, resulted in the most meaningful photos. Usually the Pearces hired a professional photographer take a formal group portrait. This last time, while still using a professional photographer, they decided to add context to the photo sessions.

Though the family home is no longer standing, most of the landscaping Dean had done in his extensive yard still exists as part of a city park. The Pearce family went to the park and had portraits of Mom and Dad taken in front of a beautiful flowering shrub Dean had planted thirty-five years ago. Each branch of the family was then photographed in front of one of the groves of trees that he had planted. In fact, each tree had been planted and named for one of his grandchildren. While the professional was at work with group photos, members of the family took candid shots of the children playing, using the neighborhood in which they had grown up as a backdrop. They also did four-generation photos, photos with Grace and Dean with each of their children, a photo of the grandchildren, and one of the great-grandchildren. One family member had a digital camera, and by the end of the day, some of the grandchildren who hadn't been able to come to the reunion were sharing in the fun via a family Web site. Looking at these pictures now, each family member is not only reminded of the people they love the most, they also remember the surrounding scenery and the places and things that were most important in the years they shared the home built and landscaped by "Dad Pearce."

The Pearce family is well on its way to creating a family photo collection that will be treasured for many years to come. Their tradition of gathering the family together at the old home site lends enthusiasm for the picture-taking sessions; the digitization efforts of other family members helps keep the distant family connected and provides an electronic archive of treasured family photos.

While the family photo collection you create may be entirely different, you'll want to determine your goals for creating a personal, family, or even an extended family photo collection. What will be the scope of your collection? Who are your best sources for photographs? What will you do to store and preserve these images for future generations, and make them accessible and presentable for your own family?

Creating a photo collection is made up of several steps and begins, simply enough, with gathering the photos. It continues as you discover clues to help identify them, and as you preserve them for posterity with digital technology. You should begin first by understanding that a picture is worth a thousand words only when you have the details of the story. Following are guidelines to creating a meaningful family photo collection.

Step 1: Decide What to Include in Your Collection

If all that survived of your life story were the photos you leave and what you have written about them, what would your descendants know about you? Professional portraits help us place our family and ourselves in a specific time; contextual photos (or snapshots) help us understand what our lives or the lives of our loved ones were like. Your collection should include a good mix of both. Include portraits so that your grandchildren can see what you looked like in your youth and why they look the way they do; include contextual snapshots to allow them to know where and how you lived, what you did, and what you loved.

HISTORICAL CONTEXT AND LIFE EVENTS

With change being the only constant in life, you need to be sure that your photos don't focus on only one time period in your life and the lives of your children. Too many family albums are full of baby pictures and birthday parties without the other photographable moments of life. As you select photographs that will be meaningful to future generations, capture each season of the lives you value. Take and keep those that represent of a broad range of events: birthdays, vacations, graduations, weddings, anniversaries, funerals, holidays, family reunions, visits to relatives, trips to the beach, and everything in between.

Our lives are less about how we looked at a particular time than what we did and what was important to us. The most meaningful photo collection goes beyond the people to include the many details of life as well. Take and look for pictures of homes, cars, places of work and worship, friends, fellow employees, teammates, pets, projects, and all the things that make up your life.

One of the most important sets of photographs one woman has is a set made by her brother. He got up on the roof of the family home and took a wide-angle photo looking in each direction. Then he went around the outside and took one of each side of the house. Looking at these pictures brings back memories of the many years spent living with her family in that home.

Step 2: Record Your Discoveries

As you find family photos, you'll want to record what you learn about them so you can pass on that information. There are many ways to approach record keeping. The one recommended here is to think of each image as a story—a news item. Not only will this help you make a good record and index, but it can be your guide as you interview people about the photos you find. The news reporter's "who, what, where, when, why, and how" technique can help you create a complete story around each piece in your collection, generating information you can use as you present and display your pictures. (This is discussed in detail in the scrapbooking chapter.)

Remember that a good photo interview is conducted in the same way as any other good interview. Ask each family member who might know something about the persons or places portrayed in the photo. You will want to record their answers on tape and transcribe the important items into a report. When done well, the interview and description can lend the "thousand words" to each of your photos, turning each of them from an image of something or someone into a rich narrative that becomes a part of your family heritage.

Another critical element of record keeping is, of course, being able to attach your

35

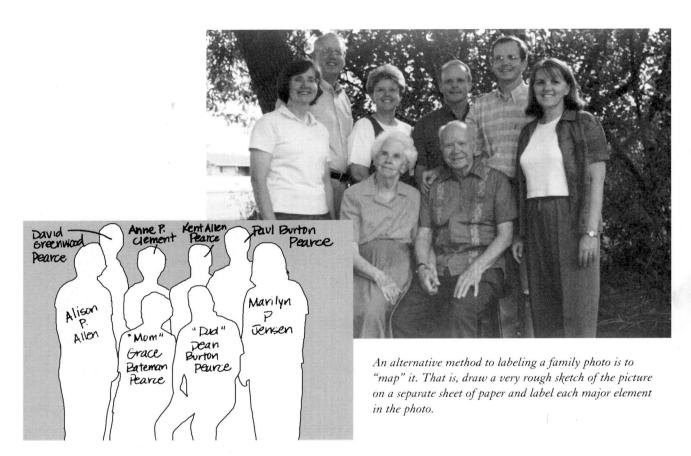

An alternative method to labeling a family photo is to "map" it. That is, draw a very rough sketch of the picture on a separate sheet of paper and label each major element in the photo.

description to the photo. A traditional method has been to write the description on the back. This is problematic for several reasons: First, space is limited, especially when you have a lot to say about a picture. Second, you will likely display your photos in an album, with the back hidden from view. Also, writing on the back with non-archival-quality ink can bleed onto the image or fade with time (refer to the "Photographs for Scrapbooks" section, starting on page 59). An easier method is to attach a copy of the photograph to the written or electronic record. (The electronic approach will be discussed more fully in the section on digital photography.)

You have probably had the experience of looking at a photograph you took and wondering where or when it was taken, or even why you took it or who was in the picture. Labeling and creating records apply every bit as much to current photos as to your historical collection. While not every photo on every roll you take requires a complete record, carefully choose a few based on some criteria of your own and make a good record about each. Making a record on several in each roll will allow you and your posterity to use them as an index to others taken at the same place and time. The more you record, the more you'll remember—and the more those who follow you will know about your life.

PHOTOGRAPH INFORMATION SHEET

Who:

Who is in the photo?

Who owns the photo?

Relationship of person to owner, e.g., great grandmother

What:

Type of photo (for example, black-and-white albumen print)

Size and description (for example, 4" x 2¹/₂" carte de visite)

Copy or original?

Framed or mounted? (yes or no and description of)

Where:

Where was the photo taken? (geographic location)

Name and place of studio and/or photographer, with address and source of knowledge.

If the subject of the photo is an object as opposed to a person, give the full address.

When:

When was the photo taken? (best guess, if unsure)

Why:

Why was the photo taken, e.g., wedding, graduation etc.?

Why is the photo important to you?

Why is this photo meaningful to your family?

How:

How did you came to have it?

How does it relate to other photos in your collection?

You will want to fill out this type of sheet for all of your important family photographs. Don't worry if you don't have an answer for every question. Just be as complete as you can.

When Jared's Grandma Hansen was diagnosed with cancer, the family knew that she would not likely live much longer. During her first hospital stay they began to clean and organize her condo, and in one closet Jared found several shoeboxes full of photos, slides, and negatives. He asked her about them during a hospital visit, and she agreed to tell him the stories behind the pictures. Unfortunately, many of the pictures, especially the faces, were small. He was not sure that Grandma, with her failing eyesight, would be able to see and identify them.

One of Jared's coworkers came up with a great solution. He suggested that Jared create digital images of his grandmother's photos and load them onto a laptop computer. With some effort, Jared did just that, and in the process he brought to life images that had not seen the light of day in years. Jared took the laptop to his grandma's bedside and spent many delightful hours listening to and recording her memories as she told story after story about the people in the photos. In some cases he zoomed in on faces, filling the screen, so she could better see who was in each photo. With the information gained from his visit, Jared wrote a description of each photo on a form he had designed, and soon had a rich family history based on her memories.

Although Grandma Hansen didn't remember some of the details of the events or a few of the people portrayed, she often knew who might. Jared expanded the scope of his laptop visits to include aunts and uncles and even printed some of the pictures and sent them with an information form to family members he couldn't visit — some of whom he had never met. He was surprised at the enthusiasm with which they responded and, in many cases, received back additional pictures that the recipients felt went along with the ones Jared had sent.

It was only two months after he finished going through all the pictures with his grandmother that she died. He misses her, but realizes that he would have missed much more had he not spent those hours with her and saved the legacy of her photograph collection — not just the pictures, but the stories — for himself, his own family and those yet to come. He also knows that the memories the pictures brought back had enriched the last few months of his grandmother's life.

Step 3: Gather Your Family Photographs

As with Jared and his grandmother, one of the greatest values of any family image collection is its power to bring generations together. Organizing, preserving, and distributing your family photos are critical steps to having a full and complete collection that you can share.

Gathering a family photo collection begins at your home and with your relatives. When you visit with your grandmother, ask her if she has pictures of herself as a child, of her graduation from high school, her wedding, reunions, funerals, or other family events.

As you collect and organize family photos you will see that they begin to cross generations and will lead you to people who will have more images of your family's past—grandparents, great-aunts and great-uncles, and long-lost cousins. Remember that family may not be the only source of family photos. Find out which friends of your older or deceased relatives may have snapshots that include your family. Check with local newspapers and libraries for photos that may include family members. Yearbooks and other records of organizations such as unions, military units, and companies where relatives worked are good sources. If a photographer's studio has existed in a family home town for more years than you can remember, ask them if they keep old negatives and if you may review them for family. Local, state, and national archives may house photos important to your family. These are often indexed, and most archives, particularly public ones, provide a way for interested patrons to get copies.

Don't limit your family photo collection to shots of people. As you build your collection, you'll want pictures of homes, schools, workplaces, neighborhoods, churches, gravestones, and all the contextual surroundings that will add richness to the lives of the people who will become more than a name and a face as your collection grows.

Step 4: Become a Photo Detective

Unfortunately, you will not always find someone who has information about the photos you find. Often, family pictures come to light as family members go through a relative's estate after a funeral, when the owner is no longer there to tell you about their photos. Sometimes items and albums are labeled, giving you a starting point for your description. If that is not the case, don't despair. The physical photograph itself contains many clues that will help you answer the details of the unidentified photos and

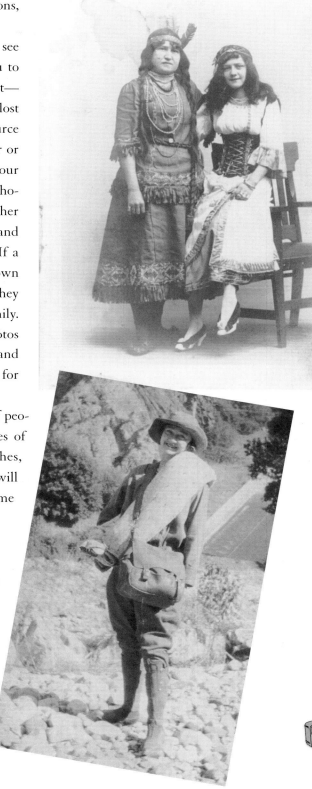

Sometimes the name of the studio in which the photo was taken will be imprinted on the matte. This labeling can yield important clues to identifying information about the time frame of and people in the photo.

with that information, you may be able to discover who the subject(s) is.

IDENTIFYING EARLY PHOTOGRAPHS

An important key to identifying early photographs is figuring out what kind of photographic process was used to create it. This may allow you to date the photograph within decades, if not more closely; figuring out approximately when a particular process was used can be easier than you might think. (See the sidebar on pages 42 and 43 for more information.)

Many of the images you come across will contain bits of information beyond the photo type that will help you place them in your family chronology.

Boxes of cased photos and card stock, paper frames, and albums containing early prints often include the name of the studio where the picture was taken. Checking city directories may reveal when and where these studios were in business. During the last years of the Civil War, the federal government placed a stamp tax on photography, so photos with a tax stamp (it looks much like a postage stamp) on the back were taken between August 1864 and August 1866.

Of course, the most interesting clues that place a scene at a particular time and place are in the photo itself. Clothing, jewelry, poses, props, hair styles, and context such as buildings, carriages, automobiles, and other objects tell their own tale. Libraries provide catalogs dating many of these details. While learning about styles and props of the past may seem like a lot of work, if you meet your great-grandmother on that journey, it will be well worth the trip.

WHO IS IN THE PHOTO?

While knowing the details of your old photos is important, you won't get very far in your collection if you don't know who is in the pictures. Sometimes the key is using the what, where, and when to lead you to that essential information. Dating a wedding picture, for example, that relates clearly to a particular branch of the family will let you know that it was you great-grandfather's wedding, not your grand-father's. Knowing the identity of one person in a group or period may provide clues to the identity of others in the same photo or another that includes the known person at a different age or in another setting. As you begin to learn about one or two images in a collection, place them on a table with others that might reflect the same branch of the family tree. Look for details that will connect them, then place them in combinations of time and place. As you do so, you may be helped (or possibly led astray by a generation or so) by that sudden recognition, "She looks just like..." If you still don't know who is in the photo, stay with it. As you collect more shots, clues will pop out, and as you interact with family members found through your research, you are sure to encounter someone who knows more about the photos in question.

Archiving Videotape

When archiving your videotapes, make sure you mark the master as such so as not to confuse it with copies. VHS loses some quality with each copy made and you want to make sure to copy from the original to preserve as much quality as possible.

Also, make sure the tape is stored on its thin edge, up and down like a book on a shelf. Avoid storing tapes on the flat side. Over time, gravity will pull the tape off the spools if it is lying flat, creating tracking problems that may be insurmountable.

Step 5: Preserve Your Photos for the Future

Much more tragic than not being able to identify the time, place, or person in a family photo is losing the photograph altogether. The chief dangers to photographs, slides, and negatives can be summarized in the phrases "fingers, fire, flood" or "handling, heat, humidity." Dirt, dust, and chemical damage complete the list of dangers. The ultimate preservation facility is probably a concrete vault full of fireproof files kept at sixty degrees Fahrenheit with a relative humidity of thirty percent, filtered air, total chemical neutrality in everything that holds or touches a photograph, and no humans (because humans are not chemically neutral). If you don't have such a place to store your family treasures—and it's more than likely that you don't—there is still hope.

Photography is a chemical process; papers and plastics treated with chemicals have been exposed to light that affects those chemicals. They are then exposed to other chemicals to complete the development process. Exposure to new chemical sources, light, or heat may reactivate some of these processes or otherwise affect image quality for the worse.

It is important that you keep photos, slides, and negatives in chemically neutral environments. This is done by using "archive-quality" storage media. If you keep your photos in albums, be sure that they are made of acid-free, archive-quality paper and bindings. Use

Types of Photographs Throughout History

Early photographs are all direct positive images—that is, the image was created by direct exposure of the image on metal or glass.

Daguerreotype. The first to achieve popularity and common usage was the daguerreotype, invented in 1839 and named after its French inventor, Louis Daguerre. These photos were made on sheets of highly polished metal and are characterized by a shiny, highly reflective surface. They are usually cased under a glass cover, often with a mat, within a brass or, later, fiber or plastic frame. Unless the cased image has an added backing, the back will be metal. The whole is referred to as a cased image. If you have a daguerreotype of your great aunt and wonder why she looks as if her cat just died, it may be in part because smiling was frowned upon; the exposure time required to create the image was so long that it was hard to hold a smile. Daguerreotypes were produced in the United States and Europe between 1840 and 1860. There is a good likelihood that your visual family history includes daguerreotypes, as millions were created—an estimated three million in 1844 alone.

Ambrotype. A second type of cased image that you might find is the ambrotype. These were produced on chemically coated glass rather than metal. The developed image was then encased with a mat against a black background to create the appearance of a positive image. Ambrotypes out of their casings appear as a piece of glass with a very light negative image on them. Ambrotypes lack the daguerreotype's shiny metallic surface, and the photo is best viewed under direct lighting. Ambrotypes were produced in the United States from 1854 to 1881, with their most popular period being 1855 to 1856.

Tintype. A third type of direct positive photograph popular in the late 1800s is the ferrotype, or as it was more commonly called, the tintype. Tintypes were made on a thin iron sheet.

They were much more resilient than daguerreotypes or ambrotypes; they didn't need to be cased to display the image, and they are more likely to be found without a casing or glass cover. They don't have the shiny surface of daguerreotypes. An easy clue that a photo on metal is a tintype is that it can be held by a magnet; the metal is iron ("ferro" is Greek for iron), not tin. Ferrotypes, or tintypes, were produced in the United States from 1856 until 1920. They were made in large numbers and were more likely to be in use in the less-settled parts of the American frontier and rural areas because their "iron constitution" allowed them to thrive where the less hardy glass and polished metal of other cased images didn't hold up.

Prints. While cased images were still in their heyday, paper-based photos were working their way onto the American scene. At first less popular because the paper was course and the images faint, by 1860, improved processes and better paper brought them to the fore. Particularly important is the albumen print. These were made by coating paper with egg white mixed with light sensitive chemicals. A print was made by placing a glass negative over this paper, leaving it in the sun for a while, and then developing the print. The thin paper print was then glued to a stiff paper backing, often with a printed edge forming a frame. With this process it was possible—for the first time—to make many copies of the same picture, and it became the rage to use one of these card-backed photos as a calling card or carte-de-visite. These prints are about 2½ inches x 4½ inches. Albums for these cards and their big sister, the cabinet print, were a household necessity for wealthy and middle-class America, and you should look for these as a possible source for family photos.

By 1880, most albumen prints were varnished, changing the surface from a soft luster to a shiny gloss much like that of the modern black-and-white glossy celluloid prints which replaced them around 1890.

Roll film. Roll film came into the photographic world about 1888 and quickly replaced the glass negative and albumen print with plastic negatives and gelatin print coatings. (Note the warning in the preservation section of this chapter concerning early negatives.) Some early Kodak film and cameras created round prints and negatives. If you find one of these—the prints are about 2½ inches in diameter—they can be dated to the 1890s.

Replaceable roll film. The twentieth century brought the greatest revolution in photography since its inception, namely the Kodak Brownie camera with replaceable roll film. At one dollar for a camera and pennies for film, the snapshot took family pictures from the studio to the backyard and to every vacation spot and birthday party in America. As you gather these expressions of what your ancestors thought important, the size, type of negative, and type of print paper can still provide important clues as to when the photo was made. The information necessary to guide you in that dating is beyond the scope of this chapter, but it is readily available in books on family and photo history that are in your library or referenced in the bibliography.

a mounting system that is also archive quality. Many glues, tapes, and other adhesives are not chemically neutral. Corner mounts have the advantage of not touching the picture itself. Storing in archive-quality plastic view sleeves adds the advantage of protection from dust, dirt, and some moisture.

Handling is another major preservation issue. As mentioned, humans are not chemically neutral (we are generally acidic), and our fingers are generally good purveyors of dirt, dust, and moisture. Prints, slides, and negatives should be handled as little as possible and should be picked up only on the edges. Fingerprints are especially bad since they attract dust and cause chemical reactions. Using photo-handling gloves or padded tweezers made specifically for this purpose is a good idea when handling your photo collection.

Once mounted in albums or protective sheets, your photos should be stored in archive-quality boxes to give added protection against dust, dirt, and water. These in turn need to be stored in a cool, dry, dark place away from possible flooding. Fire remains a danger, and the most complete protection is a fireproof safe or filing cabinet.

Warning about Old Negatives

If you have negatives in your collection that date prior to 1939, you may have a significant archiving problem. Much of the early negative media is made of nitrocellulose. This material had the advantage of being a clear, flexible, and plastic. It is also, however, the same material of which modern gunpowder is made. It is highly flammable, chemically unstable, and should not be kept or stored. If the clear edge of a plastic film negative (black and white) doesn't read "safety film," and the picture is pre-World War II, it may be this type of film. If it is pre-World War I, it likely is.

Test the negative by carefully cutting a small piece of the clear edge, placing it on a fireproof surface, and lighting it with a match. If it burns (usually quickly), as opposed to slowly melting, you have a nitro negative. Take these negatives to a photo-processing company that deals with nitrocellulose negatives and have them reproduced as new negatives. The old negative should then be destroyed. The photo-processing specialist may be willing to do this; if not, take it to your local police. If no one there knows about old negative material, tell them that the negative should be handled like old, unstable smokeless powder.

Step 6: Duplicate Your Photos

Photographs are meant to be seen. Therefore, overcoming the handling issue is critical when you reach the display process in your photo collection project. The solution is to have quality copies made of pictures you want to display. Find a source that will carefully duplicate your valuable photos and then archive the originals; this allows you to enjoy and share the photographs on your wall or in an album on the coffee table without the risk of losing them. You might even duplicate your entire collection for each sibling or child, and help them understand how to care for the collection. Always keep negatives and originals separate from the prints made from them. Duplication and separation should be an important part of your preservation plan.

Placing your photos onto alternative, nonphotographic media is also a means of duplication/separation. Numerous photo stores transfer 8mm film or slides to video. This has the advantage of ease of reproduction; once it has been done you can make duplicates for all family members. It also has the advantage of moving your images one step further away from obsolete viewing hardware. Finding working 8mm projectors and slide projectors has already become difficult and will become even more so as those formats become less and less common. Digital duplication is a possibility that will continue to develop and become easier and cheaper each year. It is discussed in more detail in the section of this chapter on digital photography and media.

RESTORING OLD AND DAMAGED PHOTOGRAPHS

Unfortunately, the family members from whom you have inherited your photos probably have not followed all the preceding steps. All too often photos are dirty, water damaged, bent, or faded. All, however, can be restored to some degree, and many to their original quality. Restoration really consists of two concepts: (1) repairing and restoring the actual photograph and (2) re-creating the image to restore its original quality. Each of these, even simply cleaning an old photo, is a fine art as well as a science.

Until recently, re-creating an image involved photographically reproducing,

This turn-of-the-century photo illustrates the benefits of photo manipulation. This process can significantly enhance the appearance of your older photos.

sometimes even redeveloping, the damaged photo, manually removing the damaged portion, and using ink and airbrush to fill in what should be there. Such cleaning and direct repair, of course, are physically intrusive. It means removing part of what is on the photo permanently. In short, image cleaning, restoration, and photographic re-creation are to be done by carefully chosen professionals who will also care for the original. Ask for recommendations from reliable photo shops and studios, research books on photo restoration; don't hesitate to carefully interview a restorer to whom you will send work.

Recently, digital imaging has dramatically changed the process of photo re-creation. Software can now do much that was once manual, mechanical, or photochemical.

Step 7: Get the Image in Digital Format

As Alison tried to think of what she could get her brothers and sisters for Christmas, she thought of all the Christmases they had shared and the memories they had in common. It struck her that there were also many Christmases that the whole family had not been able to share after they had left home to start their own families and traditions. She decided to create the ultimate photo album of Christmas memories and asked her parents, each brother and sister, and their children to send copies of their favorite Christmas photos. They cooperated beyond her wildest dreams, and she soon had hundreds of photos, black-and-white as well as color, all shapes and sizes, slides, even some digital photos sent over the Internet.

Alison soon felt she had bitten off more than she could chew. Getting copies made of all these photos and arranging them in albums for six families was a lot of work. She had an epiphany while preparing a presentation for her boss at work. He had Alison scan a photo to place on one of the presentation slides. Why not do that with all the family photos she had received? The photos scanned easily enough. Learning to scan the slides was a bit trickier, but the digital photos fit right in. The presentation software allowed her to add graphics, text, music, and spoken words, so she could label and narrate each picture to a background of Christmas music. She "burned" a copy of the whole presentation and the viewer for it onto a CD-ROM, not only for each sibling but for each niece and nephew as well. The whole thing was a lot faster than trying to put all those pictures into albums and was also a lot cheaper since she didn't have to pay to get copies made. The calls of thanks Alison received from families gathered around their computers on Christmas Day made all the effort worthwhile.

File Format Options

Format defines the way information making up the image is stored, how much information is stored, and how that information relates to the software required to display or print the image. There are many image file formats used in digital imaging, each having advantages and disadvantages. Deciding on the one you will use determines how you will have to use and display you images in the future. File size (the amount of storage space the file will take on whatever media you store it on) is a result of format and resolution. Both jpeg (.jpg) and tiff (.tif) formats have become standard, and many software applications recognize and work with them. Because a full-color, high-resolution tiff image is a very large file, it is a good format for archiving or preparing for printing but not for distributing images, especially over the Internet. You will want to store tiff images on large-volume media such as CD-ROMs, DVDs, or Zip disks. Most photo software allows easy conversion from tiff to other formats. Jpeg is a good sharing format; the files are not as large as tiff files, but the image quality remains good. In short, archive in tiff, but share and display in jpeg.

With the increased use and decreasing cost of the computer and other digital devices, it is an under-statement to say that digital photography and imaging has exploded into everyday life. Like it or not—and there are many great reasons to like it—understanding digital photography and using digital imaging will be an important part of your family photo collection.

Because digital imaging is developing so quickly, and the possibilities are so extensive, what follows must be general and simple, but should provide a starting point.

As Alison's story illustrates, computer technology and the peripherals available—cameras, scanners, printers—have added a new dimension to visual collections, with new possibilities for creating, manipulating, presenting, and storing images. You don't need a darkroom to create digital images; each image can be reproduced exactly, an infinite numbers of times, and at almost no cost; photos can be shared by e-mail or over the Internet anywhere in the world almost instantaneously; software can sometimes be used to "repair" photos without the services of a professional restorer; and digital images can be manipulated to emphasize a portion of the image, a color, or even to put something in, leave something out, or to correct mistakes in exposure or color balance in the original.

Pixels and Resolution

A pixel is any individual dot in an image that makes up colors, brightness, and other qualities. Resolution is the number of pixels in a space (per square inch). The quality of an image is in great part determined by its resolution. To print high-quality images, make sure your resolution is at least 300 dpi (dots per inch). Images placed on the Internet are usually 72 dpi.

Color in Photographs

The color quality of a digital image depends on the quantity of information that is stored about each pixel and the ability of the display mechanism to reproduce those colors. In early color computing, only sixteen color possibilities were stored. A pixel was defined as one of those sixteen colors, or, if more color information was stored, displayed in the color closest to that stored. Most modern devices are able to store "real" color, and that is a consideration as you chose how you will capture and display digital images in your visual family history.

Before you can use a digital image in your family photo collection, you need to "capture" that image. This can be done the traditional way by taking a picture of something with a digital camera. Digital camera imaging is used much like traditional photography, but it has the advantages of instant availability, ease of editing and manipulation, and ease of copying and sharing. Possible disadvantages are image quality for printing and the need to have a computer or television with appropriate software available to view the image. In considering whether and when to acquire and use a digital camera, you will need to learn about resolution (which defines the quality, sharpness, and realism of the picture) and file format (the way the image is stored and recalled by software).

To digitally capture an existing photo you'll need access to a scanner. Most print photo work can be done with a flatbed scanner. Cased images may need special attention because they are sensitive to the direction from which the light that the scanner uses comes. Experimenting should lead you to a good result.

There are also projection scanners or adapters that are specially designed for use with slides or negatives. If you are going to image large numbers of slides or negatives, one of these special scanners may be what you need.

A third and increasingly common capture device is a video capture board. This device creates a digital file, still or in video, from a standard video camera or VCR. If you have used video as part of your family photography, or converted your films or slides to video, this method allows you to bring those sources into a digital format. Video is also a way to capture three-dimensional objects such as the covers of photo albums, frames and other items that won't scan well.

Another digital capture possibility that is increasingly popular is to have your photos captured digitally when your film is developed. Images are usually supplied by CD-ROM or made available to a private Internet location. Be sure that the format supplied by your processor is compatible with your software and equipment. Some processors use a proprietary format that requires you to send the digital images to them if you want a high-quality print made, locking you in as customer.

A laptop and scanner or other method of digital imaging allows you to collect and share photos almost anywhere with quality that could otherwise be had only by sending precious photos to an expensive reproduction service.

Scanning Photographs

When scanning photos, especially for archiving, remember to preserve the context as well as the image. Scan the whole thing, including the card stock and paper frame (if there is one). If there is writing or marking on the back, such as the studio marking, scan the back as well. If you have albums with text and description around the pictures, try scanning entire pages, as well as each image.

PHOTO MANIPULATION

Another great feature of digital imaging is easy editing and manipulation. Most input devices (scanners, cameras, capture cards, and even commercial photo CD-ROMs) come with some manipulation software that allows you to crop images, label with text, and adjust or correct color, hue, and brightness. More sophisticated programs include tools that allow a person with basic computer skills and a willingness to learn to do significant image restoration such as scratch and bend elimination, exact color correction, spot removal, and most of the repairs formerly done by artistic restorers. There are now professional digital restorers, as well, to whom images can be sent in a digital format while the original is kept safe.

*Digital images can be easily
manipulated with the help
of computer software such
as Adobe Photoshop,
Microsoft Picture It!, or
Corel Photo-Paint.*

Manipulation can also be done for effect or fun. You can create multigeneration photos, combining pictures of people who lived many years or great distances apart and could
never have been photographed together, or make collages of family members without
tedious cutting and pasting. For the future family historian, this presents the quandary of
knowing that what they see in a family photo may not be "real." Be fair and include a good
fact sheet with your digital files.

Step 8: Share Your Photo Collection

One of the great advantages of digital images is the wide variety of possibilities you will have for presentation and sharing. Prints can be made on readily available, low-cost printers. You can choose the print size, crop the photo, and, with proper software, even convert and print negatives as positives.

Because a digital image can be reproduced exactly, without any loss of quality and at very low cost, it can easily be shared with all members of you family. Even large-format files can be passed along on Zip disks, CD-ROMs, or DVDs. Of course, you will need to be sure that the recipient has software that can read the format you send. One way of heading off this possible problem is using presentation software that uses a "viewer," a piece of software that you can send along which will allow the user to view the images on their computer so long as the operating system is compatible. Viewers do not, however, allow the recipient to download and manipulate the image.

One of the most popular ways to share and present images is via the Internet. You will need to decide whether to use a public site, one that can be reached by anyone on the Internet, or a private site that can only be accessed by those to whom you grant password access.

PRESERVING PHOTOS
USING CD-ROM AND DVD

Digital imaging may also be the ultimate solution to preservation and archiving. It certainly helps with the duplication and separation issue. All of the photos you are likely to own can be imaged in a high-quality format and stored on a few CD-ROMs and even fewer DVDs. You can create and keep your written forms about each image in pure electronic format. In fact, the written form can be recreated in a word processing software like Microsoft Word and the electronic image can often be dropped right onto the form in a resolution and size you chose. These forms can then be saved or reproduced in both electronic and/or hard copy and easily shared.

There are potential drawbacks with digital preservation and archiving. For starters, digital media are relatively new and no one knows how long they will last. Metal and paper photographs have lasted more than a hundred years, and some paper objects have lasted more than two thousand years. CD-ROMs and DVDs are plastic and can be scratched. Over long periods they may lose their surface properties, which may affect a drive's ability to read them. Magnetic media can be affected by magnetic fields.

Perhaps as big a problem as durability is hardware and software obsolescence. If you have had a computer with a 5¼-inch floppy drive or own a Bernoulli drive, you will understand this problem all too well. As hardware advances, media is left behind. The floppy has been replaced by the CD-ROM, which is being replaced by DVD, which will likely be replaced soon with something else. Also, software formats will change. Proprietary formats disappear as companies go out of business or find better technological solutions. Even common formats succumb to technological improvements.

Does this mean that digitization should not be an important part of your archiving? Not at all. The pros certainly outweigh the cons, and many of the cons can be overcome. Using common formats will protect your files from format obsolescence for some time. Duplicate storage on both magnetic and optical media, for example CD-ROM and Zip disks, can provide some protection against media obsolescence and media deterioration.

	File name	Name			
	0142 Name: Vedell Birthdate 12/1/1915 Photo year 1940 Photo source Violet Gold "Vedell" car, leaning		Lenard		Hatch
	0143 Name: Deverl Birthdate 5/12/1918 Photo year 1940 Photo source Violet Gold "Deverl" tent, standing, cars		Herrick		Hatch
	0144 Name: Thelma Birthdate 3/24/1920 Photo year 1935 Photo source Violet Gold "Thelma" portrait, child		Mary	Hatch	Tanner
	0145 Name: Sisson Birthdate 3/2/1879 Photo year 1940 Photo source Violet Gold "Sisson, Rose" standing, brick home		Jacob		Hatch
	0146 Name: Vedell Birthdate 12/1/1915 Photo year 1940 Photo source Violet Gold "Vedell" Army uniform, portrait		Lenard		Hatch
	0147 Name: Vedell Birthdate 12/1/1915 Photo year 1940 Photo source Violet Gold "Vedell" Army uniform, standing		Lenard		Hatch
	0148 Name: Violet Birthdate 12/2/1908 Photo year 1945 Photo source Violet Gold "Ella Vee, Vilda, Thelma, Violet" group, standing, white dresses, yard		Jane	Hatch	Gold

This photographic archive is searchable by name, date, etc. The database can be archived on CD-ROM for easy access.

Archiving Nonphotographic Documents

Photographic preservation applies as well to nonphotographic documents. The "duplicate and separate" rule applies particularly to documents that are originally on non-archival paper. Old-method photocopies (those that are probably already yellowing), "blue print" and "negative" copies, and mimeographs are particularly sensitive. These should be carefully reproduced and archived separately so their chemical deterioration won't affect other items.

Media deterioration can also be avoided by reduplication on a regular basis and upgrading to the best media available at the time. The Library of Congress is spending millions of dollars to study and resolve the media and format obsolescence issue. When they find the solution, implement it. In the meantime, using both paper archives and duplicate digital archives is the best solution. One more archival issue: digital printers use inks that are also relatively untried. While their manufacturers are confident that they will store well for at least twenty-five years, you may want to get a photographic print made of digital originals.

Digitization has had more impact on photography and imaging than anything since the Brownie camera with roll film. Take advantage, keep up as the change rolls on, and enjoy. Using digital imagining in your family history is limited only by your imagination, and you will have a hard time keeping your imagination up with the technological advances that are to come.

Now, the project is up to you. You need to determine the scope of your collection, the best sources for photographs, and the storage and preservation techniques you will use. However you go about doing it, the benefits of a photo collection outweigh the work involved. And in the end, you'll have a visual record of your family that extends well beyond the written word.

There's something about putting a name with a face —
and then reading a story or experience —
that makes family history come alive.

CHAPTER THREE

Creating a Visual Legacy
Your Heritage Scrapbook

Kimber felt very important. He was going to the store with his big sister, Ethelynne, and after much pleading and coaxing, she had allowed him to carry the grocery money—a shiny silver dollar. Kimber's chubby three-year-old fist clenched tightly around the money as the two made their way to the store.

The walk to the store didn't take long, but it felt like a lifetime to a three-year-old. Kimber's mind wandered and his grip loosened. When he and Ethelynne arrived at the store, Kimber realized that somewhere along the way, he'd dropped the precious dollar. He broke into sobs as he confessed to Ethelynne what had happened.

Eleven-year-old Ethelynne hugged her sobbing brother. "Don't cry," she said. "We'll find the money." Then she tenderly picked up her brother, carrying him on her back as the two slowly and carefully retraced their steps.

"We looked for that dollar for quite a while," Kimber recalls. "And she carried me the whole time. We never did find the money, but she didn't get angry. And back then (in the early 1940s), a dollar was an awful lot of money."

Only a year later, Ethelynne died from complications associated with diabetes. Kimber's memories of his big sister were few, but this experience remained vivid in his mind. He sometimes shared it with his own children as they looked through old family photo albums and asked about the aunt they had never known.

Recently Kimber's daughter borrowed a photo of both Ethelynne and Kimber from one of those old albums. She enlarged the photos and copied them, then typed up the story of the lost silver dollar and Ethelynne's patience with her little brother. She artfully arranged the photo and the memories on a beautiful scrapbook page and added it to her family scrapbook so her own children would come to know and love Ethelynne as she had.

For decades, people have taken photographs and faithfully stored them in photo albums. While these albums are truly family treasures, more often than not their contents can be more puzzling than enriching. Picture after picture is pasted to a page, but typically there is little else. Sometimes a name is scrawled on the back of a photo or in the narrow white border. And if you're extremely lucky, an occasional date might be included as well. But the details, the tidbits of information that make history and our ancestors come alive, are all but forgotten.

"One of my favorite examples of the lack of information with these old family photographs was an old black and white photo that someone showed me," notes Anita Hallman, author of *Self-Preservation: A Complete Guide to Keeping Your Memories Alive* and an expert in the preservation of treasured family heirlooms such as photographs. "On the back of the photo the caption simply reads, 'Me, last year.' The person who now has the photo has no idea who is in the photo or when it was taken. And that kind of lack of crucial information is typical of many of these treasured family photos."

However, recent trends have started to drastically change all that. In the last decade, scrapbooking has exploded into a $500 million industry, with tens of thousands of avid scrapbookers around the world enthusiastically preserving photos for generations to come. And the difference between these scrapbooks and the photo albums of the past is that today's scrapbookers recognize the importance of including what they call "journaling"— the who, what, where, when, why, and how behind the photos—thus creating a legacy much deeper and richer than simple pictures on a page.

Without a doubt, scrapbooking has become a form of family history that appeals to all ages and connects generations past, present, and future like few things ever have before. Putting a name with a face—and then reading a story, experience, or memory about that face—makes family history live and creates a feeling of belonging.

Remembering Ethelynne

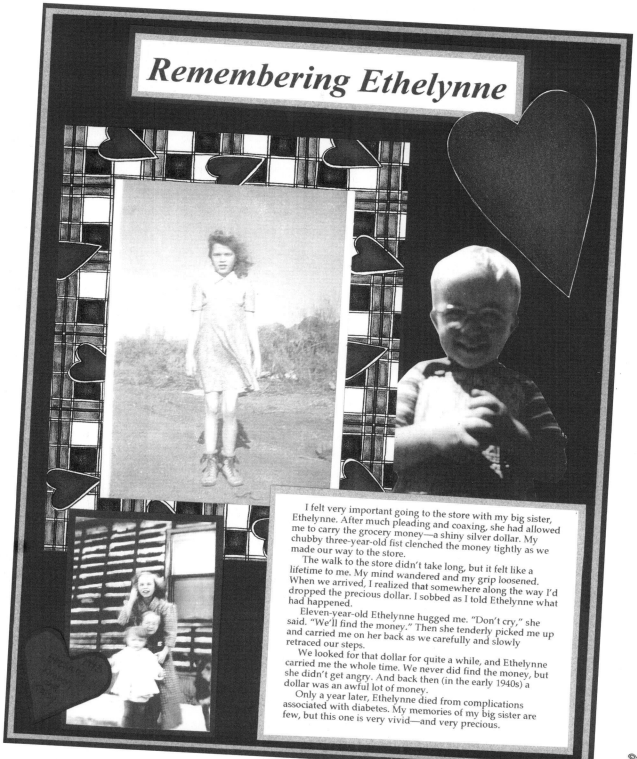

I felt very important going to the store with my big sister, Ethelynne. After much pleading and coaxing, she had allowed me to carry the grocery money—a shiny silver dollar. My chubby three-year-old fist clenched the money tightly as we made our way to the store.

The walk to the store didn't take long, but it felt like a lifetime to me. My mind wandered and my grip loosened. When we arrived, I realized that somewhere along the way I'd dropped the precious dollar. I sobbed as I told Ethelynne what had happened.

Eleven-year-old Ethelynne hugged me. "Don't cry," she said. "We'll find the money." Then she tenderly picked me up and carried me on her back as we carefully and slowly retraced our steps.

We looked for that dollar for quite a while, and Ethelynne carried me the whole time. We never did find the money, but she didn't get angry. And back then (in the early 1940s) a dollar was an awful lot of money.

Only a year later, Ethelynne died from complications associated with diabetes. My memories of my big sister are few, but this one is very vivid—and very precious.

The Basics of Scrapbooking

Debbie hung up the phone in tears. How could her dear friend Sandra possibly have cancer? It seemed impossible. Sandra was so young, and she seemed so healthy. She was the mother of three little children, aged seven months to six years old. What were those children going to do without their mother?

Over the next several months, Debbie struggled to help Sandra in any way she could. Over and over she asked her friend if there was anything she could do. She babysat the kids and helped with housework, but mostly she watched helplessly as her dear friend underwent chemotherapy and radiation, lost her hair, her energy, and finally, with the discovery of new cancer sites scattered throughout her body, her hope.

Although Sandra's attitude remained courageous, she realistically faced the fact that she was dying, and with that knowledge, she picked up the phone and called Debbie.

"Deb," she began, "you've asked several times if there was anything you could do to help me. I've never really been able to think of anything, but now I have. I want my children to remember me," Sandra whispered. "I want them to know what I looked like, to remember things we did together, to feel my love for them. I've been saving piles and piles of photos through the years, and I've been meaning to put them together, but I never took the time. Now I don't have the time. Can you help?"

Debbie was an avid scrapbooker; she knew exactly what to do. She shared the story with a few scrapbooking friends, and word spread quickly. She stopped by Sandra's home, picked up shoeboxes stuffed full of pictures and other treasured keepsakes, and left Sandra with promises that before long, her children would have tangible memories of their mother that they could hold in their hands.

Over a period of several weeks, Debbie and her scrapbooking pals gathered to work. A

local scrapbook store donated the supplies; the scrapbookers donated their time. Hundreds of photos were cropped, mounted, matted, and preserved. The scrapbookers left space on every page for Sandra to record important memories, thoughts, and feelings. Before she died, Sandra had three scrapbooks (one for each child). She spent the last few days of her life leafing through them and remembering all the good times, as her children hopefully would for many years to come.

Scrapbooks like the ones Debbie and her friends made for Sandra are absolutely irreplaceable, creating a rich legacy and history that links past generations to present and future ones. Legacy scrapbooking combines visual images with treasured keepsakes, memorabilia, and invaluable journaling, which together paint a vivid picture of your family and its history.

Photographs for Scrapbooks

Obviously, most of the visual images in a scrapbook will be photographs. Experts say that every year an estimated fourteen billion photos are taken. At least some of those photos end up in scrapbooks where they become stories to be enjoyed and treasured for generations to come.

Most photos today are resin coated, meaning that the back of the photo is shiny and smooth. Older photos, including those shot before the 1960s, are typically fiber-based. The backs of these photos look and feel just like a regular piece of paper. It's important to be able to tell the difference because you use different methods for placing these two types of photos in legacy scrapbooks.

Since resin-coated photos have slick, smooth backs, you can adhere them to your scrapbook pages with acid-free, archival-safe adhesives. Most scrapbookers agree that, for photos, you should use nonpermanent adhesive. (You can use permanent adhesives for other elements of your page if you desire.) Nonpermanent adhesives hold the photos securely to the page, yet allow you to remove them later if necessary. Fiber-based photos, or those with paper backing, are best placed in scrapbooks with corner mounts. Any kind of adhesive can tear the fragile backing of these photos and is simply not worth the risk. Knowing how to identify the type of photos you're working with and using the correct adhesives to attach them to scrapbook pages ensures that they will be preserved in pristine condition, even if they need to be removed.

Another thing to remember is that you should never write on a photo. If you must, write it on the back. Once again, being able to identify whether the photo is resin coated or fiber based comes in handy. Always use pencils to write on the back of fiber-based photos. On the other hand, the slick surface of a resin-coated photo mandates that you use a pen; pencils won't leave a mark. Be sure to use an acid-free, photo-marking pen, though. Other types of pens can leak through to the picture side of the photo.

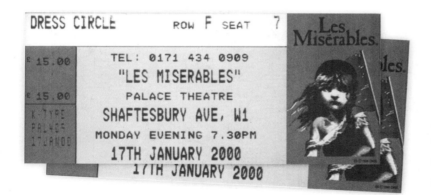

Memorabilia for Scrapbooks

Some of the most interesting elements of family history scrapbooks are the bits of memorabilia that so often get tucked away and lost in drawers, cupboards, or files. These items, whether they're newspaper clippings, tickets, programs, certificates, reports, letters, or cards, add invaluable insight and information about memorable events, yet if they're not preserved and stored in an accessible manner, that information can be lost forever.

A favorite family photo or treasured family keepsake can become meaningless if it's not identified. Suppose years from now a son or daughter stumbles across a wrinkled and torn *Les Miserables* program with two tickets slipped inside. It may be absolutely unimaginable to think that they wouldn't know that *Les Miserables* was one of the most popular shows of the

McKenna: The Perfect Medicine

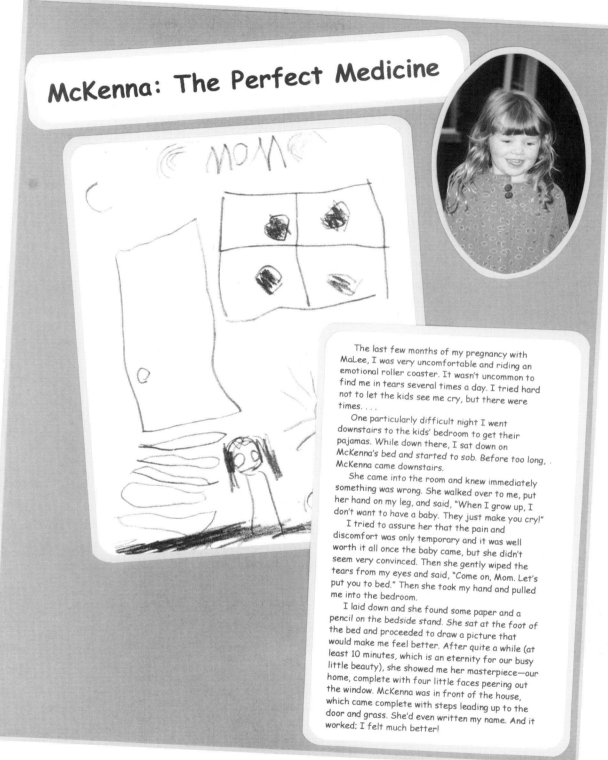

The last few months of my pregnancy with MaLee, I was very uncomfortable and riding an emotional roller coaster. It wasn't uncommon to find me in tears several times a day. I tried hard not to let the kids see me cry, but there were times. . . .

One particularly difficult night I went downstairs to the kids' bedroom to get their pajamas. While down there, I sat down on McKenna's bed and started to sob. Before too long, McKenna came downstairs.

She came into the room and knew immediately something was wrong. She walked over to me, put her hand on my leg, and said, "When I grow up, I don't want to have a baby. They just make you cry!"

I tried to assure her that the pain and discomfort was only temporary and it was well worth it all once the baby came, but she didn't seem very convinced. Then she gently wiped the tears from my eyes and said, "Come on, Mom. Let's put you to bed." Then she took my hand and pulled me into the bedroom.

I laid down and she found some paper and a pencil on the bedside stand. She sat at the foot of the bed and proceeded to draw a picture that would make me feel better. After quite a while (at least 10 minutes, which is an eternity for our busy little beauty), she showed me her masterpiece—our home, complete with four little faces peering out the window. McKenna was in front of the house, which came complete with steps leading up to the door and grass. She'd even written my name. And it worked; I felt much better!

Journaling can turn a simple photo and a child's artwork into an especially precious family keepsake. This child's drawing takes on much more meaning when you read the story behind it.

period, or that attending the production in a London theater was one of the most exciting experiences of your lifetime. Keep in mind, however, that much can happen in even a few years. Your treasured *Les Mis* ticket will be little more than a ticket if it isn't preserved, complete with dates and details about your West End experience that will make it come alive again (e.g., Did you take a cab or the Underground to the theater? Did you buy refreshments and how much did they cost? Did you wait around afterwards to get autographs from some of the performers? How long did the production last?). And of course, a photograph of you in a formal gown purchased just for the occasion would make the memory complete.

Memorabilia can present a few tricky challenges when assembling your legacy scrapbooks. One of the most important things to keep in mind when working on scrapbooks is that you want them to last a long time, and in order to ensure this, you must work with archival-safe, acid-free products. Most memorabilia does not meet those requirements. Acid and other chemicals in materials can cause deterioration. While most photos are acid-free, you must take great care to ensure that the materials you place with your photos are equally safe. You've all seen newspaper clippings that have started to curl and turn yellow, sometimes in only a matter of days. If you put newspapers in your scrapbooks, the chemicals will affect the photos, and they, too, will begin to fade. Programs, tickets, artwork, letters or notes, and certificates can be just as damaging.

Luckily, there are many options available so you can still include these materials in your scrapbooks without endangering your photographs. One of the simplest methods is to treat any item that may not be acid-free or archival safe with a deacidification spray, such as Archival Mist, Weit'o, or Bookkeeper Spray. This simple step neutralizes the acid and other chemicals contained in paper and prevents the yellowing and brittling process. Once you've done this, your materials are safe to include in your scrapbooks.

Many people opt to make color photocopies of materials they want to include in their scrapbooks. This allows them to store the old or priceless items somewhere safe, while still making the information and images available for family history.

Another challenge associated with including certain memorabilia in your scrapbooks is displaying the various items. Many of these pieces have important information on both sides, so the last thing you want to do is attach them to a page where you can only see the front. Other things, such as letters, cards, and programs, beg to be read and handled but adhering them to pages makes that an impossibility. Finally, some items are simply too heavy or too big to fit on a normal piece of card-stock. For the quick and easy solution, tuck these materials straight into a page protector. All your scrapbook audience has to do is reach in the protector to access these keepsakes.

Probably the most popular method of storing this type of material, however, is pocket pages. Depending on the size of the items you want to include in your scrapbook, you can create a pocket page on your layout that will hold just about anything. These pages can be made with card stock, vellum, or patterned paper. Some manufacturers even offer premade pocket pages in a variety of sizes. Utilizing pocket pages allows you to include journaling and photos that complement and explain the memorabilia, while at the same time permitting it to be removed, examined, read, and enjoyed.

Ideas for Creative Journaling

- Don't remember the event? Write about what you do remember, such as the clothes the people were wearing, their hairstyles, what life was like when the photo was taken, any information you recall as you look at the photo.
- Journal your hopes and dreams.
- Share your feelings about the person(s) featured in the layout.
- Journal in steps or lists.
- Add letters from family, friends, etc.
- Tell a story about the person in the layout. The story doesn't necessarily have to do with the photo at all. Any memories or information is better than nothing at all.
- List height, weight, favorite toys, favorite foods, etc.
- No photos? Make a layout anyway that includes memorabilia and journaling of an event. Decorate the page with die cuts, stickers, and other elements that tie in with the event.
- Add family newsletters to your scrapbooks.
- Include your child's unique pronunciation (or mispronunciation) of words.
- Add other people's points of view, memories, observations, stories, etc.
- Add a favorite poem or rhyme.
- Let others who were at the event do the journaling.
- Include styles of the times, prices of items, trends, popular phrases, etc.
- List headline news from the times.

Journaling for Scrapbooks

Have you ever been watching a movie when the sound suddenly stopped? It doesn't take long for the audience to get restless, and you can bet that the theater management is hustling to correct the problem. Once the problem is fixed, the movie is rewound to the point where the sound originally stopped. Simply seeing the pictures is not enough; we know that

The Five W's of Journaling

Journaling consists of five main components:

Who?
Knowing who the subjects in the photos are is crucial. Be sure to mention the key players in the photos, as well as other family and friends shown.

When?
Always list the date in layouts, even if it is small and in the corner of the page.

Where, What, and Why?
To help decide the important details to include on the page, ask yourself these questions:

- Where was this photo taken?

- What was happening? What is important for people to know about this photo?

- Why did I take this picture? Why do I want it included in my scrapbook?

we missed critical information provided through the dialogue.

Journaling provides the "sound" in our scrapbooks, the essential component that transforms simple photos into true family history. Looking at photos and memorabilia can be great, but the experience is vastly enhanced when those items are accompanied with information about who is in the shots; what is happening in them; and when, where, and why the photos were taken.

How many times have you looked through photo albums that belong to your parents or grandparents and been filled with questions about what was happening in the pictures or whom you were looking at? There's your father, looking all dashing and debonair in a black tux, and he's standing next to a woman who you're pretty sure isn't your mother. Of course, you're glad he ended up with Mom, but it might be nice to know who this high school friend was. And what about that old black-and-white ancient-looking photo that shows your grandfather as a young child, decked out in a muslin, floor-length dress and sporting shoulder-length golden ringlets. You're dying to know how old Grandpa is. He looks like he's at least four or five. Does he remember the photo? Was the dress and hair stylish for the day, or did your great-grandmother simply love to dress her little boy up as a little girl? He's with three other children about the same age, and since he was an only child, you're also curious about who those other children are. Cousins, neighbors, friends?

Journaling is important because it answers questions, provides information, fills holes, and makes photos come alive. Scrapbooking is a fun way to preserve history and to keep a diary of sorts. But history is not preserved with just a picture; the explanatory information that goes along with the photo is essential. Every page should at least identify the who, when, and what behind the photos included. This is essential information that will prove absolutely priceless to your future descendants.

DEFINING THE ELEMENTS

Many scrapbookers don't journal because they either don't understand the importance of journaling or because it seems too complicated. Basically, journaling consists of five main components: who, when, where, what, and why.

The Adams Family Pumpkin Patch

Recording your scrapbook journaling in your own handwriting adds a personal touch to the page. Years from now, your descendants will treasure your handwriting, even though it might not be perfect.

Who? This one seems pretty basic, but there are more scrapbook pages out there lacking this information than you would imagine. Certainly identifying the people in your photos is essential. One point worth noting, however, is that scrapbookers sometimes mention the main players (or family members) in their photos, but they don't always identify other people in photos. If you've got shots of your kids playing in the backyard with their neighborhood friends, don't forget to mention the names of those friends. In twenty years, chances are good neither you nor your children will remember the names, so it's good to write that information down now. And the flood of memories that your child may have when she reads about her childhood friend is worth the few seconds it takes to include that pertinent "who" information.

When? This is another seemingly obvious part of journaling. And this is probably one of the easiest bits of information to include on your pages. If nothing else, simply write the date unobtrusively in the corner of your layout. Of course this information will ideally be contained in more detailed journaling, but make a commitment right now to never do another page without at least including the date somewhere on the page.

The Ideal Scrapbook

The ideal family history or legacy scrapbook is one that people can get to easily and browse through at their leisure. Anita Hallman, author of *Self-Preservation: A Complete Guide to Keeping Your Memories Alive*, offers the following criteria for the perfect scrapbook:

Durable enough for anyone to look at. When your scrapbooks are too fragile for people to handle, they aren't serving their purpose. You want scrapbooks that are sturdy and that can be taken out and looked at over and over.

Versatile and reversible. Ensure that your photos can be removed if necessary, and that cards, programs, letters, etc., can be taken out so both sides can be looked at.

Expandable. Being able to add to your scrapbook easily and inexpensively is important. Avoid purchasing binders or materials that are not available from different sources; this could prevent you from adding to your scrapbook if you need to.

Reasonably priced. Once you begin scrapbooking, it will most likely become a lifetime pursuit. While you may choose to purchase one or two special albums for special occasions, you'll want to make sure that most of the material you work with is affordable.

Attractive and fun. You'll want your scrapbook to be visually appealing, colorful, and enjoyable to look at.

Archival quality. Ideally, you want your scrapbook to last at least one hundred years. If you're going to put the time and effort into creating a family history scrapbook, you want to make sure that it's around for generations to enjoy. Make sure that the materials and tools you use are acid-free and archival-safe.

Where, What, and Why? This is most likely the point where journaling starts to overwhelm people. The more people feel like they have to record, the more inadequate they feel.

As you venture into the why, what, and where of journaling, relax. It's not nearly as complicated as it may seem. Simply ask yourself these three questions: Where was this photo taken? What was happening? Why did I take it?

Maybe you want to start with short, two- or three-word statements. You don't need to compose a Pulitzer prize–winning novel or even the world's cleverest short story. You don't even need complete sentences.

Disneyland.
Our first vacation in seven years.
Well worth the wait.

Or maybe:
Backyard Harvest.
Our first attempt to grow our own pumpkins. Check out the results.

Even those few words communicate a world of meaning and memories. Twenty years from now, your kids may remember that trip to California, but they may have no idea at all that it was the family's first vacation in seven years. That little tidbit of information makes that trip and that memory all the more precious.

Most scrapbookers rely heavily on computer journaling in their family history albums. Typing your journaling is quick and easy, especially when you're recording lengthy stories or memories. In addition, there are a myriad of fonts available, so the typeface you use actually becomes an element of your layout. Be certain to print your journaling on acid-free paper; don't just use the regular paper found in most printers and assume it is safe.

While computer journaling is quick and easy, think about occasionally handwriting your journaling—especially if you're trying to create a family history scrapbook. Your children and grandchildren will treasure your handwriting, even if it is sloppy.

"My grandmother died when I was six months old," notes Angie Randall, editor-in-chief of *PaperKuts*® scrapbook magazine. "I never knew her personally, but my mother adored her and talks of her with such a deep respect and love that one of my deepest regrets in life is not having known her.

"However, this particular grandmother kept a diary. It wasn't a long diary, and most of her entries actually summarized the weather and the daily activities she was involved in.

But these short, even boring entries have given me great insight into my grandmother's life. As I've read her journals I've somehow felt closer to her. Through those pages, which are now decades old, I've been able to get to know her and find out about her life and the way she lived and what she thought.

"Our scrapbooks will accomplish the same thing—if we include journaling on our pages. A few short words, or in some instances longer, lengthier stories or explanations, provide the window into the past that our children and grandchildren need to get to know us better. The importance of journaling in your scrapbooks can't be emphasized enough."

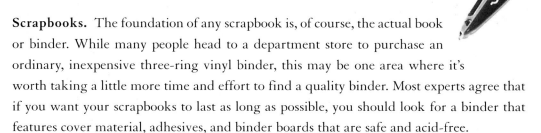

Basic Tools of the Trade

Basic Tools of the Trade:
- Scrapbooks
- Page protectors
- Scissors or trimmers
- Pens
- Adhesives

Tools of the Trade

While legacy scrapbooks are priceless, the scrapbooks themselves, and the materials you need to create them, don't have to cost a lot. In fact, you only need a few basic tools of the trade to put together stunning scrapbooks.

All of these items can be found in just about any craft or scrapbooking store; there are numerous Internet sites that sell a huge variety of scrapbooking items as well.

Scrapbooks. The foundation of any scrapbook is, of course, the actual book or binder. While many people head to a department store to purchase an ordinary, inexpensive three-ring vinyl binder, this may be one area where it's worth taking a little more time and effort to find a quality binder. Most experts agree that if you want your scrapbooks to last as long as possible, you should look for a binder that features cover material, adhesives, and binder boards that are safe and acid-free.

There are two standard sizes of scrapbook binders: 8½" x 11" or 12" x 12". You can purchase three-ring binders in either of these two sizes, or you can opt for binders that use extensions instead of rings. These are also available in both sizes.

Card Stock. After you've chosen your binder, your next basic tool will be paper. You'll be mounting your photos, journaling, memorabilia, and other elements on this paper. Regular paper is too flimsy to support the weight of photos; a heavier-weight paper, or card stock, is the safest way to go.

Only a few years ago, most scrapbook card stock was simply white or black. But in the last few years, there's been an explosion of paper choices. You can find solid-colored card stock in almost every hue of the rainbow, and there are hundreds of pattern papers available as well.

You'll probably want to begin with a basic collection of card stock; just make sure that the paper you're choosing is acid-free. Select a few sheets of primary colors, and add a few more sheets in other colors that appeal to you. You'll want to pick background paper that matches or complements colors found in your photos, so stick to common, ordinary colors. After all, even though your favorite color is fuschia, you probably don't have many photos that feature that color, so there's probably no need to stock up on fuschia card stock.

Add some white and black sheets of card stock as well; they coordinate with almost any photo and often provide the perfect background when no other color will work.

Page Protectors. To preserve your pages, it's essential that you place them in page protectors. Make sure your page protectors are made from polypropylene, polyethylene, or polyester. Avoid any products made with PVC, or polyvinyl chloride, a chemical that may actually harm your pages.

Using page protectors provides a wide array of protection. Page protectors prevent photos from touching each other when they are stored face to face in a binder. And what three-year-old can resist touching the picture of his favorite bedtime buddy or pointing out that "This baby is me when I was little." Page protectors make your pages reader-friendly, rendering oily, dirty fingerprints harmless. Page protectors also prevent pollutants and toxins in the air from reaching your photos.

Scissors and/or Trimmers. You will need to do a fair amount of cutting and cropping as you create your scrapbook pages. A high-quality pair of straight-edge scissors will do the trick. However, before you get too far into scrapbooking, you'll probably recognize the value of paper trimmers. Available in a several different sizes, this handy tool allows you to quickly and accurately cut or trim everything from small squares of cardstock to entire pages.

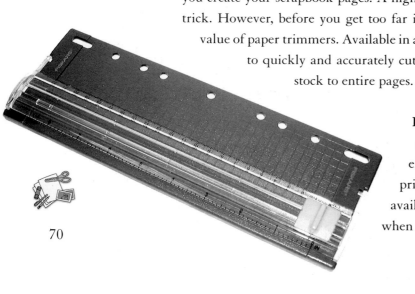

Pens. There are dozens of scrapbooking pens available, in a huge variety of colors and with several different tips. While some scrapbookers take pride in owning almost every scrapbooking pen available, there's really no need to load up, especially when you're just beginning. One black, acid-free pen

Norman Blair Hillam

Born in 1931, Uncle Blair was Mom's older brother. I never knew him; he died of aplastic anemia, a blood disease, in 1953. Every Memorial Day, however, we took flowers to his grave, so I certainly grew up knowing about him. If he was anything like the rest of Mom's family, he was certainly a wonderful man.

When information about an ancestor is scarce, a simple caption-only layout does the trick.

Decorative Options for Scrapbooks

Decorative scissors/cutters. Most scrapbooking experts discourage using decorative scissors on actual photos, but these scissors provide a quick and easy way to add variety to your mounting, borders, and other page elements.

Stickers. The variety of stickers is absolutely overwhelming; you can find a sticker for practically any occasion. In addition, a wide variety of alphabet stickers make it easy to create titles and journaling.

Punches. Many scrapbookers rely on punches to decorate their pages. With a little creativity and imagination, a basic collection of punches can yield an almost unlimited number of page embellishments.

Stamps. More and more scrapbookers are including stamping in their scrapbooks. Stamps create a whole new look and texture to pages.

Templates. Templates, or stencils, allow scrapbookers to use the same images in a wide variety of ways. Scrapbookers can also choose their own paper, which allows them to ensure that colors match and balance.

Die cuts and cut outs. A huge array of figures is available. Many scrapbookers combine these elements to create original page decorations.

Preprinted frames, page toppers, borders, etc. More and more companies are providing a variety of page elements—from frames to titles and borders to die cuts—designed to work together to create a well-coordinated page that can be assembled in minutes. Typically, these pieces are available separately, but when used together they create a visually appealing page that looks like it took much longer to create than it actually did.

enables you to do all the writing, recording, and journaling necessary to create family history scrapbooks. Of course, as your interest and expertise grows, you may want to expand your collection. Be sure that all your pens are acid-free, odorless, fade-resistant, waterproof, photo-safe, and permanent.

Adhesives. Adhesives come in a variety of forms, from glue sticks and glue "pens" to photo corners and double-sided tape. As with all your materials, what matters most is that the adhesives are acid-free and archival-safe.

Most scrapbookers own different adhesives for different purposes, often using non-permanent adhesives on photos and more permanent adhesive on other page elements such as journaling, titles, decorations, etc. As you experiment, you will no doubt decide what works best for you.

As you become more familiar with scrapbooking, you will quickly discover that these basic tools of the trade barely scratch the surface of what's available in the world of scrapbooking. While you need nothing else to create beautiful family history scrapbooks, few scrapbookers can resist the urge to try out a few other options.

Ready, Set, Go!

Kayla had literally thousands and thousands of photos. Since she'd received a camera for Christmas in junior high school, she'd always been an avid photographer. And after she got married and had children, her interest in taking pictures only intensified.

Unfortunately, she'd never established a system for organizing or preserving her pictures. In the beginning she tossed them into a few shoeboxes, and when that became inadequate, she began to pile them into larger boxes. When she desperately needed a photo, she could always find it, although sometimes it took hours. Kayla

knew that those precious memories weren't doing anyone any good on the floor of her closet, and she often wished her photographs were organized so her children and others, including herself, could look through them. But Kayla couldn't decide the best approach to getting the photos organized, and the task simply seemed too large of an undertaking. She'd toyed with the idea of scrapbooking, but she had never been "artsy-craftsy" (her interior designer sister called her "design disabled"), and she knew she could never create pages that competed with those she'd seen in her friends' albums. Consequently, she did nothing.

One day, however, one of Kayla's friends persuaded her to attend a "crop," an evening where scrapbookers got together and created pages for their scrapbooks. Although Kayla was intimidated, she agreed to go. She spent several hours pawing through her boxes of photos and came up with a handful from her daughter's recent second birthday. When she arrived at the crop, she put together what even she recognized as a ghastly few pages, combining pastel stickers with bold, primary-color backgrounds and a sparkly title that directly competed with her photos. Despite that, Kayla felt a small sense of pride in her pages. She took them home and showed them to her daughter, who carried them around for days, showing everyone over and over again the pictures from her party.

Kayla was hooked. She had actually enjoyed the process of creating the pages, and as she watched her daughter show them off, she knew her children needed that sense of family belonging that legacy scrapbooks could create. So she turned her attention to where to begin the mammoth task confronting her.

Kayla started by organizing her photos and memorabilia chronologically. First, she sorted everything into large time periods and placed them into boxes: pre-wedding, post-wedding without children, and then, because she took so many more pictures after her children arrived, she sorted the remaining photos into years.

Scrapbook and Photo Storage Tips

There are many elements that can damage or destroy your photos and scrapbooks. Consider each of these elements when you're selecting a storage area for these precious items.

Light. Light, especially ultraviolet rays from sunlight and fluorescent lighting, can be especially destructive because it is so prevalent. If you've ever placed a photograph on a wall or mantelpiece where sunlight hits every day, you've learned this lesson. The photo fades very quickly. It's essential to store your photos and scrapbooks in a dark place.

Heat. Consider the temperature where you're storing your treasured keepsakes. High temperatures cause chemical reactions that wreak havoc on paper. The Library of Congress recommends 68–70° F as the optimum temperature for paper storage. This is a fairly comfortable temperature, for most homes.

Humidity. Moisture can also be extremely destructive. Too much moisture can cause mold and mildew; not enough moisture can make paper brittle and dry. You may want to invest in humidifiers or silica gel packets to absorb excessive moisture. At the very least, ensure that your photos and scrapbooks are kept in a relatively consistent environment (i.e., avoid storing these items near air conditioning or heating vents or where they will receive direct sunlight).

Next, she went through each of the larger categories and sorted everything into smaller categories, this time placing them into file folders. She had file folders labeled "Junior High," "High School," and several different folders for college, including a favorite cross-country vacation with friends and her college graduation. Post-wedding folders included "Wedding," "Honeymoon," and various vacations, holidays, birthdays, and other memorable events. Finally, once she began organizing the photos that included her children, she found that it worked best to have a folder for every month of every year. Some months had a particularly large number of photos, so she created additional folders (e.g., "Decorating the Tree," "Christmas Eve," "Christmas Day," to divide up the photos even more).

Although it took her months to accomplish this enormous organizing project, Kayla knew every minute was worth it. She recognized that she had to begin somewhere and that putting it off would only make the task loom larger and larger.

While Kayla opted to organize her photos and memorabilia chronologically, there are other ways to begin. Some people choose to create "theme" scrapbooks. They organize materials into holidays, vacations, school, birthdays, etc., and then create scrapbooks with those themes. Other scrapbookers organize their materials according to child and then create a scrapbook for each child.

Identifying Page Elements. Once Kayla had everything organized in file folders, scrapbooking the items became much easier. Before going to the craft or scrapbooking store, Kayla selected the file to complete. She went through the items in the folder and decided what, if anything, she needed to purchase to complete the scrapbooking pages for that folder. She already had the basic scrapbooking tools on hand, so she often spent only pennies on paper and maybe a few page decorations. Since her focus was on the photos, she didn't dress up her pages much, although she always included journaling on her pages.

Gathering Journaling. Another step Kayla found valuable was recording tidbits of information about the items in the folders. She talked to family members in the photos, asking them what they remembered about the activity or event. (This was especially helpful when she worked on photos that were taken several years ago.) She showed the photos to her children and wrote down what they remembered as well, capturing their own words and expressions. She included statistics and facts where applicable; the pages recording her children's births include a copy of the hospital bill. Someday her children may be astounded that it cost so little (or so much!) to welcome them into the world.

Kayla found that when others look at her photos, they remember things she has completely forgotten. For instance, her mother remembered making the dress Kayla was

This picture of the Ho Nian LIN family was taken in 1958 in Taiwan. Clockwise, beginning from the upper left, family members are: Shin Yee, Tsung Heng, Hsin Long, Annie/Miou Chu *(LIN) *CHEN, Paul/Po Chung, Ho Nian, Ying Ming *(PAI) *LIN, and **Kathy/Ling Chu *(LIN) *YU.**

Kathy Ling Chu LIN and family

Only about a decade after these family portraits were taken, Kathy Lin and James Yu met, married, immigrated to the United States and raised their own family of five.

James Che Jen YU and family

Chinese New Years, 1963, Taoyuan, Taiwan: The YU children are wearing uniforms from their schools. The older children had already been accepted into the most elite schools in their area, based on high test scores.

L-R, back row: Jonathan/Yu Hung, **James/Che Jen**. L-R, front row: Huey Chen CHEN, Chin Yee *YU, Chih *(CHIU) *YU, Chen *MEI (father's mother), Jeff/Che Yung, and Steven/Shih Yen.

*last names are in capital letters and maiden names are in parenthesis

Scrapbook pages can easily be designed on a personal computer for ease of photo manipulation and editing.

When Kathy was growing up in Tainan, Taiwan, her father was often abroad, working as a doctor. When he brought her this doll from New York, it created quite a stir. Everyone wanted to see the doll with soft skin and blinking eyes. Kathy was an adult before this type of doll began appearing in the Taiwan markets.

1950s

James Che Jen YU and Kathy Ling Chu (LIN) YU were married August 14, 1974 in Taipei, Taiwan.

James began his education a year early because he wanted to attend school when his older brother began attending. Since his mother was his schoolteacher, he had the special privilege of riding his bicycle in this class picture.

1960s-70s

James and Kathy were in their late-teenage years when they met. They began dating in college, when they could see each other during summer vacations.

Kathy earned her degree at the College of Art, where this picture was taken on her graduation day. Her family has produced many talented artists ranging in skills from painting to sculpting to intricate crafts, all of which Kathy does well.

James earned a bachelor's degree in engineering right before he entered the Taiwan military, a mandatory duty. He is pictured here standing near his dorm unit in 1972. He later earned a master's in engineering in the United States.

wearing in one of her high school prom photos. Kayla had forgotten that, but when her mother, not an avid fan of sewing, mentioned it, the dress became an even more treasured memory than the dance, and Kayla added that to the journaling she included on that page.

Once she gathered all that information, Kayla created the journaling for her page. Like many scrapbookers, Kayla used both computer journaling and handwriting for the text. Although she didn't particularly like her handwriting, she understood the value it may have to later generations.

Assembling the Page. Once Kayla gathered all the photos, memorabilia, titles, journaling, and page embellishments together, she designed each page. This step only took a few minutes as she rearranged things a bit here and there to find a balance that appealed to her. She selected one photo as her focal point, and then arranged the rest of the page elements around that photo. With so many page decorations to choose from, it's extremely easy to overload a page. Avoid the temptation to make your page cluttered and busy. Usually, the simpler the page, the better.

When she assembled her pages, Kayla paid special attention to the way her eyes moved over the page. Generally speaking, a well-designed page will be balanced (Does one side seem heavier than the other?) and the eye will follow a natural, smooth flow from right to left, then down. She never adhered anything to the page until she made her final selection. It's much easier to make changes before anything has been pasted to the page. Kayla experimented with several different adhesives—all acid-free, of course. She tried glue sticks, double-sided tape, corner mounts, and glue pens. She now uses nonpermanent, double-sided tape on her photos and permanent glue on other page elements.

Storing and Preserving. Creating family history scrapbooks takes effort and time, and within the pages of your scrapbooks are absolutely priceless memories and mementos. When you don't make the effort to carefully store and preserve your scrapbooks, your time could be wasted and your memories lost forever.

Every finished page should be placed in a page protector to keep it safe from environmental toxins and pollutants, oily and dirty fingerprints, and other chemicals and acids that might otherwise destroy photos and family treasures. In addition, you should take great care to store your scrapbooks in a cool, dark, dry place. Of course, you want your scrapbooks to be accessible as well; many scrapbookers report that their children pull out their scrapbooks almost daily to browse through past memories and events. Look for a bookshelf in a dark corner, away from sunlight but in a room where your family often gathers, as your official scrapbook spot.

As you undertake the massive task of beginning your family scrapbooks, don't despair. Recognize that it will take time. After all, you're trying to preserve years and years of information. It only makes sense that the process will take a little time. Be patient with yourself, and break the project up into bite-size pieces.

Most scrapbookers begin family scrapbooking with the present and then work backward as they have time. They scrapbook current photos as they are developed. After all, it's much easier to include memorabilia, gather journaling, and record information when it's happening rather than trying to reconstruct it later. Approaching family history scrapbooking this way provides a sense of accomplishment and motivation. With current scrapbooks already put together, it's much easier to envision the possibilities as you work on piles from the past.

Creating Your Legacy Scrapbook

"Most people begin by scrapbooking their own pictures and their own history," notes Angie Randall. "But once they recognize the value of scrapbooks, it's almost impossible to stop at their own generation. The interest that has been sparked in their own history spreads to generations past, and they start working on their parents' history, and then their grandparents'. Scrapbooking is such an interesting and visual way to preserve family history that the need to continue backward as far as possible seems only natural."

Often the most precious family heirlooms we own are photos of our ancestors, some of whom are still living, but others who are no longer with us. These photos are best preserved—and best treasured—when they are placed in legacy scrapbooks. In scrapbooks, our ancestors' stories and faces can be easily reviewed and remembered by family members who actually knew them, as well as by later generations of people who can become familiar with them through a treasured scrapbook.

CLIMBING YOUR FAMILY TREE

Creating a legacy scrapbook is no different than putting together your own family history scrapbook—with one additional step. Begin the journey into your past by becoming familiar with your family tree. Already knowing the names of your ancestors and where they fit in the family simplifies things as you begin to sort through photos and gather information. After all, once you sit down with Great-grandma and start going through her old photos, you want to focus on what she remembers about those photos instead of trying to clarify who exactly Great-aunt Helen was and whether she was Great-uncle Norman's older or younger sister.

Of course, you probably know your parents' names and basic statistical information (date and location of birth, marriage, death, etc.) about them. Record that information on a family history sheet (located in the appendix of this book. You can also download a free copy of one from a Web site like Ancestry.com at www.ancestry.com/save/charts/ancchart.htm). Go back as far as possible, recording the pertinent information about each of your ancestors.

1918
1942
1966
1989

Some scrapbook pages are effective without journaling details. This page illustrates, without many words, four generations of women as graduating high school seniors.

When you get stumped, check with other family members to see if they can fill in the blanks. Maybe your family has an avid family historian who has already done much of the research. Contact this family member, who will most likely prove an incredibly valuable source of information during the entire process of creating your heritage scrapbook. If you're still missing information, several Internet sites offer family history research information that may provide exactly what you're looking for.

GATHERING AND ORGANIZING

Next you'll want to gather and organize the photos. While you may have a few of these photos, most likely you'll be tracking them down from parents, grandparents, aunts, uncles, and other extended family members.

Maybe your family has an avid family historian who has already done much of the family history research for you. Contact this family member; he or she will most likely prove an incredibly valuable source of information during the entire process of creating your heritage scrapbook.

Take a minute to decide exactly how far back you want to go and how far out you want to branch into heritage scrapbooking. Don't bite off more than you can chew. For instance, you may want to limit yourself to only collecting photos of and information about your parents and their parents. Or perhaps you want to go back even further, but only work on your direct ancestors.

On the other hand, you may feel a deep desire to gather and learn as much as possible about all of your family members. If so, you may find yourself with a mountain of information. Make sure you're organized from the very beginning. Label a file folder or photo box for each branch or member of the family, depending on how much material you are able to gather.

Many family members will be reluctant to give you their treasured antique photos or other family keepsakes. Thankfully, modern technology renders color photocopies that are almost exact duplicates of the originals. In fact, with some of the options now available, you may end up with a copy that's even better looking than the original. This is especially true in the case of black-and-white photos. Once again, make sure you're copying onto high-quality, acid-free, archival-safe paper.

Another option is photo-duplication machines, which can be found in many copy centers, craft and scrapbooking stores, or photo-developing stores. These machines make copies of a photo on regular photographic paper and allow you to choose the size of photo you would like, crop, reduce red eye, and adjust the contrast. The final product is an actual photograph rather than a color photocopy.

Generally speaking, color copies cost quite a bit less than creating a duplicate, and the quality is usually comparable. Experiment with both to decide which works best for you.

If you're working with original photos, keep in mind that these photos are most likely fiber-based, which means the back is simply paper. Remember, never adhere these photos

Highlights of 1941

IN THE NEWS

Roosevelt Addresses A Joint Session Of Congress And Describes The Attack On Pearl Harbor As "A Day Which Will Live In Infamy . . ."

U.S. Defense Savings Bonds Go On Sale

Librarian At University Of Michigan Announces The Highly Perishable Nature Of Wood Pulp Threatens Document Preservation And Suggests Microfilm

"Uncle Sam Needs You" Posters Appear In All Public Places

ACADEMY AWARDS

BEST MOVIE: "How Green Was My Valley"

BEST ACTOR: Gary Cooper "Sergeant York"

BEST ACTRESS: Joan Fontaine "Suspicion"

Also At The Movies: "Citizen Kane" "The Maltese Falcon" "Dumbo" "Meet John Doe" "Dr Jekyll and Mr. Hyde" "Tobacco Road" "High Sierra"

1941 PRICES

Average Family Income: $1,777

New House: $4,075

New Car: $850

Dow Jones Average: Low: 106.0 High: 133.0

Gallon Of Gas: 12¢

Loaf Of Bread: 8¢

Postage Stamp: 3¢

A Case Of Soda Sells For 49¢ And Beer Is Still 5¢

Frozen Shrimp Sells For 15¢ Per Pound

Chicken Is 23¢ Per Lb.

POLITICS

PRESIDENT: Franklin D. Roosevelt

VICE PRESIDENT: Henry A. Wallace

Japanese Attack Pearl Harbor, Hawaii, And U.S. Declares War On Japan

Draft Is Extended. Men 18-65 Must Register And Ages 20-44 May Serve

At The Beginning Of The War, The U.S. Army Ranked 18th In The World

Rubber Rationing Regulation Decreases Civilian Consumption By 80% - Tires Go First

HIT PARADE

Glenn Miller - "Chattanooga Choo Choo" and "Elmer's Tune"
Jimmy Dorsey - "Green Eyes"
The Ink Spots - "We Three" (My Echo, My Shadow, and Me)
Vaughn Monroe - "Racing With The Moon"

STUFF

"Rosie The Riveter" Becomes The Symbol Of American Women Working In Defense Industries
A New Kind Of Canned And Processed Meat Named "Spam" Appears On The Market
"Kilroy Was Here" Is New Graffiti

SPORTS

World Series: New York Yankees
NFL Champs: Chicago Bears
"Whirlaway", Ridden By Eddie Arcaro, Wins The Triple Crown
Boxer Joe Lewis, Who Defeats A Contender A Month, Becomes A National Hero

MISCELLANEOUS

Radio Favorites Include "The Red Skelton Show", "Inner Sanctum", "Duffy's Tavern", "Guiding Light"
Births Include Placido Domingo, Bob Dylan, Jesse Jackson
Deaths Include Lou Gehrig, James Joyce, Virginia Woolf

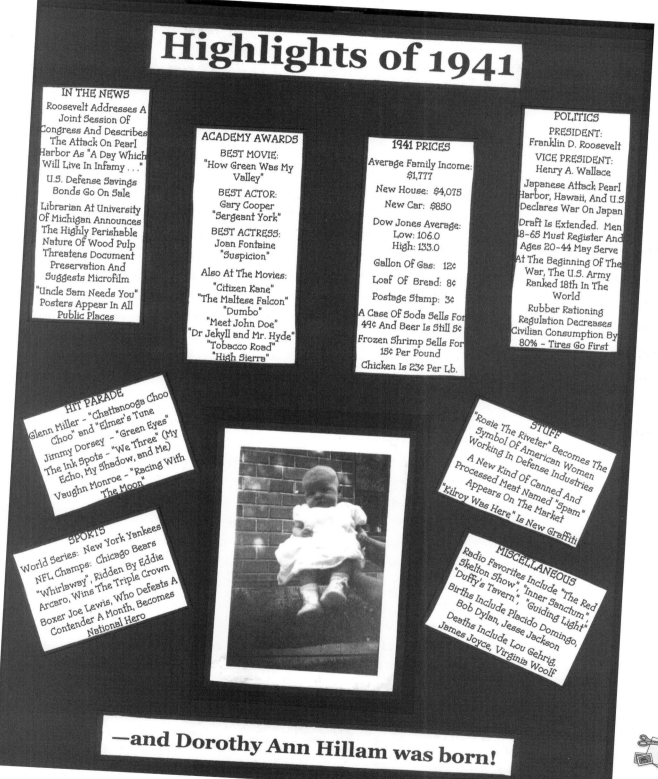

—and Dorothy Ann Hillam was born!

Including interesting tidbits about a time period can add great interest to a scrapbook page.

to your scrapbooks by putting adhesives on the back.

FINDING THE FACTS

Heritage albums present unique challenges to family history scrapbookers. Often the number of photos and keepsakes is very limited, and depending on whether the people involved are still alive, the information about the material you've found may be even more limited.

This means that creating journaling for your legacy scrapbook can be especially challenging. Begin by reviewing the photos and memorabilia you've collected and recording everything you know about them. If you've heard stories about someone in one of the photos, write those stories down. Gather diaries and family histories when you can. Pay attention to items, such as homes, cars, etc., that may help you identify dates or locations.

Next, turn to your family. Interview your relatives. This process alone can result in valuable family history information, especially if you record (either audio or video) the interview. If you can visit with your relatives face to face, take the photos you have questions about with you to help trigger their memories. Start by asking simple questions. Once they begin to warm up, chances are good that you'll get more information than you anticipated. Most people love to share their life memories with others.

If you cannot visit family members in person, talk to them on the phone or write them a letter. Send them copies of photos you're trying to find out about, and once again, ask specific questions. The more specific you are, the easier it will be for them to provide accurate information. If you simply ask "What was life like back then?" you'll most likely get "It was great" as an answer. But when you ask about a first car, first date, favorite sport, or most-hated chore, you're opening the door to a flood of memories.

Tying your heritage photos to specific eras or periods of time can create a fascinating aspect to your scrapbook. If you scrapbook a page with your uncle in his army uniform heading off to serve in World War II, that connection is made automatically. But other times, you may want to slip in information that, while not integral to the story, is interesting just the same. For instance, if you've got a picture of your dad with his first car, it might be worthwhile to find out how much that car cost. Or if you've got a photo of your grandmother during the Depression, slip in a few facts about the Depression (how long it lasted, unemployment rates, etc.) Much of this general but colorful information can be found at your local library and online.

ASSEMBLING YOUR PAGES

Now that you've got photos and memorabilia and facts and figures, you can decide what else, if anything, you need to complete your page. Depending on how much information

you were able to gather, your page may simply have a caption that includes who, when, and where journaling information. If you were able to gather a bit more information, you may include these facts in bullet format or longer captions. Finally, you can include longer stories, memories, or experiences in narrative, story, or even diary-like format.

A wealth of heritage products are available to help you design simple, elegant, yet sophisticated pages. Because most heritage pages feature black- and-white or antique photographs, many scrapbookers choose muted, rich, deep colors (although when the right colors are chosen, bright colors can be equally as impressive).

In addition, a large number of page embellishments are available to complete these heritage scrapbook pages. Typically these elements are elegant, sophisticated, soft, and subtle and can include lace borders and decorations, calligraphy fonts and alphabet lettering, and period-related die cuts, patterns, punches, stickers, etc.

Connecting the Generations

Four-year-old Abby came home from preschool one day with a "Me" bag. "I'm supposed to put something in it that represents me," she explained to her mother. "Then I get to show it to everybody at school and talk about why it's important to me."

83

Abby spent a lot of time that day wandering around her house, trying to find the perfect item for the "Me" bag. She thought about her favorite doll but decided it wouldn't work. She tried to stuff her little sister in the bag, but Zoey would have nothing to do with it. "It's just as well," Abby confided to her mother. "She wouldn't be quiet during class anyway." She gathered a few of her favorite books together, then put them away and chose some artwork instead. Eventually she put those away as well. When she went to bed that night, she still had no idea what she was going to put in the "Me" bag.

Early the next morning, Abby came dancing into her mother's bedroom with her hands hidden behind her back. "I know what I'm taking!" she announced with great enthusiasm. Then she carefully placed a scrapbook on her mother's bed. "This has everything about me in it," she explained. "My friends can see me as a baby, and they can see me when I was growing up. They'll know everything about me when they go through this book."

Later that day, when Abby pulled out her scrapbook and her friends gathered around to look through the pages, her mother was amazed at how long these four-year-olds lingered. The pictures truly did capture their attention as they asked Abby question after question about the events and memories preserved in her book.

Abby had recognized, as we do, the power of pictures and words combining to tell someone's life story. And the interest her young, typically short-attention-spanned friends showed in her scrapbook illustrates the power that pictures and words have to intrigue and interest individuals of all ages. Simply stated, scrapbooking takes family history beyond the written word into the visual world, where photos and memorabilia can tell a fuller, more complete story of our lives and the lives of those who have gone before.

In all of us there is a hunger marrow deep to know our heritage — to know who we are and where we came from.
—Alex Haley

CHAPTER FOUR

Digging for Roots
Your Family History

There was a military footlocker and a duffel bag in a cupboard high over the back stairs that Paul hadn't even realized was there, the seams of the knotty pine doors fit so closely together. The bag bore a naval insignia—that would be his uncle's. The locker that had "U.S. Army" stenciled on the side was his father's.

Inside his father's footlocker there was a dress uniform on top, a flat cap with stiff brim and gold insignia, and an olive drab coat with the red, gold, and blue 7th Army patch on the shoulder. Somebody held up the pants and laughed. They looked to be almost as wide in the waist as they were long. But that was only the beginning. The locker had been packed carefully in layers, and like an archeological dig, the layers revealed years.

Here was a photo of his father as a young man of twenty, a curl of hair that was now long gone breaking like a wave back from his forehead. He was in a suit, white shirt and narrow tie, with a serious look on his face. There was an FFA (Future Farmers of America) jacket, in heavy blue corduroy with a gold symbol on the back. His father tried it on in the kitchen, claiming it still fit—which it did, if he didn't try to bring the two halves of the zipper together up front.

"When was this?" Paul's brother was holding up a black-and-white photo that said "Chicago" on the back. There was the young man again, with the curl of hair up front, in a white dinner jacket, sitting at a banquet table. He discovered an old-fashioned hypodermic that looked as though it came out of some pioneer surgeon's office—for insulin. There were high school yearbooks, one of them with an "escape" tunnel penciled in next to the picture of the school on the back cover, and a Scout shirt with an old second-class badge stitched to the pocket. There was a young man in this box, a teenager, and Paul realized that teenager was somebody he has never really begun to know—until now...

There's an old joke that says you'll finally find something in the last place you look. The challenge for many of us who want to search for our roots, however, is deciding where the first place to look ought to be—to say nothing of the last. There are graveyards full of crumbling headstones, old churches that are keeps for vital records, libraries stuffed with books and microfilm, historical societies and family organizations and government archives, and there must be something available on the Internet. Where do you start—and where do you go from there? The good news is that you can start, and end, right in your own home.

First Things First

Family history research does not need to be complicated. You want to learn all you can about your ancestors and there are proven methods and avenues to find the information that is available. You will proceed, generally, from the present to the past, filling in a family tree chart with the names and important dates of your ancestors that you find as you search through records. This vital information will lead you to historical sources that will paint a picture of what life was like for them, and still other sources will help you place your ancestors in context. Along the way you may encounter "long-lost cousins" or other interested family members that will add to your research. This isn't to say that family history research is easy; the principles are easy enough to learn, but, since the information you want won't always be in the place you expect, you will invariably be presented with some wild twists and turns. You are bound to encounter dreaded "brick walls," or dead ends in your research.

Before you begin your family history quest you should set a research goal. Are you trying to establish a link to a famous forefather? Do you want to research your ancestors in an effort to pass on that information to your children? Maybe you have no specific research aim and your goal is to completely fill out a pedigree chart. Regardless of your goal, the first step will be to assess what you already know. You will, obviously, start with yourself and then document what you know about your parents, their parents, and so on. To fill in some of those blanks you will next search your home, your parents' home, etc. for any documents that answer your questions. You will also call or visit relatives who may have firsthand information that will be of help to you. Once you have exhausted all of your personal avenues of information, it will be time to expand the circle to include records created by federal and

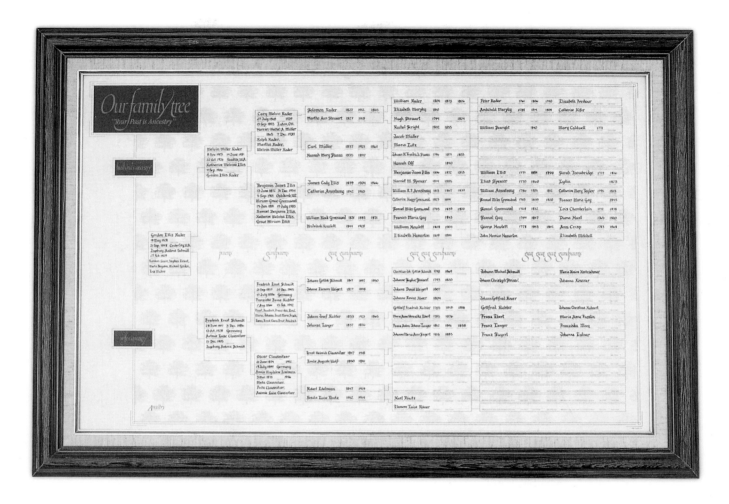

state agencies, churches, and other groups. And, as you start compiling your ancestral information, you will want to take care to organize the information you come across.

Step 1: Start with Yourself

Before you start your family history quest you need to know a few basics. If your are starting from scratch, the first step will be to photocopy a pedigree chart from the appendix of this book (or download one from the Internet at www.ancestry.com/save/charts/ancchart. htm). Write in your full name in position one and add your birth date and marriage date (if applicable). Do the same for your parents, their parents, and so on, as far back as your firsthand knowledge will take you. When you have exhausted all of your personal knowledge on the matter—whether you make it back one generation or five—it is time to expand your search. The goal is to find the tidbits of information that will take your pedigree chart back as far as you can, documenting your sources all the way, so that you can get to the bottom of where and who in the world you came from.

Step 2: Search for Home Sources

It makes sense that your own home is the best place to start your search for information about your roots. Almost every family preserves remembrances of past generations in some form; family Bibles, diaries, journals, scrapbooks, letters, and other sentimental items are obvious and rich sources of information. And there may be other, less obvious, sources in your home: certificates, newspaper clippings, school records, military records, and many other items that can offer important clues and documentation. Look for names, dates, and other clues that can lead you to other records; for example, an old letter might mention that an ancestor arrived in the United States on a certain date at a particular port. Using this

information, you could search for the ancestor's name in passenger arrival lists (we'll discuss those a little later); that list might then indicate where the person lived before emigrating.

Make sure you record any information you find and note the source it came from. You will find some tips on organizing these finds later in this chapter.

Home sources are probably the most tantalizing sources you'll encounter. It is usually from personal belongings and eyewitness accounts that we best catch the spirit and character of a family. Cherished stories, photographs, and mementos breathe life into otherwise dull statistics. And when you're discouraged because you've run out of ways to continue your research, you can always go back to your home sources for inspiration.

You'll also find it helpful to return to home sources for another reason: something that you overlooked in a document or photograph when you first saw it can have new significance after you've accumulated more information from the variety of sources available at libraries, archives, and on the Internet.

Step 3: Interview Living Relatives

The next step is to talk to relatives who may have helpful facts, artifacts, documents—and stories. Almost every family has intriguing traditions and beliefs that have been passed down through the generations. As you started filling in your family tree chart, you likely placed a call to your parents or an aunt or uncle. This is a great start. If you are fortunate enough to have older members in the family, approach them next. Make sure to take good notes or, better still, make audio or video recordings of your conversations. Keep in mind as you analyze and record information that time has a way of fogging memories, and a "fact" presented with the best of intentions may not be completely accurate. We all interpret information in our own way and tend to "twist" it in the retelling. Older family members will recall the family's weaknesses and its strengths, its happiest and saddest days—but they may be selective in disclosing the negative.

Family History Terms

Ahnentafel A numbering system used to identify each individual in a family tree. The formula states that an individual's father is twice that individual's number, and that an individual's mother is twice that individual's number plus one.

Census Official listing or counting of persons.

Emigrant One who leaves a country or region to settle in another country.

GEDCOM Acronym for GEnealogical Data COMmunication; file format supported by most genealogy database programs for the exchange of genealogy information between different programs and computers.

Immigrant One who settles in a country having emigrated from another.

Naturalization The process of becoming a citizen of the United States.

Patronymic A name formed by the addition of a prefix or suffix indicating sonship or other relationship to the name of one's father or paternal ancestors, as Johnson (son of John), MacDonald (son of Donald), etc.

Primary record A record created at the time of the event (birth, marriage, death, etc.) as opposed to records written years later.

Probate Process of legally establishing the validity of a will of a deceased person and settling an estate before a judicial authority.

Secondary record A record created some time after an event took place.

Social Security Death Index An index of records containing names of deceased Social Security recipients whose relatives applied for Social Security Death Benefits after their deaths.

Soundex A card index system prepared for the federal censuses; names are arranged by letter and number codes according to the sounds of their consonants.

Vital records Civil records of birth, marriage and death.

Most of us have heard stories of illustrious ancestors, and if you are lucky, you will be able to verify these nuggets. Other family stories are just that—stories! But all stories are worth preserving as long as you cite the source of the information and do not incorporate them into your family history as fact without documenting them first. It's often these intriguing tales that draw us into family history to begin with. And sometimes you will find that hidden in a lot of fiction is at least a touch of truth. That "touch" may be the key to making a connection that you can really prove.

When deciding which relatives to contact, don't overlook more-distant relatives. Distant relatives—both those who are geographically far afield and those who are not closely related—may have critical or helpful answers to some of your questions. It is always possible that someone in another branch of the family or in another location has inherited a document or a memory that will help you piece things together. (If you interview someone over the telephone, be especially careful about taking accurate notes, and copy them over to your family history immediately after the call while your memory is still fresh.)

These days, finding long-lost cousins may not be as difficult as you might think. With an online directory search you can look up almost anyone in the United States who has a listed telephone number.

If you are writing a letter soliciting information, it is a common courtesy, especially when you are asking for something, to send a self-addressed, stamped envelope (commonly referred to as an SASE). Your chances of getting a reply are much greater with this approach. And make every effort to keep the letter neat and brief! Long, wordy letters tend to overwhelm people and to be pushed aside. A warm, courteous, and short letter that teases a memory about names, places, and events is best.

Step 4: Find Record Sources

Once the dust settles from your initial research with home sources and relatives, it is time to take a look at your pedigree chart and see what's missing—and there is likely to be more missing than not. As you find those missing pieces, try and think of sources that might have them. For example, if you were unable to find the birth date of your paternal grandmother, you would, ideally, like to find a birth certificate. If you need to find when your maternal great-grandfather came to America, you need to find his immigration record. To find the date and cause of death for an ancestor you could try and find his or her obituary.

Much of what you will be able to determine as fact regarding your ancestors' lives will be found among the records that have been kept by government institutions, libraries and archives, churches, and the societies your relatives lived and participated in. You will want to start with original records like the vital records kept by church and government, since these are some of the most extensive and, in some instances, the best indexed. While there will obviously not be room here to go into detail on how to use many of the sources, there are several how-to guides available that cover each topic in greater depth.

Original Records

As a general rule, your ancestors were accounted for at birth, marriage, and death. They were also counted for governmental purposes, including taxation, representation in congress, and military service. The paper trail that resulted from all this accounting represents some of the best sources of genealogical information. In many cases, a phone call or letter to the appropriate agency can yield extremely valuable information about an ancestor. Copies of records can be obtained for a small fee and, in some cases, the Internet provides the capability to view them from home. Here is a listing of the major resources of original records to help you get started.

FEDERAL RECORDS

While federal records were not created for family historians, some government records are rich in historical and biographical information, and many federal records are also widely accessible. Most census, military, immigration, and land records used regularly by family historians are held by the National Archives and Records Administration (NARA) in Washington, D.C., and its regional archives: www.nara.gov. Some, in particular the U.S. Federal Census, are available on the Internet or on CD-ROM.

Steps for Using the Census

Most beginning U.S. Census researchers start with the 1930, 1920, 1910, 1900, and 1880 census records. Queries in these census records are aided by the Soundex indexing system. Below you will find five basic steps to researching these census records.

1. Identify what you know about the individual.

2. Choose a census year. Start with the most recent census your ancestor is likely to have appeared in and work backward from the known to the unknown.

3. Locate the Soundex code for the person's surname. The Soundex system indexes individuals by the sound of their last name. Each group of surnames has a code, and the library or archive will have instructions or software for learning it. Next, locate the soundex film. Many libraries with census film collections have references with the film numbers of both the Soundex and the census. These film numbers are usually arranged by state and then by Soundex code. The Soundex system indexes the surname by the sound of the last name and then lists in alphabetical order the first name.

4. Search for your ancestor. Scroll through the film until you find the Soundex code. Then look for the first name of the ancestor and search for the surname along with other identifying information such as age, sex, or name of spouse and children. Use the information you already have on the family to choose the most likely individual. Always finish scrolling through the film to see if there are other possibilities. In the upper right-hand corner of the Soundex card is the information that will lead you to the census page. Record all the information listed.

5. Search the census. Go to a separate index to find the film number. Scroll through the film until you find the correct county and city, then look for the enumeration district and sheet number. (These are generally in the upper right-hand corner of the census page.) Then look for the line number of your ancestor along the right-hand side of the page. Following the line across the page, you should locate your family. Make a copy and record the information onto a census extract sheet (see Appendix).

Census Records. Few, if any, records reveal as many details about individuals and families as do the U.S. Federal Censuses. The census population schedules make up successive "snapshots" of Americans that depict where and how they were living at particular periods. Once your home sources and library sources have been exhausted, the census is often the best starting point for further genealogical research.

Military Records. Almost every American family, in one generation or another, has seen one or more of its members serve in America's armed forces. From regimental histories, which provide blow-by-blow accounts of a unit's participation in military actions, to the

Notable People in the U.S. Federal Censuses

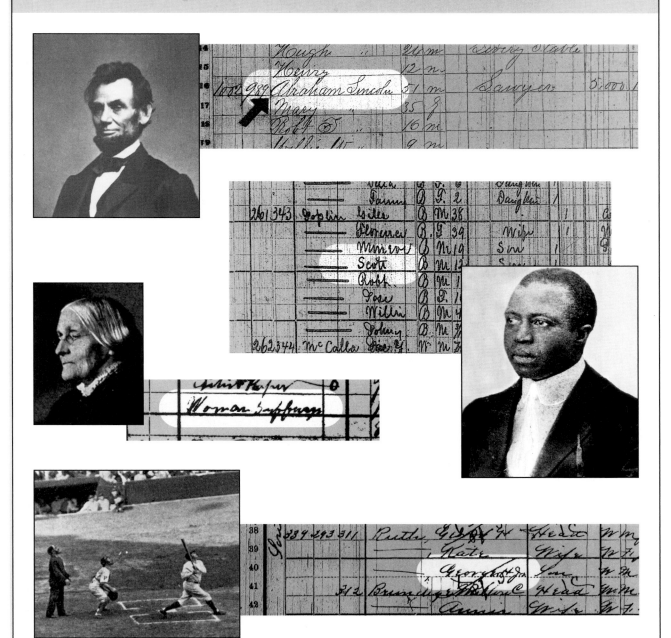

From top to bottom: Record of Abraham Lincoln and family in the 1860 Census; record of Scott Joplin in the 1880 Census; record of Susan B. Anthony (note the "women's suffrage" annotation) in the 1900 census; and record of five-year-old George "Babe" Ruth in the 1900 Census.

Locating Military Records

To locate military records for an individual, it is essential to know when and where in the armed forces he or she served and whether that person served in the enlisted ranks or was an officer. Creating a historical time line, including known dates and places of residence, can be especially useful for determining if and when someone might have served in the military. Was the individual the right age to be eligible for the draft or to serve voluntarily in the Civil War? Is it likely that the person served on the Northern rather than the Southern side, or vice versa?

Ellis Island

The Statue of Liberty-Ellis Island Foundation

The Statue of Liberty-Ellis Island Foundation was founded in 1982 to raise funds for the restoration and preservation of the Statue of Liberty and Ellis Island. By 1986, the Statue of Liberty was restored, and the Foundation moved on to renovating the buildings on Ellis Island, which were completed in 1992.

The latest Foundation project is the American Family Immigration History Center, located on Ellis Island and the World Wide Web, which makes the millions of immigrant arrival records in the Ellis Island Archives available to everyone. With these records now so easily available, family historians can more easily "jump across the pond" to research the native homelands of their immigrant ancestors. To access the American Family Immigration History Center online, visit www.ellisisland.org.

personal details contained in the service and pension files of individual men and women, military records provide valuable information concerning a significant portion of the American population.

U.S. Immigration and Naturalization Records. Citizenship records have been kept by the federal government since 1790, though it was not until 1820 that the federal government began to keep track of incoming ship passengers. For most ships entering U.S. ports between 1565 and 1954, a passenger list was compiled.

Land Records. The right to own land has always been one of the great incentives for living in the United States, and written land records go back in time further than virtually any other type of record family historians might use.

U.S. Social Security Death Index. Since President Franklin D. Roosevelt signed the Social Security Act into law in 1935, nearly 400 million Social Security cards have been issued. Close to 98 percent of the Social Security Death Index (SSDI) represents individuals who have died after 1962, when the database was started. You can search the SSDI free of charge at select libraries and online at Web sites like Ancestry.com: www.ancestry.com/SSDI.

STATE AND LOCAL RECORDS

Begin your search for records at the state or county level by writing or visiting the record-keeping agency for the area in which the event occurred. Some counties and states provide services for ordering vital records online. Indexes to some vital records for a few states are available through the office of the secretary of the state, through the state archives, or through the state genealogical society.

PETITION FOR NATURAL

[Under General Provisions of the Nationality Act of 19

Naturalization records, such as this Petition for Naturalization, applied for by actress Greta Garbo, provide important information for determining the background of an ancestor.

Searching for Naturalization Records

Here are a few tips to help out in your search for naturalization records:

- To begin, learn as much as you can about that person, including full name, approximate birth date, native country, approximately when he or she came to the United States, and where that person lived after his or her arrival here.

- Generally, the best place to begin a naturalization search is in the county in which the immigrant settled in the United States.

- Many federal and local court naturalizations and naturalization indexes have been micro-filmed and are available from the Family History Library in Salt Lake City, Utah.

- Relatively few single women became naturalized citizens before 1922, and married women could not be naturalized on their own unless they were widowed or divorced.

- Aliens from China, Japan, and other East and South Asian countries were barred from becoming citizens from 1882 to 1943.

Court Actions

Even if your ancestor is not mentioned in a probate case, consider all of the other procedures that might have resulted in him or her appearing in court records:

Admiralty courts	Judgments
Adoptions	Jury records
Affidavits	Land disputes
Apprenticeships	Marshals' records
Bankruptcies	Military
Bonds	Minutes
Chancery	Naturalization records
Civil cases	Notices
Civil War claims	Orders
Claims	Orphan records
Complaints	Petitions
Court opinions	Plaintiff
Criminal	Printed court records
Decrees	Probate
Declarations	Receipts
Defendant	Slave and slave owners
Depositions	Subpoenas
Divorce	Summons
Dockets	Testimony
Guardianship	Transcripts

Note: When requesting probate information from the county clerk, it is important not to limit yourself by asking for a person's "will." The clerk will usually take you at your word and not copy other papers in the probate file that may be equally important information.

Vital Records. Vital records are connected with central life events: birth, marriage, and death. These records often supply details on family members well back into the nineteenth century. Every state and county has a division responsible for maintaining and dispersing information from its vital record holdings. Vital records, especially those less than seventy-two years old, are protected by privacy laws.

Court and Probate Records. America's English heritage established a tradition of court processes in which the people have a right to participate actively. When a person dies, every state has laws that provide for public supervision over the estate that is left, whether or not there is a will. The term "probate records" covers all the records produced by these laws, although, strictly speaking, "probate" applies only when there is a will.

Cemetery Records. Cemetery and other sources associated with death can include biographical works, burial permits, church burial registers, cemetery records, cemetery indexes (often compiled by genealogical societies), cemetery deed and plot registers, death certificates, death indexes, funeral director's records, gravestone (monument) inscriptions, military records, necrologies, newspaper death notices, published death records, and transcriptions of cemetery inscriptions.

Historical Societies and Museums. Museum collections can include local histories, family histories, biographical collections, historical and genealogical periodicals, published local records, city directories, school records, military rosters, newspapers, yearbooks, scrapbooks, photograph collections, indexes of all sorts, and records that can't be found anywhere else.

Ethnic Research. Knowledge of an ancestor's ethnic group, its history, settlement patterns, and its laws and customs can lead you to specific and often unique record sources.

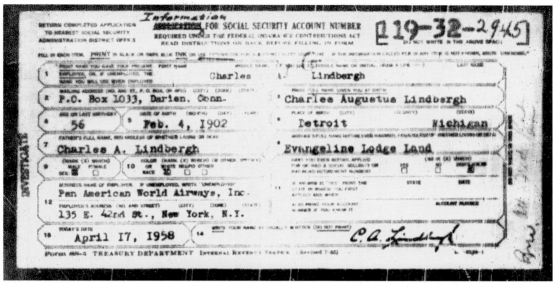

Requesting a Social Security Application of your ancestor will yield a photocopy of the document, similar to the this application by Charles Lindbergh.

Ethnic sources can also help you understand your ancestors as real people; without cultural background, we are often at a loss to understand their actions.

RELIGIOUS RECORDS

Church records rank among the most promising genealogical records available. Indeed, for periods before civil registration of vital statistics (a very late development in many American states), church records are the best available sources for information on specific vital events: birth, marriage, and death.

Baptisms recorded in church ledgers almost always list the name of the person baptized, the names of his or her parents, date and place of birth, and the date of the baptism. Most denominations have recorded marriages. Death and burial records vary from one denomination to another, and while one register will provide the name and date of death only, others may provide birth dates and even birthplaces. This information can be especially useful in cases where the birthplace is an unknown foreign place.

There are also other church records worth searching for. Confirmation records, membership rosters, church census records, historical commemorative publications, and religious newspapers can also be sources of vital information. Religious newspapers often

Ethnic Sources

One of the most definitive and useful background sources for almost every ethnic group is Stephan Thurstrom's *Harvard Encyclopedia of American Ethnic Groups*. This work contains basic information about the multitudes of people who make up the population of the United States.

Newspapers

Newspapers are useful in supplying clues about historical events, local history, probate court and legal notices, real estate transactions, political biographies, announcements, notices of new and terminated partnerships, business advertisements, and notices for settling debts. Newspapers can provide at least a partial substitute for nonexistent civil records.

How-to References

The Source: A Guidebook of American Genealogy
by Loretto D. Szucs and Sandra H. Luebking (Editors)
Ancestry Publishing

The Handybook for Genealogists: United States of America
(9th Edition)
by George B. Everton
Everton Publishers

Unpuzzling Your Past: The Best-Selling Basic Guide to Genealogy
by Emily Anne Croom
Betterway Books

The Researcher's Guide to American Genealogy
by Val D. Greenwood
Genealogical Publishing Company

contain biographical sketches and obituaries found nowhere else. Religious records often supply information not found elsewhere—even clues to former residences which may lead to the name of a town or church in the "Old Country."

PUBLISHED SOURCES

Even the smallest public libraries generally have reference sections that include major directories, indexes, and reference materials that will open new doors. And libraries in places where your ancestors once lived may have materials you won't find anywhere else.

For example, local libraries often have historical works that pertain to the immediate area and biographical sources for prominent citizens. You may find a county or town history that will give you a close look at the places and times in which your ancestors lived. These books may even name them and provide biographical sketches and portraits. Often a local library will contain bound records, newspapers, school yearbooks, and other sources from around the area. Some libraries maintain scrapbooks, photograph collections, and obituary files. Some even have large collections of genealogy and family history books, microfilm, microfiche, and CD-ROMs and other computerized sources.

State libraries, college and university libraries, and many private libraries also house treasures for family historians.

How-to Guides. Once you have acquainted yourself with the libraries, your next step is finding the records that will lead you closer to your ancestor. A wonderful array of books have been published to help you with specific research areas, and more are being published in both book and electronic form. There are guides to specific types of records (from censuses to tax records to newspapers), guides designed to help you research particular places in the United States, and still more to help you search particular ethnic groups or research in foreign countries. These instructional works can suggest unique sources, and they can save you hours of time and frustrating effort by helping to direct your search from the start. Both libraries and bookstores are good places to look for these titles.

Family Histories. Thousands of family histories have been published since the 1800s. It may be that some near or distant relative of yours has already researched and published a history about one or more of your family lines. Some of these homespun publications have not been well researched or documented, however, so while they may provide you with invaluable clues and background, use them with caution.

Not every library will have all of the works you need, but even small libraries are likely to have some of the most important genealogy and family history reference works on their shelves. Remember, too, that many local libraries are now connected to national

Genealogy Conferences and Institutes

Depending on where you live, there may be occasional genealogical lectures or regular classes—usually sponsored by public libraries, community colleges, or genealogical societies. In addition, national genealogical conferences, sponsored by national, local, and ethnic groups, are held annually in different parts of the United States. Genealogical societies usually advertise these events in their own publications, and they also distribute information about upcoming conferences to libraries, archives, and other places where family historians tend to congregate.

networks through computers. Talk to your librarian about how you might be able to search another library's collections and even borrow materials through an interlibrary loan.

Reference Works. Reference sources such as gazetteers, history books, and encyclopedias add context to your family history. Looking at trends of migration, natural disasters, and historical events, will help you understand why your ancestors made the decisions they did. Without such historical background it is impossible to truly understand our ancestors and to feel a connection to them.

Step 5: Organize Your Findings

Every family historian has unique and compelling reasons to keep family memories alive. Once you've begun discovering information about your ancestors, however, you need to organize the information and materials you collect and to preserve them as an heirloom from which future generations will benefit.

HOW TO RECORD

From the beginning of your family history project, make it a point to record all of your research activities. Write down the source of every name, date, and place as you gather

Getting Involved in a Genealogical Society

Genealogical societies represent a "living" source of like-minded people that can be an invaluable resource. Genealogical societies hold regular meetings, workshops, and conferences at which specialists speak on topics such as how to best locate and use local records and other special kinds of records most efficiently. Frequently, genealogical societies collaborate with local archives, historical societies, colleges and universities, and libraries to sponsor workshops and classes.

Most societies publish monthly newsletters to keep members current on local projects, events, and issues. In addition to newsletters, almost all genealogical societies publish quarterly journals featuring essays on research methodology. Local records, historical events, and historical figures and families are usually the predominant themes of these publications.

Because family history research relies greatly upon records found at the county level, many local genealogical societies represent counties. Organizations also form around shared interests. Ethnic or religious origins account for many groups, such as the Polish Genealogical Society of America and P.O.I.N.T. (Pursuing Our Italian Names Together), and others form around common locales of origin for members' ancestors; hence, the Palatines to America and Germans from Russia societies.

Almost every state has a state genealogical society, a state genealogical council, or both. In addition to their own work, state-level groups sometimes help coordinate the efforts of local societies within the state. At the national level, the Federation of Genealogical Societies (FGS) is an umbrella organization for local, state, and other organizations, such as genealogical societies, libraries, archives, and institutes. The National Genealogical Society (NGS) is composed of individual researchers.

information. Include the place where every piece of information was found and try to include at least a photocopied version of every record in your files. Answering and recording the following questions will help you verify and analyze the reliability of each piece of information:

- Where did you find the name or date?
- Who recorded the information?
- Was the information you collected for an individual found in a record that is entirely reliable?
- Is this piece of information from an undocumented family tradition? If so, be sure to make a record of it because it could be a valuable clue. However, be sure to note that it is only "tradition" until the story can be proved or disproved.
- Have birth dates and birthplaces been obtained from relatives—or anyone else— whose memory may not be entirely accurate? Note the circumstances of interviews.
- Was the information you have collected from a family history compiled by someone who was not careful in proving accuracy? Record the exact title of the family history, the author, and where you found it (name the library or individual who shared it with you).

RESEARCH STRATEGY

As you begin your research, remember the following hints:

- It is generally more effective to concentrate on one family at a time, beginning with your immediate family.
- Define your search objectives and think about what records could give you this information.
- List the record sources you plan to search and where they are located. Think of how you can use them most effectively.
- Log results on a research calendar or correspondence chart as your research is completed.
- If you're planning to interview someone, do a little research on interviewing strategies. One good piece of advice to always remember, though, is to make a list of important questions in advance—that way, you won't forget to ask them.

FILING AND ORGANIZING INFORMATION

Once you get started, you will be amazed at how quickly you accumulate documents and notes. The average person has 1,024 direct-line ancestors within ten generations. Of course, you will be collecting information on all their siblings (collateral lines), and you will want to keep on file all the other interesting things you run across. Expect to amass a lot of paper! It won't be a problem if you organize well from the start.

As a rule, standard-size file folders are the best way to organize and retrieve information. A single file might contain all of your findings on one surname for a time, but as the information accumulates, you'll probably find it necessary to break files down by head of family (one generation) or by individuals. All relevant documents and an inventory of what has been found on each family or individual will then be at your fingertips whenever you need it.

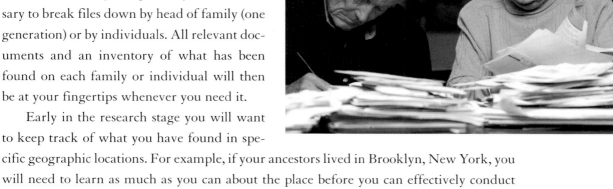

Early in the research stage you will want to keep track of what you have found in specific geographic locations. For example, if your ancestors lived in Brooklyn, New York, you will need to learn as much as you can about the place before you can effectively conduct research there. As you gather facts about Brooklyn, photocopy information pertinent to your research there and create a locality file. This is a good place to keep a list of genealogical guides, local histories, lists of records that have been microfilmed for the city, addresses and telephone numbers, and any other sources that you will need to refer to at later stages of your research. Likewise, it's a good idea to keep other subject files.

NOTE-KEEPING AND FORMS

As you begin to gather information, get into the habit of taking good notes. There are several systems for organizing genealogical information on the market, including computer software programs. Commercially produced computer programs have various methods of formatting and printing forms, but four standard genealogical forms will serve you whether you are using a computer or writing the data by hand onto preprinted forms.

The ancestral chart, or what is more often called a pedigree chart, is a record of all the generational parents of a particular person. It shows, at a glance, the progress you have made and what remains to be found and proved. It is wise to keep two charts: (1) a work chart that records the names and minimum identifying information for each person assumed to be a direct ancestor and (2) a permanent pedigree that records those ancestors who have been proved through careful research. Use a pencil on genealogical forms until you are confident about the data you have found. Most genealogical computer programs include special instructions on how to note proven information and distinguish it from undocumented sources.

The family group sheet lists the immediate family of a particular couple (whether legally married or not), including their children, their parents, and other spouses. A typical group sheet has room for considerable data on each person (in order to trace collateral lines) and a reference for the source of information. Make a family group sheet for each couple on your ancestral chart and for each of their marriages. The final result of your research efforts will be to compile complete, correct, and connected families. Using family group sheets from the beginning will make the compilation much easier.

The research calendar gives you an account of every record source you have searched and serves as a reminder of what you have already done and where you have found pertinent information.

- Use a separate research calendar for each surname.
- Describe each search you make whether it yields information or not, and indicate the results of that search.
- List author, title, publisher, date and place of publication, name and address of repository or library where the record is located, and the call number, if it has one, for every record you consult.

Forms

The forms mentioned in this chapter are included in the appendices. Feel free to photocopy and use these forms in compiling your family history.

104

- Note missing or torn pages, blurred entries, foreign languages, and indexes.
- Note personal visits while traveling. If you interview a relative, record the date of the interview and where the interview notes can be found.

A correspondence log can help you keep track of those whom you have contacted, the reasons for writing, and whether or not you have received an answer.

- Note each letter written, the address, the purpose, and the date the letter was sent, whether it was by mail, e-mail, fax, or personally delivered.
- As you receive answers to these letters, note the date and the information gleaned from them.

A looseleaf binder can be divided into sections for ancestral charts, group sheets, vital research notes, correspondence, and other materials. If you carry the binder with you while researching, you will have a quick reference to use for yourself and anyone from whom you seek help. As research continues and the files grow, you may want to have a binder for each surname.

Another likely destination for your family history research is family history software or an online family tree (see the section about computers and the Internet, starting on page 106, for more information).

CONTRIBUTING YOUR FAMILY HISTORY TO NATIONAL HISTORY

Maybe you have one ancestor about whom you want to write a biography. Maybe you are searching for a birth mother. Maybe you simply want to give a little historical sketch at the next family reunion. Keep in mind that one of the joys that comes with tracing a family history is sharing your research and discoveries with others. The Library of Congress actively seeks to acquire copies of every family history that is published. There are online sites, as well, that gather family histories to post and share. In this way, your work becomes a gift, not only to yourself and your family, but to the global community.

Computers and the Internet: A Whole New World of Family History

While most good family historians haven't stopped using paper to document their genealogical finds, almost all have converted their research to digital format for ease of use in recording, viewing, and displaying their family histories. The impact of technology on family history is increasing, it seems, on a daily basis with new Web sites, services, and gadgets becoming available to aid researchers. Advances in technology are particularly helpful to beginners, as records that once required several trips to the library and hours of scrolling through microfilm are now accessible through keyword searches on the Internet.

COMPUTER SOFTWARE

Most genealogical software is GEDCOM-based. GEDCOM stands for Genealogical Data Communications, which is a computer standard for formatting genealogical data that enables users to transfer information among different software programs. A number of genealogical computer programs are available to help you record, index, and preserve information. Each program has its strengths and limitations; however, because of the rate at which genealogical programs appear and are upgraded, the best way to determine which of these programs suit your needs is to read the latest software reviews in genealogical publications.

THE INTERNET

Investigating ancestors on the computer can become a great adventure. Ellen Militello, of Italian descent, became interested in connecting with her lost heritage when her youngest child entered first grade and she suddenly had a few discretionary hours.

Responding to her yearning to know more about her Italian ancestors, she turned to the Internet and found she needed a few solid facts to begin her research. She called her mom, asked where her family had come from, and was given the name of a little town in Sicily.

Her mother, who had never thought much about their Italian roots until now, seemed delighted with Ellen's new interest. Her mother had ample information about the three generations of their family since they had come to America in the early 1900s. However, she knew little about why the family had left Italy or exactly when they came. She had no information about the family before they came to America—not even her great-grandparents' names. She began to share her daughter Ellen's feeling that it was urgent to find out.

Family History Software

If you are interested in trying out several family history software programs before making a decision on which works best for your needs, several quality shareware and freeware versions are currently available for your use. Among the most popular are Personal Ancestral File (downloadable at www.familysearch.org), Ancestry Family Tree (downloadable at www.ancestry.com), and Legacy Family Tree (downloadable at www.legacyfamilytree.com).

Armed only with the names of her grandparents and her ancestral home, Ellen discovered a Web site called RootsWeb.com that had an e-mail mailing list specifically for people researching ancestors from Sicily. From it, she learned about all kinds of resources, including a family history center right in her home town. When she went there, kind staff members helped her decide where to start. They suggested she order reels of microfilm of the 1920 census. A few days later when she was notified that the microfilm had arrived, Ellen hurried down to the center and began perusing the names on the census. Much to her delight she found her great-grandparents listed with all their children, including her grandma, who was only a baby at the time. The census gave her several clues that helped her in her search.

Next she was directed to send a request to the National Archives for passenger lists, hoping to learn when her family had come to America. They sent her documents showing the name of the ship the family had traveled on and their date of processing through Ellis Island when they arrived. She located firsthand accounts of what it was like to travel by ship in those days and to be processed into the country through Ellis Island.

On the Internet she also found a form letter written in Italian. She filled in known family facts and sent the form to the civil records office in Sicily. Several weeks later she received a printout containing birth dates, marriage dates, and immigration dates for her great-grandmother's family. The facts she gathered eventually led her to contact living relatives in Sicily, whom she recruited to help in her investigative efforts.

Ellen's interest fanned the coals of family interest into a flame and started a family-wide two-continent search through boxes and drawers for pictures, letters, certificates, and diaries. She eventually ended up with enough information to write a very definitive family history that tied the generations together and created a closer bond with her living family.

Internet Access

If you don't have Internet access from your home, most public libraries offer Internet access and have telephone directories on CD-ROM.

The Internet is opening up a whole new world of research possibilities for family historians. Federal, state, and county agencies, genealogical societies, historical societies, and individuals have Web sites where you can discover the scope of a collection, how to access more information, complete mailing addresses, telephone numbers, and, sometimes, downloadable forms and databases.

Libraries and publishers have posted a vast array of guides and databases on their home pages. With the click of a button, you can check the card catalog of a distant library, exchange research notes with a newly found cousin, download files from some sleepy town halfway across the world, or see photographs taken in the very time and place where your ancestors lived. Even the U.S. Federal Census is available for searching, viewing, and printing from the comfort of your own home.

No matter what you are looking for, a well-planned strategy can save both the experienced and the novice researcher valuable time. With literally millions of people and sources on the Internet, and more being added daily, a visit to the Internet can be like a visit to the jungle. It's easy to get lost.

Search Engines. For starters, all search engines are not equal. In doing a search, it is important to note that the criteria entered may bring up different results on different search engines. A search for "naturalizations" may produce different results than a search for "naturalization records." So don't give up if your first search doesn't result in the information that you need. Try some variations and/or experiment with a different search engine.

FamilySearch®. FamilySearch is the official family history Web site of The Church of Jesus Christ of Latter-day Saints. Accessible at The Family History Library and its centers, as well as on the World Wide Web, the site offers a vast collection of record sources and guidance for researchers including research guides on many topics. Through it you can also search the holdings of the Family History Library.

Directories. Whether you're looking for a long-lost cousin or the address of a library in your ancestor's hometown, there are many online directories to assist in your search, both locally and internationally.

The Library of Congress. The Library of Congress Web site (lcweb.loc.gov/) is a valuable tool for family historians. Its catalogs are extraordinary helpful in finding publications. For information on ancestors who lived in the United States, the Library of Congress's American Memory Project is another outstanding resource.

Maps. There are many Web sites with interactive atlases from today and yesterday for both the United States and abroad. Many countries' boundaries have changed—in some cases more than once—and it is important to know exactly where ancestors were living in a given time in order to find their records. In the United States, state and county borders have changed, as have town names (some towns have ceased to exist altogether). These are just a few of the problems that can be solved by using maps.

The best way to get started using historical maps is by performing a search for your area of interest using your favorite search engine.

The Family History Library and its Centers

The Family History Library is home to the world's largest collection of genealogical information. The scope of the Family History Library's collections, as well as the easy access provided by its thousands of branch libraries, make it an outstanding resource. Since 1938, the library has been microfilming birth, marriage, death, probate, immigration, military, and many other records in more than fifty countries. While the library is maintained by The Church of Jesus Christ of Latter-day Saints, anyone is welcome to visit the library and use its collections and services at no charge.

The library's collection includes approximately two million rolls of microfilmed records and more than 500,000 microfiche. These records were created by governments, churches of many denominations, other organizations, and individuals from all over the world. The library also has copies of church registers, census records, passenger lists, military records, land records, and probate records. Most of the records date from around 1550 to about 1920. The Family History Library is located at 35 North West Temple Street, Salt Lake City, UT 84150 (telephone: 801-240-2331).

Book and Other Collections

The library has more than a quarter of a million books, including published family histories, local histories, indexes, periodicals, and other research aids. Many of these are obscure books not easily found in other libraries and which may have been out of print for decades. The library also has a useful collection of maps. The library's Automated Resource Center houses electronic materials the library has collected, and the collection of CD-ROMs represents virtually every title available that pertains to local or family history.

The Family History Library Catalog (available online at www.familysearch.org) is your key to understanding the library's growing collections, as it lists and describes the records in the library. The library has "open stacks," meaning that patrons can retrieve and use almost all of the materials personally. Copies of most of the microfilms are immediately available in the library.

Preparing to Visit the Library

You will have a more successful visit to the library if you are prepared to use its resources effectively. To do this, gather all of the background information you can beforehand, and familiarize yourself with the records you'll need to access in your research. If possible, visit a local family history center before you visit the library. Also note that, while most of the microfilms you'll want to use are kept at the library, some are housed in a different location. Contact the library to check on availability, or write to the library at least two weeks in advance and request the films you need.

Family History Centers

The Family History Library currently supports more than 2,500 branch libraries, called family history centers, throughout the world. These centers have been provided as a way for the public to use the resources of the Family History Library (at no charge) without having to travel to Salt Lake City, and they can provide access to almost all of the microfilm and microfiche maintained at the main library for a small handling fee.

While most centers have a small collection of general reference books, centers do not collect records of the area where they are located. However, because of the size of the Family History Library's collection, most sources you might be looking for are available on microfilm or microfiche and can be sent to any center. Proselyting is not allowed in family history centers, and, on average, more than half of their patrons are not members of the LDS church.

You can locate a family history center near you on the FamilySearch.org Web site: www.familysearch.org/Eng/Library/FHC/frameset_fhc.asp

Online Genealogy Classes. There are now a number of genealogy classes available on the Internet. Ancestry.com (www.ancestry.com) offers lessons on a variety of topics, such as "Genealogy for Beginners," "Using LDS Family History Centers," "Let's Get Organized," and "U.S. Genealogy State Lessons."

Another good source is the International Internet Genealogical Society's University (www.iigs.org/university). It has classes for general instruction and some classes arranged by geographic region.

RootsWeb.com (rwguide.rootsweb.com) offers a free, step-by-step guide to basic family history research as well as direction on how to use various types of record sources.

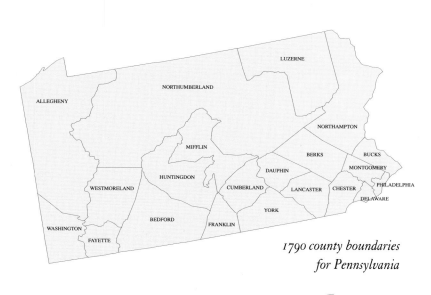

*1790 county boundaries
for Pennsylvania*

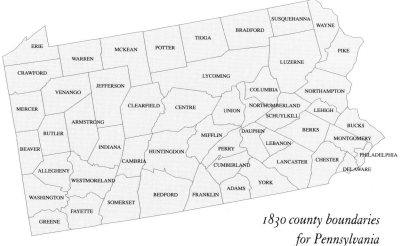

*1830 county boundaries
for Pennsylvania*

The USGenWeb Project. This outstanding resource (www.usgenweb.com) is the work of volunteers who are creating sites for every state and county in the United States. On the main page you'll find links to state pages that lead to many state resources, as well as links to various county pages. The county pages vary in content and are as individual as the volunteers who create them. Many contain databases, directories, and indexes of various types, including cemetery transcriptions, Civil War rosters, census records, and more. They also contain links and addresses for other local resources, as well as a query page and/or surname directory where you can submit your own queries or surnames.

Mailing Lists and Newsgroups. The Internet is home to many useful mailing lists and newsgroups for family historians. Some are broken down by geographic region, ethnic group, surnames, or any number of research levels and types. There are software and commercial lists, immigrant lists, "newbie" (beginner) lists, and many more.

These groups are wonderful sources for making contact with other researchers who have similar research interests, or for learning of new resources, and maybe even for finding that long-lost cousin! Remember, though: a lot of misinformation can be passed around in these forums.

Indexes and Databases. Genealogical and historical organizations, genealogical companies, individuals, and, as mentioned before, the USGenWeb Project have all been building databases, any of which may contain the unique piece of information you need to complete the biography of an individual or the history of a family. It's very important to remember that information on the Internet is not monitored and thus may not always be entirely accurate or complete. Verify any information you obtain from a database by comparing it with actual records.

Government Agencies. Government Web pages are excellent sources for information on the federal, state, and local levels. The National Archives and Records Administration (NARA) (www.nara.gov) has an elaborate system of pages with extensive information. Although it will be years before a significant portion of the genealogical records available from NARA are online, there are numerous research guides that can help you prepare for a trip to one of the many facilities.

Every state has a Web page at www.state.___.us. (Insert the appropriate two-letter state abbreviation in the blank.) This page usually provides links to many state agencies, including those responsible for vital records (which sometimes contain downloadable forms for requesting various vital records) and the state library (which often provides a directory of libraries in the state, genealogical research guides, online catalogs, state historical societies, and more). The Web pages of many state archives can also provide valuable information

regarding the collections they hold, and many are now offering online databases. Much information can be found at the county level as well. Foreign government Web sites can also be a great source of information.

Libraries and Online Catalogs. How many times have you gone to a library and spent hours poring over a computerized catalog or card index looking for holdings that pertain to your research? Many libraries' Web sites offer access to these valuable catalogs, and even if the entire catalog is not available, many times an overview of the collection is. Before a research trip, it is always helpful to check the Web page. Often, you can contact the library by e-mail ahead of time to find out if the resources in question are available.

Ready for Success

So now you are ready to succeed with researching your family history project. Your journey can be like none other you have experienced, a true-life detective story that, as it unfolds, leads not only to your ancestors but also to you. This is your past, your heritage, your source; these are your people; and there is nothing quite like feeling part of a family that stretches back in time and touches history.

It is too bad that a requirement for living is not leaving a record of it.
—Lynda Rutledge Stephenson

CHAPTER FIVE

Preserving the Story
Your Written Family History

Lorie Davis was intensely nervous as she knocked at the strange door in Vienna in 1987. She had met her grandmother only once—in 1972—and had found her rather frightening, stern, and opinionated.

Lorie had written with apprehension to ask if she could visit Grandmother Rosa in Vienna to learn details about her mother's childhood. Lorie's mom, who had died when Lorie was thirty-one, had rarely spoken of her growing-up years—only occasionally dropping a tantalizing hint. She had left no diaries or journals.

Since her mother's death, a yearning had grown within Lorie to know and understand this almost hidden woman. Her works and abilities showed enormous strength, compassion, and faith. Yet her mother had shared few of her feelings and almost none of her past. Lorie wanted to know her mother's story, and to document it for her own children.

Lorie had started her quest by writing and phoning her brothers and sisters to collect stories they remembered about their mother—which did not yield many more than Lorie already knew. Next Lorie wrote to her mother's old friends in Austria and America, which got her a few more stories, but not nearly enough.

Finally she realized that only her Grandmother Rosa knew the details of her mother's childhood. Any valid investigation would lead her directly there. Lorie was grateful that her grandmother was still alive and, from all reports, extremely bright and lucid. Still, she was a bit afraid to confront Rosa face to face.

As little as Lorie knew about her mother, she knew even less about her grandmother—only that when Lorie talked back as a teenager, her mother's response had been, "If I had said that to *my* mother, she would have slapped me on the mouth!" So the one thing Lorie knew for sure about her grandmother was that she had been strict and scary.

Consequently, she trembled in front of Rosa's door in Vienna. The door opened to show a very small woman with a firm, resolute mouth, her hair covered with a bandanna.

"So! You are finally here! Come in! Come in!"

After she fed Lorie a fine dinner, Rosa finally asked, "Now, what was it you wanted to ask me?"

Lorie replied, "I wanted to have you tell me about my mother's childhood. I know nothing about it, and she rarely spoke of it. I thought you would know the details." Lorie reached into her pocket and gently pressed the record button on her tape recorder.

Rosa, puzzled, then incensed, blurted out, "Your *mother's* childhood? Why, her childhood was nothing!" She gave a dismissive wave of her hand. "Now MY childhood! That was something! I'll tell you!"

And tell her she did. Rosa spoke without pause for nearly three hours, relating stories that were almost unbelievable. She spoke in a lively voice, acting out the stories, mimicking different voices as she went.

Lorie returned over the next three days, and again the next year, for repeat performances. She recorded many hours of detailed information concerning her mother's and grandmother's lives and began spending an hour each morning transcribing the tapes. Lorie had unearthed the perfect resource on the life stories of these two women—and she later wrote a series of historical novels based on those stories. Yet she had never suspected that her knock on her grandmother's door would begin an adventure that added unimaginable richness to her life and the lives of many others.

Thomas Carlyle said, "All that a person has done, thought, gained, or learned, is lying as in magic preservation in the pages of his book. They are the chosen possessions of man. But if he kept no book, it is as if he never was." Lorie's mother and grandmother had "kept no book," but Lorie came along and kept it for them, saving their amazing life stories for posterity. You can be the one to "keep the book" of your own life and the lives of your ancestors.

Getting Started

One key to getting your personal or family history in writing is to start with a clear idea in mind of what you want to end up with. This requires that you consider your emphasis and starting point, audience, and format.

EMPHASIS AND STARTING POINT

Deciding whether to emphasize one person—a personal history—or highlight the whole family will help you choose your starting point. Personal life stories keep the focus on the individual, although they cannot avoid dealing with family. Family histories do not have a main character; instead, they profile the family as a unit as illustrated by the interactions of family members.

Whatever excites you most should probably be your starting place, whether that is your own personal history, the history of your current family, the history of your family of origin, or the history of your ancestors as far back as you can go. Some writers like to start with their own story because it is easiest to write what they know the most about it. Also, it is wise to record your personal knowledge of your own living family while you still remember details that make a story rich and deep.

If you are more excited about recording the stories of ancestors who have passed on, however, there is nothing to stop you from starting there. Many people make this decision if they have journals or other first-hand accounts, such as the recorded interviews like those Lorie Davis obtained with her grandparents.

Formats for Your Written History

Like choosing a destination before you begin your journey, consider which format will best suit your talents, interests, and material. Some of your options include:

Narrative genealogy Recounting your ancestral information in story form. This is possible only when sufficient details are available.

Memoir Personal memories; a family history version of an autobiography.

Biography A factual life story of an interesting relative who left ample documentation such as diaries or journals, and who lived in a historical setting that can be readily researched.

Family profiles A collection of current family stories about nuclear and extended family, along with stories of family members of the past. These are "word snapshots" of random but meaningful life moments.

Literary snapshots Creative nonfiction that brings the past to life with imagined dialogue, setting, and three-dimensional characters. It is the "rest of the story" based on careful research and logical assumptions.

Cookbook family history Adding family stories to family recipes. This is especially appropriate when cooking and eating together have been popular family traditions.

Family documentary Using your written history as a script for a family history video. Include images that are directly related to the written history, such as schools, homes, tombstones, churches, farms, businesses, photographs, and more.

Family journalism Family stories and profiles written in newspaper/magazine style.

Pictorial history Incorporating family snapshots into a family history or, when plentiful, making the photos the center of the story.

It is also helpful to decide who your audience is. The format you choose may be very different if you are doing the writing only for yourself and immediate family—even to distribute at a family reunion—than it would be if you plan to publish it for libraries or historical societies.

An 8-Step Plan for Writing Personal and Family Histories

Even after you have an idea of what you want to write, it can be hard to know where to start a project like writing your family history. Following is a step-by-step plan for compiling the information for a family history and getting it into writing. This is just an example; you may find success by taking a different approach. Also keep in mind that, as with any new venture, you can expect there to be a learning curve. The important thing is to keep at it; writing a personal or family history only gets easier the more you do it.

Step 1: Gather the Material. Start with an empty box. Gather notes, photos, letters, journals, documents, and memorabilia from every nook and cranny in the house. (You may need a separate box for each family member, or perhaps for each generation.) Extend the search to living relatives who may have received letters from your ancestors or have inherited their journals, etc. Like Lorie Davis, you may choose to write letters, make phone calls, and personally visit relatives, tape recording and then writing down their recollections to preserve them for posterity. The Internet may be another good aid for beginning your research. Little by little, collect all the information you can, including anecdotes, recordings, videotapes, photos, and notes from interviews.

If you want to add cultural and historical detail to your history, research the background of the story so you can add essential, contextual information for your readers. Learn all you can of the area's historical and geographic setting. Study the culture's prevailing attitudes, customs, and costumes. Read local histories, books, magazines, and diaries of the era to pick up the flavor of the times.

Step 2: Organize Your Findings. Create a filing system that works for you. You may organize your information chronologically, topically, or by individual or family. With your materials organized you can focus on each section individually and avoid feeling over-whelmed. Take a good look—one section at a time. Assess how complete your information is and make a plan for filling in gaps. When scant information is available, you can still compile an interesting history by researching the major conditions and events of the times and suggesting how they may have impacted the individual or family.

Step 3: Create a Timeline. Once you have enough information gathered, you may find it helpful to create a timeline of the most momentous events in the life you are writing about, e.g. birth, baptism, education, moves to different houses, marriage, birth of children, etc. This will help you keep chronology straight and also pro-

> ## Sample Timeline
>
> 1943–48: Childhood
>
> 1949–54: Grade school days
>
> 1955–61: Jr. high and high school
>
> 1961–65: College years
>
> 1966–68: Marriage and newlywed years
>
> 1969–77: Birth of children
>
> 1983–88: Years when all the children were in school but living at home
>
> 1989–95: Accounts of each child leaving home
>
> 1996–present: Empty nest years
>
> Note: You may wish to make your timeline more detailed.

vide optional divisions for your filing system. You may wish to label a hanging file folder for each time period of your timeline and organize your materials into these folders.

Step 4: Create an Outline. Make an organized outline of all the information you have gathered. A card file or word processing outline template may be helpful, but neither is essential.

Creating an outline does not have to be a difficult job. An outline is only a skeleton of your project made up of its potential significant parts. (And remember the word "potential." Nothing in an outline is for sure. You can change it any moment you choose.) Feel free to throw out formal outline formatting you may have learned from a high school English teacher; just do your outline your own way. A simple list of stories or topics that you don't want to forget may suffice. (See page 120 for a sample outline.)

Another approach to outlining and organization is detailed in Richard Simon's unpublished guide to writing a family history. In it he divides life into four general periods: birth to twelve years, twelve years to courtship, marriage through parenthood, and later years.

With his approach, Simon attempts to organize memories and statistics chronologically, yet group them by topics in the gathering stages. He suggests starting each section with a page

Sample Outline

Birth in a maternity home that later becomes a restaurant

Trip to San Diego at 18 months

Seriously burned, six-week stay in hospital

Moves with family to Preston, paints neighbor's dog blue

Moves with family to Burley, then to Moscow—finds ashes in attic

Starts school, has tonsils out

Moves with family to Idaho Falls, attends 5th and 6th grades

Orchestrates neighborhood circus and newspaper

Moves with family to Ammon, starts 7th grade

Starts high school in new Bonneville High

Sophomore year—lead in school play

Junior year—attends girl state, elected Girl's Fed. President

Senior year—chosen Idaho Falls Jr. Miss, wins oratory contest

Attends college at USU—chosen Lambda Delta Sigma sweetheart

Junior year—chosen Sponsor Corps colonel, attends MP Institute in Detroit

Gets married in Idaho Falls, moves to California

of statistics such as names, dates, and places to keep the chronology of the text straight and to serve as a good source of information for future references. Grouping statistics on an introductory page also prevents encumbering your text with them. He then suggests organizing and outlining the topics within each period of time in the following categories:

personal

family

friends and other people

religious

educational

activities

personal and group

employment

environment

politics

health concerns

There may be overlap in topics, in which case you'll need to decide where that information will be placed.

Step 5: Choose an Outline Entry That Interests You and Begin Writing. When fleshing out the skeleton of your outline choose any item on your outline and flesh it out by telling the story. If the anecdote about your mother as a three-year-old painting a purebred dog bright blue makes you laugh every time you think about it, begin by writing that story. Just starting to write will get your creative juices flowing.

When you have enough information to begin any section of your outline or timeline, have fun with the writing. Chloe Vroman, who taught personal history writing classes for many years, suggests building your complete history out of short vignettes or "verbal snapshots." This approach sidesteps the problems of large organizational challenges, and these vignettes have a basic advantage. Chloe says, "[Vignettes] tend to focus on important moments in life—instants of discovery, turning points, moments of awareness and decision, in short, the essence of living."

She suggests that you consider including in your personal history relationships, challenges and struggles, difficulties overcome, your deepest thoughts, faith-promoting incidents, your blessings, what you believe, your heartbreaks and tragedies, and your impressions of places, things, and people. The resulting history can be compellingly interesting and eye-opening for your posterity.

Step 6: Keep Writing. It is inevitable that the more you write and revise, the better you will become at it. Choosing a place and time to write is a vital step in making it finally happen. Some sort of schedule—a time set aside just for you and your writing in a comfortable, well-lighted place—can make all the difference.

> *The man who writes about himself and his own time is the only man who writes about all people and about all time.*
>
> —Bernard Shaw

In order to motivate yourself to keep writing, always remember the most encouraging truth: a step is a step is a step. If you find it impossible to take a big step today, take a tiny one. Any forward movement—even the smallest—will move you closer to your goal of a finished, written personal or family history. Imagine how you would feel holding that treasure in your hands! That visualization can be a powerful motivation to get you started and keep you moving.

WRITING AND STYLE TIPS

Just write. Whenever you sit down to write, pick a place in your outline and write a draft of that small portion. Spill it out! Write down everything that comes to mind. Don't analyze or criticize your work at this point.

Remember, your efforts are a work in progress. Label your writing "rough draft" or "draft working paper," and remember that good writing is rewriting and only that which has been drafted once can be rewritten. Only when your work exists in writing can you finish, refine, focus, deepen, expand, or improve your work.

Hush your internal nitpicker. The inner nagging voice of perfectionism can discourage you by constantly telling you that your work is "not good enough." Lynda Rutledge Stephenson says, "Ignore any inner voices that make you doubt yourself. No one feels confident starting a new project, especially a big one. … Keep working on your outline as you begin to write

Famous Memoirs

St. Augustine—*Confessions*

Russell Baker—*Growing Up*

Isak Dinesen—*Out of Africa*

Anne Frank—*Anne Frank: Diary of a Young Girl*

Benjamin Franklin—*The Autobiography of Benjamin Franklin*

Ernest Hemingway—*A Moveable Feast*

Helen Keller—*The Story of My Life*

Meriwether Lewis—*The Journals of Lewis and Clark*

George Orwell—*Homage to Catalonia*

Samuel Pepys—*The Diary of Samual Pepys*

Eleanor Roosevelt—*The Autobiography of Eleanor Roosevelt*

Mark Twain—*Roughing It, Innocents Abroad,* and *Life on the Mississippi*

Henry David Thoreau—*Walden*

Eudora Welty—*One Writer's Beginnings*

Elie Wiesel—*Night*

Malcolm X—*The Autobiography of Malcolm X*

parts of the whole, and believe that you'll be able to do what it takes to get it on paper. Small steps, remember, are the key." (From *The Complete Idiot's Guide to Writing Your Family History,* page 328)

Decide your purpose. You can't say all you know if your history is for the public. You should say it all if the purpose of your work is information preserving. Be aware of whose privacy you must protect and who might be hurt by revealing family secrets.

Let your style show. Lorie Davis says, "Your true voice will come by itself, or it will be phony. You do have a style whether you like it or not. To imagine that you can write anything without a style is like thinking you can have a body without having looks. Your style is there. It will come out. As you keep on writing and keep on redoing what you wrote the day before, your true voice will become more clearly and distinctly yours."

Show, don't tell. Do not tell the reader about the person or family; instead, reveal them to the reader by directing attention to experience. Sinclair Lewis put it this way, "Don't explain your characters—make 'em live!" The writer can do this by showing the reader what the person did and said so the reader feels he is present and can feel what the subject may have felt.

TELLING: "As a teenager, Rachel was willful and stubborn. She firmly resisted her mother's constant wheedling to get her to conform to convention."

SHOWING: Rachel wore short shorts to school in the winter, T-shirts and jeans to formal gatherings, and flannel PJs and floppy bunny slippers to family parties. "Oh Rachel," her mother would always say, wringing her hands. "What will people think? It's just not proper."

Use words that are specific, definite, and concrete. The best writing deals in particulars and gives details that matter. If you record specific, definite, concrete details that can be seen, smelled, tasted, or touched, your writing will come to life.

Interview Questions to Help Jog the Memory

Where did you live as a child?

What are your most vivid childhood memories?

Were you close to any of your grandparents?

If so, what are your favorite memories of them?

What was the most serious illness you had as a child?

What do you remember best about your grade school years?

What did you do as a child that got you in the most trouble?

How did your parents handle it?

What were your mother's best and worst traits?

Which of these traits do you share with your mother?

What were your father's best and worst traits?

Which of these traits do you share with your father?

What do you remember best about your brothers and sisters?

In what ways did they influence your growing up years?

What stories do you remember about things you did with them?

Was religion important in your home?

If so, which practices made it important?

Did you have a favorite uncle or aunt?

What do you best remember about them?

Which of your neighbors were memorable?

What stories do you remember about them?

Was junior high a hard transition time?

What activities did you love most in high school?

How well do you remember your first real romance?

What was your most embarrassing moment?

What things do your enjoy doing today that you also enjoyed in your youth?

What things do your remember about being a teenager?

What was important to you then—dreams, goals, etc.?

What family traditions do you still remember?

What holidays were special in your family?

What did you do to celebrate them?

What do you remember about your first job?

How much did you make and how did you spend your money?

How did you meet your spouse?

What made you decide to marry him/her?

What events most changed your life?

Was higher education important to you?

If so, what educational experiences were pivotal in your life?

How did you decide what to study?

How did you choose your vocation and how much have you liked it?

How many jobs have you had and which did you like most? Least?

NONSPECIFIC: "Mark woke up one morning, looked at his wife and baby, and realized that he loved them very much."

SPECIFIC, DEFINITE, CONCRETE: "Mark, suddenly aware of soft rain on the roof, opened his eyes and turned to his wife Sarah. Her dark eyes were open, reflecting stars of light. She smiled at him. When the baby fussed she arose, brought the tiny, warm bundle and placed it between them in the bed. Carl reached out and pulled both soft, sweet-smelling bodies into his embrace. This, he thought is wholeness; this is love."

Writing Resources

A few basic writing resources can add accuracy, consistency, and creativity to your writing experience. Have these within reach while you are writing:

- Dictionary
- Thesaurus
- Atlas and gazetteer
- Almanac
- *The Associated Press Stylebook and Briefing on Media Law* or *The Chicago Manual of Style*
- *Evidence! Citation and Analysis for the Family Historian* by Elizabeth Shown Mills

Nouns and verbs are pure metal; adjectives and adverbs are cheaper ore.

—Robert Frost

Use specific nouns and vigorous verbs. Instead of writing "He walked down the street," try big-muscled verbs such as ambled, strolled, dashed, charged. Instead of writing, "She played the piano loudly," try, "She pounded out tunes on the piano." Instead of saying "There were many things she enjoyed in her life," say "She embraced many aspects of life."

Remember the strength of single-syllable words. Never use a long word when a short one will do. Short words are like bright sparks that glow in the night, terse like the dart and sting of a bee. (Notice that every word in that sentence was a single-syllable word.)

Use the active voice, where the action indicated by the verb is performed by the subject of the sentence, not the passive. Avoid *am, was,* and *were* whenever possible. They are passive.

ACTIVE: The boy grabbed the snake.
PASSIVE: The snake was grabbed by the boy.

Use adjectives sparingly. Keep only adjectives that denote qualities that can be perceived, that show rather than tell.

TOO MANY ADJECTIVES: "The long, flowing, glittering train of the glowing, happy bride made a soft, funny swishing sound as it followed her down the isle.

BETTER: The radiant bride's flowing train glittered and swished behind her.

Write what you know. But don't try to jam everything you know into your story. Be selective.

Interview yourself. Ask yourself pertinent questions in regard to the individuals you are writing about, such as "How did they look?" "How did they act?" or "What did they say?"

Think of your life stories like scenes in a movie. When Lorie Davis was asked "How do you write your stuff?" she said, "I look at the facts and ask myself, 'How could this have come to pass? What must have happened to make her feel that way or do that thing?' Then I close my eyes and imagine a movie of it in my brain. And I play each character in the scene to internalize their emotions and motivations. Maybe I try several movies of the same basic facts until one seems right and logical. Then, I write what I saw in the movie."

Use titillating transitions. A transition is the word, phrase, or idea that connects one sentence, paragraph, or chapter part to another. Improving transitions can be one of the most important parts of the revision process. Good transitions keep the reader reading.

Three kinds of transitions are
   1. Conjunctions, such as *and*, *but*, and *however.*
   2. Time passages, such as "ten years before," "the night after," etc.
   3. Questions. A thought-provoking question at the end of a paragraph, chapter, or section can pique your readers' curiosity and keep their interest.

Don't be afraid to delete part of what you write. Many editors share the opinion that you can tell a good story by the amount of good stuff that is thrown away. Too many words often muddy the stream.

Step 7: Fill in the Gaps with Historical Information. Research can help you tell family stories using the tiniest clues. Sometimes there is nothing at all available about the daily lives of ancestors long dead, yet sparse tidbits of information can be the key to unlocking whole decades of family history. For example, from translating entries in the ancient family Bible, Lars Johnson learned that his Finnish ancestors earned their living by growing and selling flax. His research of the flax industry in the eighteenth and nineteenth centuries unearthed a wealth of detail about the political, cultural, and day-to-day influences on his ancestors that enabled him to put together a fascinating story of what their lives were probably like.

Also, abundant information exists on the daily life and conditions of those who came to America on ships, entered the country through Ellis Island, settled in various parts of the country, traveled across the plains, etc. This information can flesh out the skeleton of basic

Rewriting, rereading, reviewing, rethinking, repairing, restructuring, reevaluating, tightening, rearranging, sharpening, deleting, transposing, expanding, condensing, pruning, polishing, perfecting. Rewriting is all of these and more. It is the secret weapon of the professional writer, the thing that separates the real writers from the 'wannabes,' the acceptable writing from the incredible writing, the average book from the page-turner. Rewriting is revision. This is the moment in your writing in which you can make your work sing.

—Lynda Rutledge Stephenson

facts to make a great story. Such research and writing experiences can be as much fun as looking through an old photo album or going through an ancestor's trunk in the attic.

Step 8: Rewrite Later. If you get bogged down in one episode and can't finish your draft, set it aside and start on another. Let the first one ripen a day, a week, a month. In the meantime, you can be rewriting another section you have fleshed out from your outline.

Revise and Polish

Whatever you write today, revise and improve tomorrow. When rewriting, keep in mind the qualities of good writing: economy, simplicity, and clarity. Reread what you wrote, and rewrite, cut, add, clarify, and make it better. Then pick another place in your outline and repeat the process.

After a week or so, go back to the first thing you wrote and improve it again. You may see more clearly where you want to go and what you want to say. If you feel like tossing a segment out and completely rewriting it, go ahead and do it.

Rewriting can actually be fun, and by doing a good job of it you can avoid the dead giveaways typical of inexperienced writers. As you read and reread, you will instinctively know what is too wordy or too vague, and you will get better at correcting these flaws. When deciding what to put in and what to leave out, it is important to keep a history as factual as possible; photos, documents, pedigree and family group sheets and other memorabilia can add color and insight to your written history. And be careful which topics you consider too uninteresting to include. Personality quirks, medical history, or favorite foods are the sorts of things that make a person unique. You may hesitate to add some details that may be just the ones that give your story zest. On the other hand, be cautious not to include details that may be offensive or that make the history cumbersome to read.

ADVANTAGES OF TECHNOLOGY

Writers of personal and family histories in the new millennium have advantages that their grandparents would hardly believe possible. Particularly in the rewriting and revision process, computers can be your best friend.

"Recent advances in personal computing, specifically with the numerous excellent word-processing programs available, make the checking of spelling, the movement of sections of text, the reduction and expansion of sentences and ideas, and the final preparation of a cam-

Getting Motivated to Write Your Family History

Why Not Start—NOW?

You may be one of those who have chosen the exciting goal of recording family histories (or it has chosen you) and even decided where to start, yet can't seem to get started. Following are ways to pop your procrastination balloons.

Can't Find the Time?

"Give Me Five." If you write no more than five minutes, five lines, five paragraphs, or five pages, if you write five you will eventually reach your goal. The "give me five" commitment is the prediction of success. Those who "give five" consistently will experience a growing sense of excitement and progress as their project becomes increasingly real and obviously possible.

Intimidated by the Immensity of the Project?

Start small, but start. Begin wherever your interest leads you. Remember that a little effort on a fairly consistent basis can reap an amazing result in a year's time. If you write just one page a week, at the end of a year you will have produced fifty-two pages of copy! Twice a week and you'll have twice that number. Why not start today?

Paralyzed by Perfectionism?

Settle in your mind that your first efforts are just that—first efforts. They may even be bad, but that doesn't matter at all. Once you've got something down you can find an infinite number of ways to improve it. However, you can't improve what doesn't exist. Read the following words over and over until you believe them: perfection is not possible, but good writing is.

Lack Information?

Turn to living relatives first. Lorie Davis, whose mother had told her nothing about her early life or her ancestors, was fortunate to have a living relative who was a veritable storehouse of information. But if you have no living relatives to turn to, don't despair.

Throughout history many people—including your ancestors—have kept all kinds of records. History itself is based, in a large part, on the records kept by individuals. Personal journals are the firsthand accounts of individuals who lived the experiences and bear witness to what they saw and heard. They should be your next consideration. If your parents, grandparents, or great-grandparents kept journals, cherish them. If journals were kept, the history usually becomes an abridgement of the journals, supplemented by other research. If no journals are available, more research will be necessary to write the story.

era-ready copy a cinch." says Lawrence P. Goldrup, Ph.D in *Writing the Family Narrative*.

In addition, there are family history computer programs that help speed and smooth the process of writing family history. For example, several programs available today ask you to simply fill in the blanks; then they write the story based on that information. This method is less personal and more prone to inaccuracies because these programs do not always interpret information correctly. However, a fill-in-the-blank writing program could be especially helpful for those who have not found the time to write a more personal story, or for those who need a jumping-off point. These computer programs are available from most major genealogy companies. Just make sure to double-check the computer program's story as carefully as you would your own work.

THE VALUE OF KINDLY FEEDBACK

All writers reach a point where they are too close to the forest to see the trees. Choosing a trusted reader for feedback can be one of the most helpful things you do.

Chloe Vroman says, "If you are working by yourself, it is easy to run dry and become discouraged. Writing is communicating, and if there is no reader to interact with, it is virtually impossible to know whether you are getting your message across. If you are work-

ing on your own, enlarge your circle by reading from your work to your children and friends. Get together with like-minded friends and set a time to meet and read to each other what you have written."

Sharing can be intimidating, but honest feedback can let you know whether you are hitting the mark in reader interest. Be careful to avoid sharing your work with those who may be too critical or negative. Find friends or relatives who are interested enough that they will not only give you helpful suggestions, but will mention your strengths and encourage you as well.

A Family History Case Study

Fern Larsen used the plan outlined in this chapter to create a personal and family history that has become a great treasure to her family. She initially chose the picture history format and determined that the books she created would be strictly for the family.

When sorting and packing Fern's possessions in order to move her from a condo into her own home, her daughter Darla gathered all Fern's journals, photo albums, slides, and important papers into labeled boxes. Later, she and Fern created a timeline of the most important periods and events of Fern's life. Together they labeled one hanging file folder for each time period (such as "school years"), then sorted her materials and photos into the appropriate folders. When they could

see what they had to work with, they made a fairly detailed outline.

They scoured Fern's diaries and journals, highlighting and marking important information for inclusion in her written history, and then pulled the best pictures from her lifelong collection. They focused on one time period, organized the pictures they had pulled from old albums and loose collections, and entered information for that time period on the computer. When the information from her journals proved to be inadequate, Fern would dictate other memories and details, and Darla would type them into the computer, then revise and polish the words.

Fern had no photos, journal entries, or letters, and very few specific memories of her early childhood. However, using many

Outline of Fern's Life

Fern's large nuclear family
Her childhood
Summers on the farm
School days
Her father's untimely death
Move to Mantua and newfound popularity
Dating, dances, plays, graduation
Becoming a housemaid
Unpleasant dating experiences, discouragement, fear of never marrying
Meeting Arland, courtship, engagement
Arland's family and youth
Marriage, settling down
First baby, health problems
Second baby, sharing daily life with friends
Buying ice cream store in Blackfoot, having to work there
Third baby, joy at staying home with children
Death of baby, loneliness, expecting another baby gives her hope
Birth of fourth baby, World War II, Arland drafted
Trip to San Diego, joy interrupted when baby seriously injured
War over, Arland discharged, move to Burley, Idaho
Birth of fifth baby, his long illness and hospitalization
Move to Moscow, Idaho, birth of sixth baby

of the ideas in this chapter, the history of her childhood (1910-1920) became a fascinating part of her history. She and Darla found pictures and written information about the time period, and Fern related what it was like to live as a child in a house with no electricity or indoor plumbing. She remembered traveling by horse and buggy before the first automobiles and described how farming was done with horses before the first tractor. She told of churning butter, washing clothes on a board, and taking Saturday night baths in a big, tin tub. She remembered the first record player, first radio, first Model T, first airplane. They are all part of her childhood, and now documented with her words and pictures from various sources, they have become intensely interesting to her posterity who can hardly imagine such a different way of life.

When they came to the last decade of Fern's life, they asked her children and grandchildren for pictures of events she had been involved in as well as for pictures

of their own families. Designing pages that were mostly pictures was a creative and fun part of the process. Sharing the work with others and getting enthusiastic feedback kept them going. Because of Fern's advanced age, they never worked more than an hour or two a day. Many times health challenges kept them from their pet project for days on end, but they always came back to it. The stack of finished pages grew, and Fern took great delight in sharing her story with friends and relatives who visited.

Publishing and Distribution Possibilities

Fern had no desire to have her books copied, printed, or published, but you might. When

your writing is finished, printing and/or publishing your work can be your next great adventure. Your options include having it copied and bound at a copy shop, self-publishing, or submitting it to a publisher interested in family histories. Desktop publishing programs abound, and you can make your manuscript look like a book by using a typesetting program and creating front and back matter such as a table of contents, title page, and index.

You should be proud of your work and you can easily find outlets for sharing it beyond your family and friends. "Check with your local genealogical organizations and online genealogical chat groups… historical museums, genealogical societies, and even libraries offer contests and fairs to showcase your work, as well as chances to see what others are doing with their family histories," suggests Lynda Rutledge Stephenson in The Complete Idiot's Guide to Writing Your Family History. She says that new genealogical magazines and journals are hungry for interesting work. "Keep your eyes open as you enjoy your family's response, and be proud enough of your work to take advantage of any and all chances for "sharing and showing" that you can. . .

You've done a marvelous piece of creative research, which will become more of a family treasure as the years go by."

Roots Give Wings

Writing down who we are, what we think, and what we do has always been the means of transmitting the story of what it means to be human. In 1862, a *Deseret News* journalist powerfully summarized the importance of keeping a diary. His words provide a perfect motivation for recording personal and family histories as well: "If a man keeps no diary [or fails to record his personal and family histories], the path crumbles away behind him as his feet leave it; and days gone by are but little more than a blank, broken by a few distorted shadows. His life is all confined within limits of today . . . There must be a richness about the life of a person who keeps a diary . . . And a million more little links and ties must bind him to the members of his family circle, and to all among whom he lives." (*Deseret News*, July 16, 1862.)

There are two lasting bequests we can give our children: One is roots, the other is wings.

—Hodding Carter, Jr.

There is no way to adequately stress the vast importance of recording your own history and the history of those who have gone before. Humanity yearns for ties that bind. Few of us truly wish to be alone, disconnected, without knowledge of or connection to a family. The written word can bind us to each other like little else we know. When you write about your life, about your ancestors' lives, you create ties that keep on binding, glue that keeps on sticking your family together for as long as your words can be read.

Lorie Davis, speaking of the family histories and novels she has written based on the life stories of her mother and grandmother said, "The personal triumph is that writing my mother's and grandmother's histories has brought me closer to my ancestors. Their lives have been an astonishing revelation to my own brothers and sisters, and shown the grandchildren and great-grandchildren the amazing richness of their heritage. Perhaps best of all, they have caused a great many people to take a closer look at ancestors of their own."

Even if not one other person benefitted, your work on personal and family histories can still be enormously rewarding. You need to know that untold benefits are waiting for you, too. You may be the one who will get the most out of this project.

In 1999, Fern Larsen, soon to celebrate her ninetieth birthday, found herself the last surviving sibling of her large family. The final weeks of her life became a treasured story that completed her extensive family history like frosting on a delicious cake.

Three weeks before she died, Fern had a premonition that her time was very short. She was ready for her next great adventure and excited to go. She planned

131

her funeral and gathered her family around her. She lovingly went through her treasures one last time, giving many of them to children and grandchildren. As she grew weaker and was unable to get out of bed, she asked her daughter Darla to read to her from her proudest achievement: two thick volumes that comprised the extensive picture history of her family. No precious knowledge of her family would die with her. She had documented it well and left a legacy that would continue. She was content, satisfied she had done her part. She died peacefully, certain that her influence would live on.

Using this chapter as a guide and motivation, you can be just as certain that your influence will live on. You too can create a lasting record of your personal and family history for generations to enjoy.

Study the past, if you would divine the future.
—Confucius

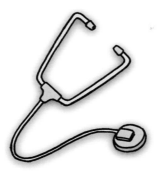

CHAPTER SIX

Decoding Genetics

Your Family Health History

Six-year-old Henry Strongin-Goldberg gives all the appearances of being just like any other kid his age. Though he may be smaller than most, he loves Batman and soccer, wrestles with his younger brother, and thinks Walt Disney World is the greatest place on earth. But Henry is not typical. He has spent much of his life in waiting rooms, doctor's offices, and hospitals.

Henry suffers from a rare disease known as Fanconi anemia, a chronic disorder associated with small stature, bone marrow failure, congenital malformations, and a predisposition to leukemia. The condition may also cause learning disabilities or mental retardation. About one thousand suffer from it, but about one in one hundred to one in six hundred carry the trait. Because it's a recessive disorder, if two carriers have offspring, the child has a 25 percent chance of inheriting the disease itself. Fanconi anemia affects every ethnic group, but among Ashkenazic Jews, like the Strongin-Goldbergs, the incidence is about one in ninety.

Henry's diagnosis spurred his grandmother, Phyllis Goldberg, into action. She was told the disease was caused by a founder effect—a mutation that occurred in one person in the fourteenth or fifteenth century in Eastern Europe and then was passed down from generation to generation. "This could be traced through family history research," Phyllis thought to herself. She set out to try and find potential carriers and have them tested. And she made a promise to Henry that she would leave no stone unturned until she found every member of their family at risk.

Armed with the rallying cry "Knowledge is power," Phyllis began researching her family's history. She found that her own family as well as that of her daughter-in-law came from the same area in the former Austro-Hungarian Empire.

Phyllis is just one of a growing breed of family historians reaching back into the past to get a better understanding of her family's health and its associated risks. According to the American Medical Association (AMA), "gathering a complete family history is becoming more important as genetic medicine explains more diseases. As a patient realizes the connection within their family, he or she undoubtedly seeks to gather, perhaps informally, perhaps not, more personal information regarding risk to develop particular diseases." The AMA supports research initiatives with Web-based tools, including a genetic screening questionnaire, a pediatric clinical genetics questionnaire, a sample pedigree and an adult family history form. One of its committees is developing a universal family history tool for patients.

"In the last ten years, a scientific and healthcare revolution has been occurring," says Joan Kirchman Mitchell, National Genealogical Society (NGS) Family Health and Heredity Committee member and health care educator. "New studies and research in genetics, including the Human Genome Project, have made the public more conscious of our health. Combine that with the increase in the number of people tracing their family history and there's a need to know what genetics is about and how it relates to your family."

Genetic disorders affect every family. There isn't anyone who doesn't have cancer, heart disease, or high cholesterol somewhere in his or her family.

—Bea Leopold,
executive director,
National Society of Genetic Counselors

Researching your medical history can help you and medical professionals preserve your family's health for generations to come. As many as half of all health conditions may have a genetic component, passed down within families from generation to generation. A recent issue of the *Mayo Clinic Health Letter* points out that it's important to remember that many significant medical problems have familial tendencies, including heart disease, high blood pressure, diabetes, some cancers, and certain psychiatric disorders. "Genetic disorders affect every family," adds Bea Leopold, executive director of the National Society of Genetic Counselors. "There isn't anyone who doesn't have cancer, heart disease, or high cholesterol somewhere in his or her family."

It's never been easier to trace your family's health history. Legislation like the Health and Human Services Health Insurance Portability and Accountability Act (HIPAA) ensures that you can access your private medical records, and an increasing number of Web-based sites and tools and software capabilities can help you learn and document your medical history.

The Human Genome Project

The Human Genome Project, a massive international scientific effort formally begun in 1990, has a goal to complete the identification of our approximately 100,000 genes by 2003. It has also sparked great interest in what makes us human as well as a general interest in genetics.

A "genome" is a term used to describe the total genetic material contained in a full set of an organism's chromosomes. Genomes vary in size, ranging from about 600,000 DNA base pairs for a bacterium to some three billion for human and mouse genomes. Sequencing has identified more than 30,000 human genes, some of which are responsible for diseases.

Researchers have collected blood samples from women and sperm samples from men to be processed as DNA resources in sequencing. Five donors representing Hispanic, Asian, Caucasian, and African-American backgrounds provided samples to the private genomics company, Celera, for this purpose.

The small genomes of several viruses and bacteria have been completely sequenced. The much larger genomes of three higher organisms—baker's yeast, the roundworm, and the fruit fly—have also been sequenced. In December 2000, the first full sequencing of a complete plant genome, *Arabidopsis thaliana*, a weed in the mustard family, was completed. Humans share most of the same protein families with worms, flies, and plants. In the case of the mustard plant weed, thirty-six of its genes are similar to those causing our genetic diseases.

As a result of the Human Genome Project, the total number of genes has been estimated to be much lower than previous estimates of 80,000 to 140,000. Scientists have also identified about 1.4 million locations where single-base DNA differences occur in humans, which promises to "revolutionize the processes of finding chromosomal locations for disease-associated sequences." The Project issued its draft sequence in February 2001 and is already having impact finding genes associated with disease. More than thirty genes have been pinpointed and associated with breast cancer, muscle disease, deafness, and blindness. Also, finding the DNA sequences underlying common diseases such as cardiovascular disease, diabetes, arthritis, and cancers is aided by the human variation maps generated by the Project in cooperation with the private sector. The genes and maps serve as targets for the development of effective new therapies.

The Basics of Genetic Inheritance

Genetic inheritance begins with DNA, the genetic code for all living things. DNA is broken up into four subunits, called bases, that are arranged in a specific order, such as ATTCCGGA: A for adenine, T for thymine, C for cytosine, and G for guanine. The order of the bases provides the code for our genes and gives us our unique traits. Our genes are arranged in rows on chromosomes. A chromosome is a DNA molecule that contains the genetic information for an organism. The human genome is estimated to contain 30,000 to 40,000 genes, which provide codes for making the proteins that perform most of the life functions in our bodies.

Each of us inherits two copies of each gene, one from our father and one from our mother. Each of us also has twenty-three pairs of chromosomes in each cell of our body except the egg and sperm, which have only one copy of each chromosome. Twenty-two pairs of our chromosomes are called non-sex chromosomes, or autosomes. The twenty-third pair is

Glossary of Genetic and Medical Terms

Autosomal dominant   An inheritance pattern in which only one copy of a gene pair needs to be abnormal in order for the disorder to appear.

Autosomal recessive   An inheritance pattern in which both copies of a gene pair carry the abnormal gene.

Autosome   A chromosome not involved in sex determination.

Carrier testing   Determines whether an individual has an abnormal gene which would, when expressed in his or her offspring, lead to a genetic disorder.

Chromosome   A DNA molecule that contains the genetic information for an organism.

Direct testing   Process of finding specific mutations or alterations in the gene's DNA.

Deoxyribonucleic acid (DNA)   The genetic code for all living things.

Gene   The basic chemical element of heredity.

Gene mapping   The process of identifying the relative positions of genes on a DNA molecule and the distance between them.

Gene therapy   Process of inserting normal DNA directly into cells to correct a genetic defect.

Genome   All the genetic material contained in a full set of chromosomes of an organism.

Linkage testing   Process that assesses the likelihood that a form of the gene has been inherited along with the marker.

Marker   An identifiable physical location on a chromosome whose inheritance can be monitored.

Multifactorial disorders   Genetic disorders brought on by the combination of multiple factors, including several different genes as well as environmental influence.

Mutation   Any permanent change in DNA sequence.

Prenatal testing   Process that determines whether a child will be at risk for disorders through the use of amniocentesis, ultrasound, or expanded feto protein procedures.

Presymptomatic testing   Conducted for conditions we have in our genes that predispose us, such as prostate or breast cancer, because these diseases run in families.

Sequencing   The process of examining DNA to see if it is coded correctly.

Sex chromosomes   X and Y chromosomes.

Single gene disorder   Hereditary disorder caused by abnormality in a single gene.

Susceptibility testing   Process that searches for a gene whose presence can increase the chances of developing a health problem later in life.

X-linked dominant   An inheritance pattern in which one copy of the gene for that disorder is present on the X chromosome.

X-linked recessive   An inheritance pattern in which both copies of the gene for that disorder present on the X chromosome will cause the disease in females. In males, since there is only one X chromosome, a single recessive gene will cause the disease.

known as the sex chromosome and consists of a combination of the X and/or Y chromosomes. Females have two X chromosomes, and males have one X and one Y chromosome.

Changes to our DNA, chromosomes, or genes may cause certain diseases or disorders. Large changes may involve having either too few or too many chromosomes—such as Down syndrome, a disorder in which an individual's cells contain a third copy of chromosome twenty-one—or a rearrangement, such as a gene that is normally linked to chromosome one but shows up on chromosome four. More subtle changes at the DNA level can cause hereditary abnormal mutations such as cystic fibrosis and sickle cell anemia, or may predispose you to cancer, major psychiatric diseases, and other disorders.

Patterns of Inheritance

In the nineteenth century, the Austrian monk Gregor Mendel experimented with inheritance patterns in plants, making careful observations of traits passed from parent to offspring. Although his work was largely neglected at the time, it nonetheless forms the foundation of modern genetics.

Disorders caused by changes in single genes follow certain patterns described by Mendel; these are labeled autosomal dominant, autosomal recessive, and X-linked. Other diseases are caused by a combination of genetics and environmental factors. These are known as multifactorial disorders.

What is meant by dominant and recessive? To put it simply, you inherit a dominant disorder if you receive one copy of an abnormal gene. You inherit a recessive disorder if you receive two copies of the abnormal gene. If your parents each had a dominant gene, however, it doesn't necessarily mean you inherited it. Likewise, if they each carried a recessive gene, it could still be passed on to you.

This five-generation photograph shows the obvious physical characteristics that are passed from one generation to the next. It also serves as a reminder that medical characteristics can be passed on just as easily.

AUTOSOMAL DOMINANT AND RECESSIVE

Autosomal dominant conditions involve having one copy of an abnormal gene and one copy of a normal gene. There's a 50 percent chance of passing the abnormal gene on to your children. Men and women can be equally affected by autosomal dominant conditions. When looking at dominant patterns in your family's history, you'll see that the condition is inherited from both males and females, it affects multiple generations, and the severity of the symptoms can vary. Examples of autosomal dominant conditions include Huntington's disease, and neurofibromatosis.

Autosomal recessive conditions involve having two copies of the abnormal gene—one from each of your parents. If you inherit only one copy of the abnormal gene, you will carry the trait but will not be personally affected. When looking at recessive patterns in your family history, you'll see multiple individuals within a single generation who are affected, either male or female. For many of these disorders, members of a particular set of ethnic groups may be at higher risk than the general population. Examples of autosomal recessive conditions include phenylketonuria, sickle-cell anemia, Tay-Sachs disease, and thalassemia.

X-LINKED (ALSO KNOWN AS SEX-LINKED)

Because each female carries two X chromosomes at the twenty-third pair, she can only pass on the X chromosome. The male's sperm determines the sex of the child, depending on whether it carries an X chromosome (female) or Y (male). In the X-linked recessive inheritance pattern, the disease-causing gene is on the X chromosome. For a female to inherit the disease, both of her X chromosomes have to have the abnormal gene. Women typically are only carriers for the trait—meaning they don't exhibit the actual disorder—because their

second X chromosome most likely contains normal genes from the father. A male will inherit the disease when his one X chromosome has the abnormal gene. Men cannot simply be carriers because they only have one X chromosome.

If a male with an X-linked recessive condition such as hemophilia and Duchenne muscular dystrophy has children and the female with whom he has children is not a carrier, any daughters he has will be carriers and any sons he has will not be at risk.

When you look at your family history for patterns of X-linked recessive conditions, you'll see a predominance of affected males and you'd typically see male-to-male transmission throughout multiple generations.

OTHER INHERITANCE PATTERNS

Three other patterns are extremely rare but should be mentioned: X-linked dominant patterns, involving one copy of an abnormal gene on the X chromosome; mitochondrial DNA patterns, causing conditions that are only inherited from the mother from outside the cell's nucleus; and Y-linked patterns, involving abnormal genes on the Y chromosome.

It's also important to remember that if blood relatives marry and have children, the risk of recessive traits and diseases increases because genes will be common between the parents.

Understanding the basics of genetic inheritance can prepare you to both understand your family's medical history and to understand the contributions genetic counseling and genetic testing can offer.

Genetic Testing

Often, when meeting with medical practitioners about genetic testing, you'll be asked to provide the family's medical history. Typically, there's no expectation of format unless you're given a questionnaire in advance. However, it is important to know your family structure for at least three generations, including siblings, aunts, uncles, and cousins.

Through genetic testing, genetic counselors can help you interpret your history to understand where health risks might lie and to identify ways to further define these risks relative to the general population. They can help you prevent future onset, monitor changes, and detect symptoms at early stages. Many counselors or the institutions they are associated with may send you a questionnaire to complete so that your first meeting can be informed and productive. Being as specific as you can and providing documentation are critical.

"One goal of many counselors is to help promote an individual's long-term health so he or she can take a more proactive role in health promotion and disease prevention," says Jennifer Farmer, genetic counselor and clinical coordinator at the University of Pennsylvania Hospital. "Knowing your family's history helps you be more proactive. It can be a means to empower people with information."

Because documentation is so important, counselors can help you access medical records, autopsy reports, and sometimes death certificates. The more detailed the information, the better. Let's suppose someone in your family had cancer. In order to accurately determine your risk, the counselor needs to know the specific types of tumors and age of onset. If someone had "stomach cancer," was it kidney cancer or pancreatic cancer? If someone had "female problems," was it uterine cancer, ovarian cancer, cervical cancer, or something else? If you know where someone was diagnosed and treated and

Questions for a Health History Interview

When did your relative die, at what age, what was the cause of death?

Where were they born and where did they later live?

Are there any unusual traits in our family?

Have there been miscarriages or stillbirths in our family?

Was anyone in the family extremely obese or thin?

Who suffered from major diseases, such as cancer, heart disease, diabetes, or Alzheimer's?

At was age were they diagnosed?

Has anyone had reconstructive surgery?

Who has been hospitalized, for what condition, and for how long?

Have cousins married cousins in our family?

Has anyone abused alcohol or drugs?

Has anyone suffered from recurring maladies, such as allergies (and to what), headaches, and others?

Do we have a history of mental illness or institutionalization in the family?

What was your relative's race and ethnicity? (Some ethnic groups are more predisposed towards certain conditions than others.)

can provide the physician's name, that can be of significant value.

It's also important to document your findings so you can share them with your relatives.

"Accurate knowledge of one's family history is an important prerequisite for susceptibility gene testing," says Dr. Doris Teichler Zallen, an expert in genetic technologies at Virginia Tech University and author of *Does It Run in the Family: A Consumer's Guide to DNA Testing for Genetic Disorders*. "The health problems experienced by older family members may herald the kinds of health problems that younger members of the family may face. Layers of confusion may need to be penetrated before the real family medical history becomes clear and a pattern emerges that points to the possible involvement of a susceptibility gene."

Dr. Ronald Bachman of the Department of Genetics at Oakland Kaiser Permanente Hospital in California, agrees. "We use any clues we can get to understand what you're predisposed to, from hemophilia to cancer."

According to Dr. Bachman, there are some five hundred to one thousand genetic tests that can be performed. The specific tests for an individual vary based on that person's heredity. "You can't come in and say I want all these tests," he says. "It depends on your background. Everything has to be identified. If you're African-American, we'd likely test for sickle-cell anemia. If you have a Jewish background, we'd test for Tay-Sachs."

Four different types of genetic testing can be performed: direct, linking, susceptibility, and carrier. Direct testing can find specific mutations or alterations in a gene's DNA. Linkage testing assesses the likelihood that a form of the gene has been inherited along with the marker, a reference point that distinguishes one DNA pattern from another. Susceptibility testing looks for a gene whose presence can increase the chances of developing a health problem later in life. And carrier testing, a very difficult process, which some people undergo at a premarital or preconception stage, is perhaps the most controversial; it can help identify potential risks so the couple can decide how to proceed before any harmful family legacies continue. Tests are currently available for Tay-Sachs, thalassemia, sickle-cell disease, hemophilia, and others.

DNA samples can also help explore the presence of a susceptibility gene in a deceased person. Stored tissue is critical if linkage testing is being considered in families where the affected members have died.

Genetic testing can be performed for multiple purposes: prenatal, presymptomatic, and diagnostic. Prenatal testing is accomplished through the expanded alpha-fetoprotein test, amniocentesis, and ultrasound—all help to determine whether your child might be at risk for disorders like Down syndrome, spina bifida, neural tube defects, cleft lip and cleft palate, congenital heart disease, club foot, and hydrocephalus.

Presymptomatic testing is conducted because some of us may be predisposed toward certain conditions (such as breast or prostate cancer) since they run in families. For instance, 5 percent to 10 percent of women with breast cancer inherited a predisposition to develop the disease.

This 1933 photograph depicts seven sisters, four of whom died of cancer, as did their mother. A health history was created for the family, and the children and grandchildren of these women now know that regular visits to the doctor are necessary to protect them from the deadly disease.

Finally, diagnostic testing is used to help understand a specific problem. For instance, when a child has a developmental delay or a birth defect, genetic testing can get to the root cause of what's going on. It can be used in an adult onset condition as well.

13 Places to Research Your Family's Health History

"For any genetic assessment to be carried out, it is necessary to find out who the members are in the nuclear family and in the extended family and exactly how they are related," Dr. Zallen says. "Further, it is important to know what health problems they have, or, if they have died, what did they have. Genetic specialists use the family history, which they organize into a diagram, as the basis for identifying what the genetic problems may be and for providing estimates of risk."

Your first step in researching your family's health history is to gather information from a variety of sources, beginning with those closest to you—your relatives.

1. Interviews. You know the scene: a family gathering where your relatives are comparing notes on their latest ailments. Listen carefully. They're revealing much about their health histories. Such a scene can provide a terrific opportunity to find out that Aunt Sally, her mother, and her mother's mother all suffered from diabetes. Or maybe Uncle Joe had cleft palate reconstructive surgery before he entered kindergarten. As Phyllis Goldberg says, "Talking to members of your family about health history is the first and most important step as well as the most valuable."

It's always best to start with your immediate family, those you know best. Arm yourself with a list of questions (see page 142), and you'll be on your way. Start with your parents, brothers and sisters, and children, either directly or indirectly. Then add data from and about grandparents, aunts and uncles, cousins, nieces, and nephews. Take note of any inconsistencies or gaps so you can research them later. Be sympathetic to and honor the need for privacy because requesting medical information requires diplomacy and sensitivity. Some relatives will probably be reluctant to admit there are certain familial traits and tendencies. They may be considered skeletons in the closet and that's where they'd like them to stay.

Because the interview process is so important and provides the basis for more detailed and specific research, it's a good idea to

- Know in advance what you want to ask. Have your list of questions ready along with some idea of family medical conditions you want to know more about.
- Begin with the family members you think will provide the most information and can guide or refer you to others. Getting a referral may also help you get past some of the more sensitive issues. Pay attention to those who you think can provide you with the key leads for expanding your search.

A Case Study: Genetic Inheritance of Familial Mediterranean Fever

Nancy Sparks Morrison of Roanoke, Virginia, suffered for years. From the time she was eight years old, she remembers attacks of high fever and pain in her lower right side. Her mother detailed attacks Nancy had even in infancy. Doctors told them she might have a mild case of polio or appendicitis. As she grew older, her health worsened. She began to suffer from depression in elementary school. In her thirties, her depression deepened and fibromyalgia, a painful muscle condition that affects millions of Americans with no known cause or cure, set in. By her late forties, periods of wellness were few and far between.

"By this time, my doctors and many of my family thought I was a hypochondriac, because of the many and varied symptoms I presented," Nancy says. "I was diagnosed previously and erroneously, it turns out, with fibromyalgia." She was later diagnosed through blood tests as having rheumatoid arthritis. She had X-rays that showed osteoarthritis. Diagnoses abounded and the list grew longer.

Nancy had been researching her family's history for decades. Forced to take disability-related early retirement, she found refuge on the Internet—continuing research to break through the brick wall after tracing her family to Kentucky in the 1800s. Another researcher suggested she check into a group known as the Melungeons—a people of Mediterranean descent who settled in the Appalachians in the 1500s. Morrison attended a nearby "reunion" of Melungeons. She says, "It was at that reunion that I heard Dr. N. Brent Kennedy speak about his tentative diagnosis of Familial Mediterranean Fever and I knew from his symptoms that this is exactly what I had."

She asked her doctor for a trial prescription of the medicine colchicine to treat Family Mediterranean Fever. Nancy says, "At the point when I took the medicine, I could not rise from a seated position without pushing or pulling myself up with my hands. I moaned and groaned as I came down the steps in the morning. I had trouble doing simple arithmetic in order to balance a checkbook. I waited to die. My life was miserable."

By researching her family's medical history, she found a clue to resolving her health problems. Once diagnosed with a variant of Familial Mediterranean Fever, she was able to reclaim her life with proper medication. She says, "If I had not found the Melungeon connection to my family, and thereby my inherited illness, Familial Mediterranean Fever, I would be dead now. I was a wreck. But I am beginning to improve. It is a miracle."

- Don't take anything for granted. People often don't know or cannot remember their exact medical condition. Probe and ask for proof and documentation. Try asking, "How do you know that?" and keep asking until you get something concrete and tangible. Ask for permission to talk to family doctors or anyone who has been involved with the family's health. This is particularly relevant when tracking genetic traits that can be a potential disaster for future generations, as not everyone will recognize or accept the implications of the trait they carry.

- Encourage the person you're interviewing to be as specific as possible. Details do matter.

- Ask for any supporting documentation. Photographs, records, and/or correspondence can all be valuable. Offer to make copies.

- Offer to share the results. Your research can help the family as a whole, so it's important to document it and then communicate it as widely as you can.
- Enlist others in the family, particularly doctors and other medical professionals who understand and support the aims of your research.

Information on any medical ailment may prove useful. Pay special attention to serious conditions such as cancer, high blood pressure, heart disease, diabetes, depression, and alcoholism. Be sure to also jot down your relative's age when an illness was diagnosed.

Aim to collect information on three or four generations. This information will make it much easier for your medical professional to be in a good position to help you and your family. And don't forget to ask for photographs, especially for disorders that are physically discernible.

What your family tells you can be helpful and revealing, but not everything you hear may be fact. Oral history is likely to be distorted. The other items in this list will help to fill in the gaps and verify critical medical information.

2. Death Certificates. Usually an attending physician lists the primary cause of death and contributing factors on a death certificate. Ask your relatives about medical conditions, when the deceased first got sick, how long the illness lasted, the duration of the hospital stay, etc. There could be more to the story than the death certificate indicates because it reflects only the terminal event. For instance, your father's death certificate may give heart failure as the cause of death, but you know he suffered from diabetes-related kidney failure and was on dialysis for some time. Or, in another example, an elderly woman died from a fall down the stairs. Her granddaughter stated that she had Alzheimer's. Which was really the cause of death? Also be sure to question "old age" or "natural causes" as a cause of death.

You can request death certificates from the town, county, or state where your family member died. Cyndi's List, a Web site with more than 100,000 links to family history sites, can lead you to the appropriate vital record office, organized by state (http://www.cyndis-list.com/usvital.htm#States). When requesting a death certificate, you may be required to provide proof of relationship. If you don't know the date or place of death, you can visit a Web site like RootsWeb.com to conduct a name search using the Social Security Death Index.

If you find yourself stumped by old medical terms used to describe the cause of death, consult the online "Glossary of Ancient Diseases" or "Old Diseases and Their Modern Definition" listed in the Appendix (page 224).

3. Obituaries. An obituary can pinpoint the date and place of death, the age at death, and the identity of spouse, children, and siblings. It can also help identify useful medical facts. Read it carefully and look for clues, such as the person died "after a long illness" or the person "lost the battle against cancer." Sometimes a foundation or memorial fund is mentioned in case readers want to send donations. These can provide additional insights. The more prominent the person was, the more information the obituary will contain. Your local librarian can help you determine whether the newspaper you're

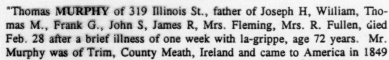

"Thomas **MURPHY** of 319 Illinois St., father of Joseph H, William, Thomas M., Frank G., John S, James R, Mrs. Fleming, Mrs. R. Fullen, died Feb. 28 after a brief illness of one week with la-grippe, age 72 years. Mr. Murphy was of Trim, County Meath, Ireland and came to America in 1849 and had been a resident of Chicago and the Cathedral Parish since 1853. He was engaged for a number of years in the ice business and won for himself hosts of friends in social and business circles. He retired from active business a few years ago. A peculiar incident in connection with Mr. Murphy's death was the fact that he died on the same day, date and hour that his wife died eleven years ago. The funeral took place at the Holy Name Cathedral Wednesday morning March 2, at 10:30 o'clock where Solemn High Mass of Requiem was celebrated by the Reverend J.M. Scanlan; Reverend J.P. Dorr, deacon; and Reverend F.J. Barry, subdeacon. The eulogy over the remains was delivered by the Rev. J.M. Scanlan who paid a well merited tribute to the departed and revered father. The remains were laid to rest in the family lot in Calvary, Reverend J.P. Dorr officiating at the grave. The pall-bearers were: Messrs. James Healy, William Walsh, Thomas Duggan, Martin Cooney, Thomas Drurry, and William Spain. May he rest in peace."

looking for has been microfilmed or exists in its original form. Obituaries for some newspapers, such as the *New York Times*, are indexed.

You might also want to visit the Web site for the USGenWeb Project (www.usgen-web.com), which has an obituary project underway. You can view the state and county pages for the obituary you're looking for and see if it's been published. This is by no means an exhaustive site, but it can be helpful.

Phyllis Goldberg was concerned about her husband's health since he had had a very serious heart attack at the age of fifty. "It seemed obvious that there was an inherited problem, but we didn't know where it was coming from," she says. "I was lucky enough to find full-text obituaries of a family of my mother-in-law's first cousins. The family owned a department store and was prominent enough in the community to warrant stories in the

Software to Document Your Health History

Many standard genealogical programs allow you to capture your family's health history. In addition, specialized programs help you chart your history.

Cyrillic 3

www.cyrillicsoftware.com/products/cyril3.htm

Cyrillic 3 from Cherwell Scientific is intended for use by research labs and clinics. It allows genetic counselors and others to draw and edit pedigrees. Cyrillic 2 allows these professionals to use genetic marker data in their analysis. These software packages can also help calculate risk of breast cancer.

Family Tree Maker

www.familytreemaker.com

From an individual's "More" page, click on Medical Information. The Medical Information Dialog Box enables you to record height, weight, cause of death, and any other medical information—illnesses, allergies, genetic diseases. Be sure to use the Source Dialog Box so you can document where you found the information. You can also create a pre-designed Medical Information Report—including an individual's name, birth date, and information from the Medical Information Dialog Box—or you can customize your own report.

Genelines

www.progenysoftware.com

Genelines features a health category that you can add to your genealogical information. An individual's bar chart will plot his or her health-related events according to a timeline. You can also compare the events of two individuals in a single chart. This would be especially useful to monitor the ages at which family members contracted a particular disease, for example.

Genetic Analysis Package (GAP)

icarus2.hsc.usc.edu/epicenter/gap.html

A management and analysis tool for professionals, GAP automatically draws pedigrees, allows for input of diagnosis codes, and can sort by genotype.

Geneweaver

www.geneweaveronline.com

Newly available, this software program from Genes & Things is specifically designed with the family historian in mind. Working with the standardized file formats from popular family history software, it allows for your personal and family health history, including documentation and medical pedigree chart. It also includes a check-list of resources for

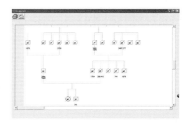

finding health information and a list of obsolete disease names.

GenoPro

www.genopro.com

A free, downloadable package to help you map out medical information.

Lifelinks International

www.lifelinks.mb.ca

Starting out as an educational initiative by the Manitoba Schizophrenia Society, this software package can be used to input family data that can generate a "no names" medical history that includes a relationship report.

Progeny

www.progeny2000.com/index.shtml

Designed for medical professional, this software package helps you draw a medical pedigree using a relational database and cut-and-paste applications with popular programs such as Microsoft Word and Powerpoint. A joint venture with DFR Group provides the ability to record family history using a toll-free number or a Web-based form, resulting in a pedigree that can be easily faxed or e-mailed.

paper when they died." Tragically, there were five brothers, and all died in their fifties as a result of heart attacks.

4. Hospital and Doctor's Records. You may be able to get medical information if you know the name of a recently deceased family member's physician and the hospital where he or she died. Even if this doesn't apply to you right now, it's a good idea to start keeping track of physician and hospital names associated with each family member. In Texas, for instance, medical record requests are guaranteed under state law, including access to records of deceased or incompetent patients. A parent, spouse, or adult child making the request in writing, according to the law, must be accommodated.

The federal antidumping law, part of the Consolidated Omnibus Reconciliation Act of 1986, requires all hospitals that participate in Medicare to maintain medical and other records for at least five years for patients transferred to, or from, another hospital. The American Hospital Association, the American Medical Record Association, and many professional societies recommend retaining original or reproduced records in electronic format for ten years for adults and even longer for children. If and when you change doctors, make sure your records are sent to your new physician or to you. It's important to hold on to those medical documents. They can be invaluable.

Medical documentation can be either in print or electronic form and can include pathology reports, radiology reports, patient intake forms, summary chart notes (either outpatient or inpatient), lab reports, physician correspondence, admission records, and insurance and billing information. You may need to ask your own physician to help you gain access, and bear in mind that obtaining these records can be costly.

5. Previous Genetic Testing Results. Have any family members been tested before? If so, providing the results of those tests can be extremely helpful to your history. Stanley Diamond's experience (see pages 154–155), for example, helped him notify his family of which tests to get and the results to look for.

Preserving Your DNA

Services are available to help you preserve your ancestor's DNA and to enable you to store DNA samples so future generations can protect their health. One such service is GeneSaver. Says its cofounder, retired pathologist Dr. Edwin Knights, "DNA fingerprinting can trace ancestry and we can find diseases, such as cancer of the breast or prostate." Blood samples satisfy the requirements. Samples can even be saved from the deceased with the help of a pathologist or funeral director, though it must be authorized by written permission by the next of kin. Because the blood has already congealed, DNA samples can be taken from inside the cheek or through needle biopsies from the liver or other organs.

6. Autopsy Reports. If anyone in your family underwent an autopsy, the resulting report may provide the most complete records you could find, including disease history, anatomical and laboratory findings, and every abnormality found at the time of death. An autopsy report is a permanent record retained by the hospital's pathology department. It might help to have your physician request a copy of the report.

7. Medical Examiner or Coroner Records. These are probably less useful than autopsies mainly because they are also found when the person's death was accidental, intentional, or clouded by suspicion.

8. Cemetery and Funeral Records. Using a map of Chicago's Waldheim Cemetery, Stanley Diamond was able to locate the gravestones of two immigrant family members—first cousins who married each other. With the help of a supportive cemetery staff member, Diamond contacted the man responsible for the graves' perpetual care. In this way he met

his cousin, Alex, also diagnosed as a beta-thalassemia carrier, and was able to move the genesis of the trait back one more generation in Poland.

9. Mortality Schedules. These will probably only be helpful if your family came to America before the massive wave of immigration that began in about 1880. The federal government kept these lists between 1850 and 1885 and included information on cause of death for twelve-month periods before the census (1 June through 31 May 1849, 1859, 1869, 1879, 1884), organized by state. Not all deaths are represented, but the schedules should be consulted, especially if you have no other vital records. You can find them in state archives, the Daughters of the American Revolution Library in Washington, D.C., the National Archives in Washington, D.C., and the Family History Library in Salt Lake City, Utah and its Family History Centers.

10. Insurance Records. As you rummage through family papers and interview relatives, carefully consider any information you may find about insurance policies and the issuing insurance company. Beginning as early as 1865, medical information was attached to the policy. Because of industry changes, you may need to conduct some research to determine which company may now have the records, as many of them have combined with other companies and now operate under a different name. Though it may be difficult to obtain, there might be more detailed medical information held by the company.

11. Military Service and Pension Records. Why might a family member have been rated "4F" in World War II? If he served, did he receive any special compensation as a result of injury? Checking service and pension records can turn up details not easily found elsewhere.

You can request twentieth-century service records, using Form 180 (downloadable from www.nara.gov/regional/mpr.html) for soldiers serving in the U.S. armed forces, from the National Personnel Records Center, 9700 Page Boulevard, St. Louis, MO 63132. Please note that due to a 1973 fire, a large amount of information has been lost. Eighty percent of the information on Army personnel discharged between 1 November 1912 and 1 January 1960 no longer exists. The same goes for seventy-five percent of the information on Air Force personnel discharged between 25 September 1947 and 1 January 1964 (with alphabetic names after Hubbard, James E). If you had family members who served in the Army and Army Air Corps during World War II or in the Army from 1950–54, the National Personnel Records Center has hospital and treatment facility admissions records. Visit www.nara.gov/regional/mpralts.html for more information.

12. Employment Records. To the extent you can get them, employee files may reveal conditions you may not know about. For instance, a supervisor may have recommended psychological testing; the diagnosis may be in the files and could have genetic ties. A relative may have suffered an on-the-job injury and that could be documented, too.

13. Correspondence and Photographs. When letter writing was in vogue, your relatives may have shared information about their own illnesses as well as those within their families. You may be able to pick up some useful clues here, so check your attics and basements, file cabinets and dresser drawers. And while you're looking, see what photographs you may be able to turn up. Disorders with a physically discernible element may show up.

Creating Your Health History

Following an "intake" session, your medical professional may document and organize your data into a picture—a sort of family tree with all relevant medical information—your medical pedigree. But you can create a similar picture yourself and share it with your family and/or present it to your health professional.

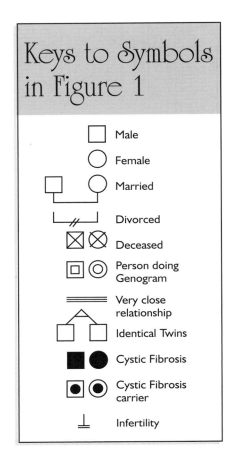

Keys to Symbols in Figure 1

- Male
- Female
- Married
- Divorced
- Deceased
- Person doing Genogram
- Very close relationship
- Identical Twins
- Cystic Fibrosis
- Cystic Fibrosis carrier
- Infertility

What is a medical pedigree exactly? It's a chart that uses standardized symbols to indicate gender and relationships (e.g., biological and nonbiological). Names are not necessary for your medical professional, but they are necessary to you as a family researcher. Unlike a standard genealogy pedigree, your medical pedigree needs to show brothers and sisters, because of the way genetic disorders are inherited. For that reason, it's also important to note in the case of twins whether they are identical or fraternal. Charting your family's medical conditions can also help you and your doctor visualize the patterns that can sometimes get lost in lists of names, dates, and places.

With a "medical pedigree" in your files, your medical professional can get an immediate picture of your family history.

Using a series of basic symbols and lines shown in Figure 1 (opposite), you can draw your pedigree. Figure 2 (opposite) shows an example of a family with diabetes. Once you have the basic layout, jot down names and birth, marriage, and death dates. You'll want to note the ages at the time of marriage and death.

Other information, such as the responses received during your family health interviews, can be noted in one of three ways: by the appropriate family member's box or circle, in the margin, or even on a separate piece of paper. You might find it useful to construct a family chronology—a listing of critical events impacting the family—to help put things into perspective. Often, providing a broader context helps as well. For instance, did anyone in your family die of lung cancer? If so, did they work in a mine or factory? Were they exposed to excessive smoke?

Discovering the Patterns

When you put your family's health information into a single pedigree, you'll find that a picture is worth a thousand words. Patterns may become obvious. Consider the case of the following family: paternal grandmother had diabetes, father had adult onset hypoglycemia that led to diabetes and ultimately death twenty years later, and uncle, his younger brother, also had diabetes that led to death. The person exploring her family history was diagnosed with hypoglycemia at the age of thirty-one. The family medical pedigree indicated that the risk of diabetes is overwhelming.

Enlist the aid of a medical professional to help you determine the patterns. While there may be some very clear trends, it's up to a professional to put all the facts together to determine your risk. Some conditions may be linked in ways we don't fully understand. You don't have to be diagnosed with a disease or disorder in order to proactively explore your health options.

Figure 1

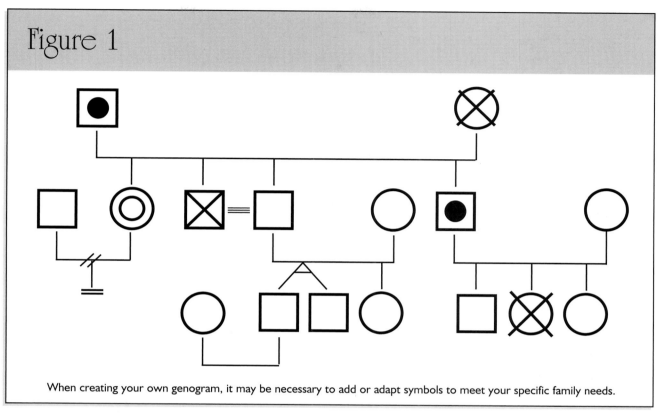

When creating your own genogram, it may be necessary to add or adapt symbols to meet your specific family needs.

Figure 2

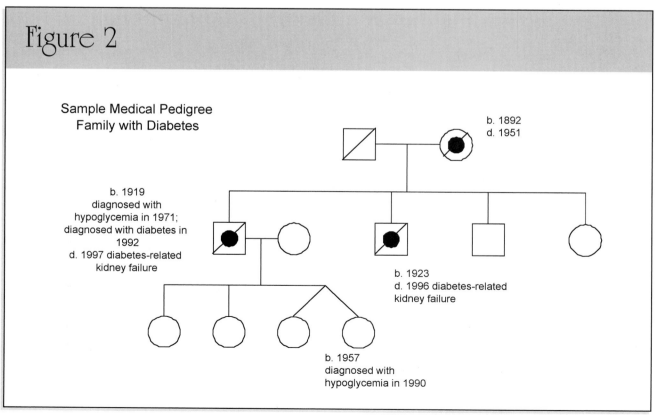

Sample Medical Pedigree
Family with Diabetes

b. 1892
d. 1951

b. 1919
diagnosed with
hypoglycemia in 1971;
diagnosed with diabetes in
1992
d. 1997 diabetes-related
kidney failure

b. 1923
d. 1996 diabetes-related
kidney failure

b. 1957
diagnosed with
hypoglycemia in 1990

Genetics Study Identifies At-risk Relatives

In 1977, Stanley Diamond of Montreal learned he carried the beta-thalassemia genetic trait. Though common among people of Mediterranean, Middle Eastern, Southeast Asian and African descent, the trait is rare among descendants of eastern European Jews like Stan. His doctor made a full study of the family and identified Stanley's father as the source.

Stan was spurred to action by a letter his brother received in 1991 from a previously unknown first cousin. Stan asked the cousin, "Do you carry the beta-thalassemia trait?" Though the answer was no, Stan began his journey to find out what other members of his family might be unsuspecting carriers. Later that year, Stan found a relative from his paternal grandmother's family, the Widelitz family. Again he asked, "Is there any incidence of anemia in your family?" His newfound cousin answered, "Oh, you mean beta-thalassemia? It's all over the family!"

There was no question now that the trait could now be traced to Stan's grandmother, Masha Widelitz Diamond and that Masha's older brother Aaron also had to have been a carrier. Stan's next question: who passed the trait onto Masha and Aaron? Was it their mother, Sura Nowes, or their father, Jankiel Widelec?

At the 1992 annual summer seminar on Jewish genealogy in New York City, Stan conferred with Dr. Robert Desnick, who suggested that Stan's first step should be to determine whether the trait was related to a known mutation or a gene unique to his family. He advised Stan to seek out another Montrealer, Dr. Charles Scriver of McGill University—Montreal Children's Hospital. With the help of a grant, Dr. Scriver undertook the necessary DNA screening with the goal of determining the beta-thalassemia mutation.

During this time, Stan began to research his family's history in earnest and identified their nineteenth century home town of Ostrow Mazowiecka in Poland. With the help of birth, marriage, and death records for the Jewish population of Ostrow Mazowiecka filmed by The Church of Jesus Christ of Latter-day Saints (LDS), Stan was able to construct his family tree.

Late in 1993, Dr. Scriver faxed the news that the mutation had been identified and that it was, in fact, a novel mutation. Independently, Dr. Ariella Oppenheim at Jerusalem's Hebrew University-Hadassah Hospital made a similar discovery about a woman who had recently emigrated from the former Soviet Union.

"The likelihood that we were witnessing a DNA region 'identical by descent' in the two families was impressive. We had apparently discovered a familial relationship between Stanley and the woman in Jerusalem, previously unknown to either family," says Dr. Scriver.

It wasn't very long ago when children born with thalassemia major seldom made it past the age of ten. Recent advances have increased life span but, to stay alive, these children must undergo blood transfusions every two to four weeks. And every night, they must receive painful transfusions of a special drug for up to twelve hours.

The repeated blood transfusions lead to a buildup of iron in the body that can damage the heart, liver, and other organs. That's why, when the disease is misdiagnosed as mild chronic anemia, the prescription of additional iron is even more harmful. Right now, no cure exists for the disease, though medical experts say experimental bone-marrow transplants and gene-therapy procedures may one day lead to one.

Stan's primary concern is that carriers of thalassemia trait may marry, often unaware that their mild chronic anemia may be something else. To aid in his search for carriers of his family's gene mutation of the beta-thalassemia trait, he founded and coordinates an initiative known as Jewish Records Indexing—Poland, an award-winning Internet-based index of Jewish vital records in Poland, with more than one million references. This database is helping Jewish families, particularly those at increased risk for hereditary conditions and diseases, trace their medical histories, as well as geneticists.

Says Dr. Robert Burk, professor of epidemiology at the Albert Einstein College of Medicine at Yeshiva University, and principal investigator for the Cancer Longevity, Ancestry and Lifestyle (CLAL) study in the Jewish population (currently focusing on prostate cancer), "Through the establishment of a searchable database from Poland, careful analysis of the relationship between individuals will be possible at both the familial and the molecular level. This will afford us the opportunity to learn not only more about the Creator's great work, but will also allow (us) researchers new opportunities to dissect the cause of many diseases in large established pedigrees." Several other medical institutions, including Yale University's Cancer Genetics Program, the Epidemiology-Genetics Program at the Johns Hopkins School of Medicine, and Mount Sinai Hospital's School of Medicine have recognized Diamond's work as an outstanding application of knowing one's family history and as a guide to others who may be trying to trace their medical histories, particularly those at increased risk for hereditary conditions and diseases.

In February 1998, in a breakthrough effort, Stan discovered another member of his family who carried the trait. He found the descendants of Jankiel's niece and nephew—first cousins who married—David Lustig and his wife, Fanny Bengelsdorf. This was no ordinary find—he located the graves by using a map of the Ostrow Mazowiecka section of Chicago's Waldheim Cemetery and contacted the person listed as the one paying for perpetual care, David and Fanny's grandson, Alex. It turned out Alex, too, had been diagnosed as a beta-thalassemia carrier by his personal physician fifteen years earlier. The discovery that David and Fanny's descendants were carri-

ers of the beta-thalassemia trait convinced Stan, Dr. Scriver, and Dr. Oppenheim that Hersz Widelec, born in 1785, must be the source of the family's novel mutation.

This groundbreaking work helps geneticists all over the world understand the trait and its effects on one family. Says Dr. Oppenheim, "A most important contribution of Stanley Diamond's work is increasing the awareness among his relatives and others to the possibility that they carry a genetic trait which, with proper measures, can be prevented in future generations. In addition, the work has demonstrated the power of modern genetics in identifying distant relatives, and helps to clarify how genetic diseases are being spread throughout the world."

For more information about thalassemia, contact Cooley's Anemia Foundation (129-09 26th Avenue, Flushing, New York, 11354; by phone 800-522-7222; or online at www.cooleysanemia.org). For more about Stanley Diamond's research, visit his Web site (www.geocities.com/Heartland/Pointe/1439).

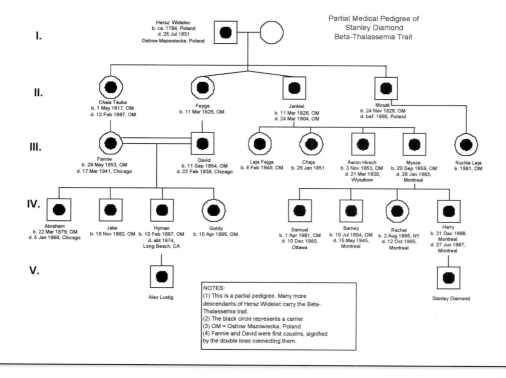

Partial Medical Pedigree of
Stanley Diamond
Beta-Thalassemia Trait

NOTES:
(1) This is a partial pedigree. Many more descendants of Hersz Widelec carry the Beta-Thalassemia trait.
(2) The black circle represents a carrier.
(3) OM = Ostrow Mazowiecka, Poland
(4) Fannie and David were first cousins, signified by the double lines connecting them.

Creating a Community

In November 1999, researcher Roni Seibel Liebowitz of Scarsdale, New York, posted the following message about a young man we will call "John" to the Jewish Records Indexing–Poland project online discussion group:

"The next time someone asks us why we are wasting our time looking for dead people, we can tell them about our efforts to save the lives of the living. The international cooperation of family historians searching for descendants of John's ancestors is remarkable. ... Family historians were contacted in the hopes of locating the best donors for a potential bone marrow transplant for this twenty-nine-year-old doctor recently diagnosed with leukemia.

"Within days, family historians in the United States, Canada, Poland, Israel, and Australia—to name a few—sprang into action. Synagogues, newspapers, Jewish organizations, *landsmanshaftn* [town-based societies], radio and TV stations were contacted. In the process of searching for family for a potential bone marrow match, an impressive tree of John's ancestors has been compiled. Through vital records and family reports John's tree is growing. Living, descendants are being contacted and made aware of the need for a genetically linked donor for John. Both guest books linked from the Web page have messages from other Bornsteins, and a few people have made genealogical connections.

"As family historians, I think we can all feel very proud of the work that continues to be done not only for John but for all those waiting for bone marrow transplants. Please encourage others to take this simple blood test and enter the bone marrow registry. Even if you can't attend a bone marrow drive, the simple blood test can be done at your local bone marrow facilities or ask your physician . . . What better use of family history than this!!!"

Dr. Simon Kreindler, a psychiatrist in Toronto and the father of a friend of John's, turned to Montreal Jewish Genealogical Society president Stanley Diamond, whose reputation as a lay expert on genealogical research for medical purposes is widely known. When Diamond learned that John's roots were in Poland, the Jewish Records Indexing–Poland project sprang into action and got results with the help of Shirley Flaum, who was managing the indexing of Jewish vital records for Lodz, an ancestral home to John, Stanley, and herself. Flaum told Diamond, "I am a breast cancer survivor… I understand what is involved and I will do everything I can to help John." Through the efforts of Flaum, Liebowitz, and Kreindler, more than twelve thousand people turned up at donor drives in Toronto, Montreal, and Israel to help John and others.

Reaching out to others is a well-understood coping mechanism for dealing with trauma and tragedy. It can also help you understand more about your family's health conditions and may even help others in the process. As you learn more about your family's genetic make-up, the information should be shared widely within your family and with your medical practitioners.

It is also important to remember that you're not alone. There are more than one hundred volunteer health organizations that have been formed to raise awareness among researchers and to raise funds for research, ranging from the Alzheimer's Association to the United Parkinson's Foundation. "Support groups are extremely important. They provide practical information,

---

Web Resources

Generational Health
www.generationalhealth.com
Pfizer Women's Health developed this educational site that enables you to build a family health history online in a step-by-step approach. Descriptions of several diseases and afflictions like Alzheimer's, breast cancer, high blood pressure, and migraines.

American Medical Association
www.ama-assn.org/ama/pub/category/2380.html
The AMA offers a Family History Tools Web page, mainly intended for health care professionals, that includes question-naires and a sample pedigree.

Texas Agricultural Extension Service
http://fcs.tamu.edu/health/health_record/medrecord_contents.htm
This online Family Health and Medical Record brochure includes worksheets for your personal health history, your spouse's history, and childhood immunizations.

---

more than I can do as a medical doctor, because they live with it," says Dr. Bachman.

And now support groups come in different forms, thanks to the Internet. The Web has made it easier to reach out through e-mails and mailing list messages such as the one Liebowitz sent out. Participants in locality and surname-based message boards such as those at http://boards.ancestry.com often discuss their family genetic traits. On one family board, a few exchanged messages about their familial cystic fibrosis and found they were connected to each other. In addition, some families like the Strongin-Goldbergs (discussed on pages 135–136) have set up their own Web sites as educational tools. Henry's site (www.hsg.org) features links to his story, photographs, information about Fanconi anemia, and more.

Another useful activity is to enroll in a registry so genetic researchers can find you and your family. The registry collects information on a number of families with a certain medical condition or genetic disorder, keeping track of affected family members and those who are at risk. Several registries have Web sites like the University of Texas M.D. Anderson

Keys to a Successful Outreach Campaign

Use the following ideas to create an effective network:
- Establish a family connection first—make sure you understand how the receiver is related to you.
- Establish rapport—what you are about to tell them will not be easy.
- Telephone—Use letter writing only when you need to reach more people than you could effectively reach through other communications media.

SAMPLE SCRIPT/LETTER
(Courtesy of Phyllis Goldberg)

Dear Members of the Zwet(s)chkenbaum Family,

My name is Phyllis Baum Goldberg. I am the daughter of Nathan Z. Baum, son of Wolf Z. Baum, son of Hirsch Kalman Zwetschkenbaum, son of Solomon Zwetschkenbaum who was born before 1820 in Kolbuszowa or Majdan in that part of Austria-Hungary which is now Poland. As some of you may know, my grandson Henry was born with a fatal genetic disease called Fanconi Anemia. When Henry was born I promised that that I would warn everyone in the family who might be at risk for having a child with this disease.

Geneticists believe that Fanconi anemia in Ashkenazi Jews is caused by a spontaneous mutation, which occurred in the fourteenth or fifteenth century. My son Allen carries a gene inherited from me and his wife Laurie carries a gene from one of her parents. My father's first cousin is also a carrier and this points to the fact that the mutation can be traced through my Zwetschkenbaum branch to my great grandfather Hirsch Kalman Zwetschkenbaum or his wife Rachel. I had been researching the Zwet(s)chkenbaum family before Henry was born and collected a great deal of information about its origins in Europe and its history in the United States. As I learned more about the Zwet(s)chkenbaums, their common heritage and their practice of cousins marrying, I was concerned that the risk of a genetic disease extended into more than just my branch of the family.

I believe that all the descendants of the Zwet(s)chkenbaum lines are related; they came from the same area in Austro Hungary, most of them from the same town. When members of different branches in the United States visited each other earlier in this century, they knew they were cousins. This may mean that other Zwet(s)chkenbaum family descendants are also Fanconi Anemia carriers. The disease does not happen unless two carriers marry, so that the existence of the mutation is concealed until a child is born. The fact that this disease has not occurred in your families does not mean that you are not a carrier or that your children or grandchildren are not at risk.

The mutation is easily detected with a blood test. Modern medicine makes this situation relatively easy to deal with if there is prior knowledge of risk. Had we known that I was a carrier before Henry was conceived, we could have conducted genetic tests. But since Fanconi is rare, those tests are not done routinely. I have enclosed an article from Washington Jewish Week, which describes the disease and recommends genetic counseling where there has been an occurrence in the family.

Testing for Fanconi Anemia is done at Rockefeller University by Dr. Arleen Auerbach. She has been doing research on the disease for many years. If you are concerned please get in touch with me and I will tell you how to contact her. Blood for testing can be drawn anywhere in the country and mailed to her lab following some simple instructions.

If you are into cyberspace then check out Henry's home page on the internet at www.hsg.org. You will find a detailed description of the disease and links to the Fanconi Anemia Foundation, which may also be of some interest.

I had never planned this letter as my first communication with you but some things have to come first. I was planning to ask you for all kinds of information about your branches of the family so that I could complete a large family tree and develop a directory. Living in Washington has given me access to the National Archives and I have early census documents for most of the Zwet(s)chkenbaums in this country. The family is diverse and interesting and its history is worth recounting. Some of us had even talked about having a reunion. Please send me the information about your branches. I will compile it and use it to produce a directory, which I will send to you. I believe that when we connect all the loose threads using the information and legends we have, we can weave a fascinating story to leave to our children.

Sincerely,

PHYLLIS B. GOLDBERG

P. S.: I know that I have not reached everyone. Please help buy circulating this information to those appropriate members of your family who I did not contact.

Cancer Center's Familial Brain Tumor Registry (www.epigenetic.org), aimed at identifying families at high risk for brain tumors and multiple cancers. The Cleveland Clinic Cancer Center (www.ccf.org/cc/medgen/diseasereg.htm) offers the Familial Cancer Registry for families with breast, ovarian, prostate, colon, and other cancers. Your medical professional can guide you to appropriate registries that focus on your family's condition.

Use the Past to Ensure a Healthy Future

Henry Strongin-Goldberg has just started school, but the future of his health is uncertain. Phyllis now hopes to work with the Fanconi anemia support community to discover her mutation's geographic roots. Her own experience suggests that others should "always do a genetic profile of your family when researching, if at all possible. There are so many things in my own family that will be significant for future generations."

When you are armed with your family's health history, you can take a proactive role in maintaining your own health and take steps toward prevention. So as Dr. Bachman says, "Go for it. Too many people don't talk to relatives until it's too late."

*There are two lasting bequests we can give
our children: one is roots, the other is wings.*
—Hodding Carter, Jr.

CHAPTER SEVEN

Connecting the Generations

Your Children and Family History

Janet Mallory first began to hope that her eleven-year-old daughter might share her interest in family history one rainy Saturday afternoon. Finished with her homework and bored by television, Megan picked up one of the framed photographs on the fireplace mantel while she cradled her cat in her other arm. "Mom, who's this in the old-fashioned dress with the cat?" Megan asked curiously.

Janet glanced at the early twentieth-century picture of her great-grandmother holding a fishbowl with her cat inside. She recalled with amusement her great-grandmother and great-aunts and the dry sense of humor that had seemed infectious among their family. She casually explained that it was a picture of Grandma Farnsworth, who was actually Megan's great-great-grandmother.

Janet also spoke of the faded patchwork quilt, torn in places and fraying at the edges, that hung on the wall over the sofa in the family room. Pointing out several squares that were stitched with initials, she told Megan how Isabelle Farnsworth had made the quilt with the help of her daughters when they were teenagers not much older than Megan was now. Her daughter's surprise at the age of the quilt made Janet smile as she remembered

how many times she had told Megan its history. Clearly she now had her daughter's full attention.

Megan continued to study the photograph. Finally she asked why her great-great-grandmother's hair appeared black while her face was so lined and withered and she looked so old. Janet explained that Grandma Farnsworth had been half Iroquois Indian, another fact that surprised Megan.

"Tell me more about her," she asked.

Setting aside her dishtowel, Janet went to her desk and pulled out the small family history chart that she used for research purposes. If Megan really wanted to learn more about Grandma Farnsworth, it was time to take a little trip.

With physical characteristics and personality traits inherited from their ancestors, our children represent more than our family's heritage. They also represent its future. Because memories connect families as strongly as pedigree charts do, instilling and nurturing children's interest in family history at a young age can be important to maintaining their interest in later years and a key to passing the family torch on to the next generation. Sharing memories and stories of their heritage can create a fascination with their forefathers that lasts a lifetime. Involving your children in family traditions personalizes the experience for them and makes such occasions unique, as well as providing a touchstone with the past. Becoming acquainted with their ancestors as well as their living relatives creates an appreciation of family history.

As a parent or grandparent you can ensure that your child's interest in the past continues into the future. Creating a reverence for the past begins with a basic introduction to ancestors along with an understanding of history to provide a context in which to place those ancestors. Giving relevance to historical events helps children build a framework for their ancestors' lives and gives them a clearer, stronger sense of identity.

One way children or grandchildren can come to appreciate their heritage is by being able to put it into historical perspective. Once they feel the importance of history, they will be able to see the value of learning how their own family fits into it—and vice versa.

Bringing History to Life

For many children, history can be a dry subject filled with meaningless dates and outdated information. How important can Gettysburg be to an eleven-year-old boy who can't wait to get to soccer practice? In his eyes, not very. Yet it's probably quite important to his grandfather who learned firsthand how the 20th Maine defeated a superior force of Alabama troops in a battle that changed the outcome of the Civil War and the direction of the country through hearing stories of the battle told by his own grandfather who fought there.

Children need to learn that their forefathers lived in a time very different from the twenty-first century. Their ancestors made decisions that are not always easily understood in today's world. As teenagers begin to realize that their ancestors' lives were influenced by financial and social pressures as well as other concerns, it leads to a deeper appreciation of history and especially family history. Parents must first do their homework so they can help their children recognize the historical differences of the world in which their great-great-grandparents lived. By doing so you help your children build a framework and create a context in which to place their ancestors. You also give history relevance to your child's life by making family connections.

Claire V. Brisson-Banks, director of the Providence, Rhode Island Family History Center of The Church of Jesus Christ of Latter-day Saints, suggests telling children about their grandparents' lives as an introduction to their family history. "Tell them what jobs they held, what they did with their lives," she advises. "Whether a grandfather helped build a railroad or was a baker, that's a valuable contribution. Finding out Grandpa was a fireman in his younger days is a badge of honor for a child." Or you might show your son his great-grandmother's grade school diploma and explain that the reason the document is so large and elaborate is that it was a great honor to graduate from grade school before 1920 because so many children were forced to enter the workplace at a young age.

Brisson-Banks also suggests using census records to learn about ancestors' occupations. For generations, the men in her husband's family were agricultural laborers. Eventually military service took its place, followed by employment as electricians, representing a

change in tradition. "Some people are pre-destined toward certain fields," she notes. "It's eye-opening for children to realize that their family has a long history of working in a certain area or specialty."

Brisson-Banks recommends that parents take children to places associated with their grandparents' lives. Show them the houses they lived in and the places they worked. If families cannot actually visit, try to provide pictures of the ancestral homeland abroad or the immigrants' first home in America. "If they were immigrants, go to the library to learn more about their journey, their culture, and their struggle," she advises. "Children need to know they have a heritage."

History can indeed capture a child's imagination. Having a hook will help to draw in your son or daughter. Look among your ancestors for a striking resemblance, a common interest, a name-sake, or a colorful story that will surprise and delight your child. Find something interesting in the past and focus on that, advises Brisson-Banks.

"Children have a deeper interest in the past than we realize," she says. "The secrets to the future are held in the past. It works when you show them your family history and explain to them how everyone is connected." Once your children gain a better understanding of their ancestors, you can connect your family with all the generations you've discovered to date.

Teaching Your Child about the Past

To take a child's ancestors from being mere names to being people of flesh and blood with personalities and emotions, he or she needs to get to know them. Whether your family is descended from John Adams or your great-great-aunt was the first woman in your state to obtain a driver's license, your family history is uniquely yours and should be celebrated as such.

Fortunately for the family historian, children are extremely open to new information. Make the process fun for them. Let them play detective. Offer them clues to the mysteries of your family history by including them when talking with relatives and looking at family mementoes and photographs. Family history is most effective with children when it intrigues them, piques their curiosity, and stimulates their imaginations. To get your children intrigued, tell them about their most interesting ancestors to bring their relatives' lives into focus.

For David Lambert, a library manager at the New England Historic Genealogical Society, it was his grandmother's stories of his great-grandfather's days on board a whaling ship that led to an enduring fascination with family history. What began as a hobby in childhood became a profession in adulthood. As a teenager he had attempted to visit the New England Historic Genealogical Society and found he needed a parent or guardian to be admitted. "I had the last laugh in that I ended up working in a library in which my parents had no interest when I was young," he says.

Lambert notes that because he was born late in his parents' lives, his four grandparents would be over a hundred years old today. One of his most fascinating discoveries was that his grandmother was born while her great-great-grandmother was still alive. "That means she was held by someone who was held by someone during the Revolutionary War," he notes.

Your ancestors needn't be famous to make them exciting, alive, and colorful. Share with your children the contributions their ancestors made, stories that have been told about them over the years, and the characteristics people remember most about them, such as a sense of humor or unusual eyes. Let them know their ancestors' accomplishments and details of their lives. Have them consider the various roles their ancestors played: daughter, sister, worker, parent, widow.

Make the picture clear by increasing your child's awareness of historical events and their significance. If you're Irish, for example, tell them that the potato famine was what led many Irish immigrants to come to America. Explain how their grandfather couldn't find work in the 1930s because of the Great Depression. Fill in the blanks with what you know from history. Girls working in the mills in Lowell, Massachusetts, in the 1840s, for instance, made around four dollars per week, about a hundred times less than factory workers make today. Those kinds of facts will help your children put their ancestors' lives in perspective.

Helping Children with an Interview

Once you've encouraged your children's curiosity about their family history, your son or daughter will naturally have many questions and want to know more. Let them ask questions of those who have the answers. "Interviewing grandparents is better than any video game or Internet Web site," says David Lambert.

Don't underestimate the importance of allowing your children to ask questions as they search for answers. If their great-grandparents came to America, did parents or siblings come with them? Did they already have family waiting for them?

It is a good idea to videotape the interview. Not only will this provide your child with a lasting remembrance of the interview, it is also quicker than writing, keeps the dialogue flowing, and provides a more accurate account of the events being described. Remember as you talk with relatives that you and your child are relying on memory, which can sometimes be faulty or selective. Family history often has more than two sides to every story. It might take a few interviews and several versions of the same story to get to the truth. In situations where a second marriage occurred, great confusion can ensue among family historians trying to sort it out several generations later. Sometimes the stories Aunt Edna tells about her sister Loretta might reveal more about Edna's personality than Loretta's. Always check dates twice to confirm accuracy. Keep your perspective, along with a sense of humor, throughout the discovery process.

Interview Questions

Basic interview questions for children to ask grandparents can get them started on the process and thinking in the right direction:

Where and when were you born?

What were your hobbies when you were little?

How many sisters or brothers do you have?

Did you work outside the home?

What was your favorite subject in school?

What sports did you like?

What pets did you have?

What are your funniest memories of growing up?

Who were your favorite relatives?

What were your favorite foods?

How did your family celebrate birthdays? Holidays?

What did your parents look like?

The following sections will give you specific hints and suggestions for involving your child in his or her family history in compelling ways. Family history is a learning process, a very effective one if you allow your child to find information and share the fun of making new discoveries along with you. You'll find that your own enthusiasm will become infectious.

Family History for Children Under Ten

Because young children are so receptive to learning, they are ideal vessels into which to pour information about their family. It's never too early to begin encouraging their interest in family history. Younger children can more easily be enticed into a fascination with genealogy than teenagers who might rather be doing something else. "Between the ages of seven and thirteen there's an open window," David Lambert suggests.

The classroom can also play an important role in shaping children's knowledge of history. The countries in which our ancestors were born make ideal subjects for school book reports. For younger children, family history can be incorporated into classroom activities in social studies classes. Claire Brisson-Banks notes that simple projects that take children back two or three generations are helpful in raising their awareness of their family's heritage.

There are many ways for parents to interest children in history outside the classroom as well. The Boy Scouts offer a genealogy merit badge, historical sites abound across America, and historical reenactments and living history museums provide a firsthand glimpse of life in another time. Family history will have the most meaning to a child if it is part of his or her upbringing and if it is personalized enough to catch his or her interest. Experts agree that the most important thing parents can do is to make an impression while their children are young.

MEMENTOS PROVIDE CLUES FOR KIDS

Claire Brisson-Banks notes that young children are more receptive to the physical aspects of genealogy, particularly the things they can see, hear, and touch. For this reason, photographs and heirlooms are especially effective with children.

Showing them objects that belonged to their ancestors makes a deep impression. Give children access to their grandmother's old trunk or their grandfather's collection of fishing rods. An old doll or stuffed animal that belonged to a parent or grandparent can become a cherished possession for a thoughtful, sensitive child.

Familiarizing children with their family's belongings at a young age heightens their interest in mementoes, valuable or otherwise, and keeps them interested in learning about their family. Tangible things that remind them of family serve as a positive presence in their lives now and will likely do so in later years.

Acquainting children with their family history in this way also gives them a sense of identity. On a trip to England, Brisson-Banks and her family took advantage of the opportunity to visit cemeteries in which her husband's ancestors were buried. They explored gravestones together with their children, aged two through eleven, all of whom were thrilled to be part of the expedition.

"The children participated as we looked for familiar last names on the stones," she says. "They had a ball and even took pictures standing next to the tombstones they found. It took away their fear of cemeteries."

Appoint your child to be the family historian of his age. Encourage him or her to keep a record of individuals and their countries of origin, family vacations, activities, favorite occasions. Imagine your child's feeling of satisfaction upon opening the journal years from now and reflecting back on the growth of your family.

As your child begins to investigate your family, give him or her clues in the form of ancestors' belongings and other family keepsakes. The collectibles a great-grandmother left behind reveal a great deal about her personality and concerns. Articles in your possession that have lived on long after their owners were gone can prove a source of great fun for your elementary-age child.

Whether elegant or functional, the stuff of our ancestors' lives represents clues to their interests and lifestyles. A photograph of a great-great-grandmother surrounded by cats, for instance, tells you what her favorite pet probably was. Your great-grandmother's fraternal jewelry shows that she was associated with a community group. A scrapbook might reveal the sentimental nature of a great-aunt, while a coin or stamp collection tells you what your great-grandfather's hobby was. The fact that an ancestor inscribed his name in the front of a book might mean that he could read in an age when many were illiterate.

Many articles around the house that we take for granted are objects of fascination to our children. An attachment forged in childhood is likely to last into adulthood and produce even deeper ties to the past. Let them see and play with knick-knacks and other items from ages past, provided they aren't truly valuable heirlooms.

Claire Brisson-Banks recommends keeping family photographs close at hand. Setting them out so children can see them is likely to elicit questions about the identity of subjects they don't recognize, especially those in old-fashioned clothing. "For young children, point out similarities in facial features," she advises. "Make note of things like noses and mannerisms. These things give children a sense of family continuity."

Children are intrigued, she notes, when you show them an old picture of your mother, someone they know as their grandmother. Seeing people at different ages fascinates them. "Genes organize themselves in amazing ways," says Brisson-Banks. "Kids want to understand why a daughter looks just like her mother's grandmother."

The perspective gained from seeing relatives at different ages in old photographs can be both fascinating and confusing to a child. David Lambert's interest in genealogy began in childhood when he picked up a tintype that fell from the pages of a published genealogy his grandmother was holding. "Nana, who's this?" he asked, not realizing he was holding a picture of her grandfather. "The fact that an eighty-year-old woman could have a father who was a child in this picture was mind-boggling," he says.

"Be sure to write the first and last names on photographs," says Brisson-Banks. "Children find it funny that their parents don't always know who people are in photos."

David Lambert agrees. He has found that countless photographs are disinherited by families ignorant of their identities. "When Mom and Dad die, their kids face an arduous task," he says. "A child goes back to the old homestead and cleans out their things, much of which isn't going to fit into their condo. Unidentified photos get tossed out because no one knows who they are."

For all the unidentified photographs that are lost to their families, he notes, there are as many family historians looking for them. "These photographs turn up on e-Bay or at church yard sales," he says. "Along with people who don't care, there are people who are searching to find them."

THE IMPORTANCE OF FAMILY STORIES

The heart of genealogy for children lies in family stories. "Photos fade, documents are lost, gravestones topple," says David Lambert. "Only the stories remain. That's what keeps children interested in their family history when they're ninety years old." Because grade school children are intrigued by family stories, he recommends weaving those stories into daily life. "Parents often get tired of telling the same old bedtime stories," he says. "Instead tell them about your life or the lives of your parents. We tell family stories now, not bedtime stories."

Parents must be the chroniclers of the past. Take every opportunity to listen to the stories your elderly relatives have to tell. Often these stories mention events and individuals that are not famous enough to be in the newspaper. That is why stories are so valuable, he notes. While the fact that an ancestor arrived on the *Empress of Britain* in 1907 might not be significant enough to make it into print, such information is invaluable to the family historian.

Family history and the stories that accompany one's heritage play an important role tradition and identity, according to Rabbi Jonathan Blake of Temple Beth-El in Providence, Rhode Island. "I don't remember living in a *shtetl* in Poland, but I've heard my grandmother's stories," he says. "Our family stories are a part of our identity. There's a wish to preserve continuity through memory." Since Judaism is more than a religion, he notes, Jews have a sense of belonging to a worldwide historical community because they have occupied so much of the globe at various times. This sense of belonging comes, in great part, through stories shared and remembered.

Family stories keep memories alive. Parents need to pass on the torch, advises David Lambert. "We are the oral historians today, the by-products of the storytellers of old," he emphasizes. "We need to pass all this on to our children."

FAMILY HISTORY PROJECTS FOR YOUNG CHILDREN

Every parent knows best what will appeal to his or her child. Try using some of these ideas as a springboard to stimulate your child's interest in his or her family history.

- Have your child make his or her family tree. Give all family members their own "leaves" on the tree on which their names and photos appear. Photocopy or scan and print out pictures of relatives to save money.
- Teach your children how to hunt for clues to their ancestors' lives by telling them stories about their backgrounds. Show them old photographs, family heirlooms, houses they lived in, churches where they worshiped, factories where they worked.
- Incorporate your family history into your daily life: place old photographs at eye-level for your child; use dishes that belonged to your grandmother; remind a child that his predecessors of a hundred fifty years ago had to live without electricity.
- Use a globe to make your children geographically aware of their ancestral homelands.
- Create models of what your ancestor's homes may have looked like using Lincoln Logs, Victorian dollhouses, medieval castles, or other historic "toy" buildings, and

purchase store-bought dolls or make clothespin dolls to occupy them.

- Re-create an old-fashioned tea party. Invite your great-aunts. Make it a dress-up occasion.
- Create historic Halloween costumes based on other time periods.
- Encourage your children to keep their own autograph books. At family get-togethers they can ask relatives to sign the books and write something special about their family. This will be a treasured keepsake for your children as they get older.
- Make historic paper dolls to use with your child. Photocopy ancestors' faces from old photographs; reduce or enlarge them to the appropriate size to fit your dolls. Use fabric to create costumes from the appropriate era.
- Read historical fiction and nonfiction to your children to give them a sense of how people lived in other times.
- Build a dollhouse that is a replica of your grandparents' or great-grandparents' first American home (it helps if someone is handy with woodworking, but you can also have a dollhouse custom-built from old photos). You might fill the house with Victorian or colonial furnishings if you have records of a family home that far back in time.

- Play games of imagination related to history by pretending to be pirates or knights. You could even make it closer to the truth of your family's history by acting as a pioneer family or shipboard traveler in the nineteenth century.
- Give your child dolls dressed in period clothing. Design and hand-sew the costumes to suit the period if they aren't sold in stores.
- Buy reproductions of antique toys from earlier centuries. Let your child imagine what it was like to be a child in other times.
- Find a hobby that was shared by your child and an ancestor. Show your children their ancestors' various collections.
- Have your children's grandparents demonstrate games from their own childhood. This is a great way to connect the generations and is a sure way to please all ages.

As Janet Mallory slowed the car before the historic cemetery she hoped her daughter wouldn't dislike the adventure they'd begun. But instead of being squeamish, Megan paid even more attention as she glanced at the aging headstones beyond the wrought iron fence. Nor had Megan objected when, at the end of their cemetery visit, Janet had suggested they continue on to the local historical society library. Once there, Janet could show her some documents connected with Megan's great-great-grandfather.

"Mom, how come Grandpa Farnsworth ran off to join the war? Why didn't he just enlist?" she asked as they entered the library.

By now they had exhausted Janet's supply of stories about Grandma Farnsworth, and they had moved on to Grandpa Farnsworth, who seemed equally fascinating in Megan's eyes. Janet explained that Grandpa Farnsworth had been too young to join the Union effort in the Civil War but that he had served as a drummer boy during some of the final campaigns in the last year of the war.

Megan was intrigued as Janet laid a heavy volume entitled Personal War Sketches *on the table before them. She turned to the page on which Grandpa Farnsworth, along with other veterans, had written his reminiscences of the war.*

Although Janet had never known her great-grandfather, he had always seemed real to her and remained vivid in her memory because of the stories his daughters—her great-aunts—had told about him.

Now, much to Janet's delight, Megan was exhibiting the same excitement about an ancestor too distant for her to have known, yet whose life was too absorbing for her to forget.

Family History for Preteens and Teenagers

Exploring your family history is a constant process of discovering and learning. For many parents, the hobby can provide their kids with a positive distraction from the negative influences that abound during the teenage years. Teens and pre-teens can benefit from the adult learning game of finding clues to the backgrounds of their ancestors. There is an undeniable challenge and intrigue in solving real-life mysteries with sometimes seemingly unanswerable questions. When our children look for clues among their ancestors, they find the answers in their own past.

The photographs you treasure are often a mere backdrop in the lives of your children for whom little can match the excitement of playing soccer with friends, listening to the latest CD, or attending the high school's varsity football game. Take comfort from the fact that while your children probably take much of their lifestyle for granted now, it is the familiar comforts of home that they remember most as they age. And there are strategies that will help you convince your child that a study of family history is not only worthwhile but "cool."

The key to getting young adults interested in their family history involves dealing with in-depth issues related to their own identity. Consider asking them to delve into their ancestors' lives and find similarities between generations, help create family tree wall charts, or work on family research projects independently; all of these are excellent ways for teenagers to discover a fascination with genealogy they didn't know they had.

Claire Brisson-Banks has taught genealogy to teenagers in private and public schools. Though family history was a subject to which most had received little exposure, she found all of the children receptive as they learned to use generational charts and discover information they had never known about their families. "Teenagers have the ability to grasp family history on a larger level," she says. "It can be more difficult for some, depending on their family structure, but it helps them to realize they are part of something larger and that they are here for a purpose."

To give them a deeper understanding of their own backgrounds, Brisson-Banks directed students to focus on several projects related to their families. In a class of eleventh-graders who were facing career decisions, she suggested that students write to various relatives and ask them what led to their career decisions or what inspired them to start a business. "Learning things they didn't know about their relatives' accomplishments gave them a new respect for their families," she says. "Many had started companies years ago. If [these kids] can be inspired by something an ancestor has done, they want to be part of the experience."

Another assignment involved asking students how they would choose to be remembered. "I asked them how they would want their obituaries to read," she says. "Students wrote up their ideas and shared them with the class. They gained a lot from that experience. It raised issues they'd never thought about before."

Years later, she still runs into students who remember her. "It's clear that they were affected by the experience of learning about their family history in a positive manner," Brisson-Banks says. "It's important to get them thinking about things other than themselves. They need to see the bigger picture."

Impressing Teenagers with Family History

The cooperation you'll receive from your teenagers and preteens with these ideas will vary according to their degree of enthusiasm. Yet whether or not they like family history, some of the projects could appeal to them on another level. And some might succeed on a rainy day or in the middle of winter when they're bored and have nothing else to do.

- Call your teenager's attention to similarities between himself and a relative from another generation. Exploring the lives of their ancestors can give teens a real sense of identity at a time when they need it most.
- If you've collected information on several generations and you have a child who has no interest in family history but leans more toward the arts, let your child create the family-tree wall chart you've always wanted. What could be a nicer collaboration than pairing your discoveries with your child's talents?
- Ask your computer-literate teen to help you assemble and enter your family history notes. You'll both learn something in the process as you experiment with the many programs available and enter information you might have overlooked.
- Have your teenager create an "album" of family photos that you can give as a Christmas gift. Give your creative child the challenge of designing and preparing

a compilation of 8 1/2" x 11" pages filled with ancestral pictures from your collection that are photocopied and bound together.

- Discouraged with your research of a particular line of your family tree? Share your frustration with your teenage son or daughter. Let him or her show you how smart they are by reviewing your records. Perhaps a fresh eye will spot something you missed.

- Create a treasure box, photo collage, or family quilt. It will get your teen thinking about what matters most today and what mattered in the past.

- Ask your teenager to make a scrapbook of newspaper clippings and other family memorabilia and encourage him or her to design a border around the edges of the pages.

- Create a time capsule. It will be fun to select items that are of great importance to a young teen today and see how important they are five years from now when he or she opens it. This experiment is bound to give your family a few laughs.

- Ask your son or daughter who might not be in the mood for socializing to videotape a family reunion or holiday gathering.

- Conduct cemetery searches with your son or daughter. Walking through quaint old cemeteries is both spiritual and spooky and might appeal to your teenagers. Suggest taking photographs or doing a grave rubbing.

- Have your child create a family newsletter. Whether you send it just at Christmas or in every season, make it funny and informative. Colorful graphics and desktop publishing programs make it easy. All you add is the news. Think of it as a chronicle of your family's life, a journal you'll enjoy looking back on. Include things you want to preserve such as your toddler's cutest expressions; vacation or holiday plans; church, school, and social activities; and progress made on your house or garden.

- Ask your child to write a family history from notes you've compiled. Use a computer program designed for the purpose, or let him or her write something more elaborate if so inclined.

- Suggest that your teen or preteen volunteer in a historical society library or local history museum. Besides exposing them to history, it gives teenagers valuable experience for entrance to college and possible future jobs.

- Have your child develop a questionnaire to send relatives. Brainstorm questions together for information you'd like to get from relatives. Then have him or her write up the questionnaire on the computer and mail out copies to family scattered around the country. You'll both have fun when the replies start coming in.

- Attend cultural events with your teenager, or encourage him or her to go with friends. An Irish music concert, a Polish heritage festival, or an Italian Pride Day are all great opportunities for your teen to discover your family's heritage.
- Rent historical videos you can watch together.

Opportunities for Adult Children

Don't give up on your adult children, even if they haven't shown any interest in their family history to date. The pressures of adolescence, college, and the job market are all stages of life that demand more time and effort than more settled periods do.

Take heart. Phases later in life present their own opportunities for reconnecting your adult children with their ancestors. The birth of children introduces a new generation that often changes a parent's perspective and stimulates a new interest in the past. As they come

full circle, parents want their child to have the same sense of security and belonging that they knew while growing up—the gift that you as a parent wisely gave them in childhood.

The long branches of their family tree that were so unimportant a few short years ago often take on greater significance now. The unappealing memories of car trips where restless teenagers were crowded in the backseat for what seemed endless hours often disappear when they reach adulthood and begin their own families. E-mail makes it more convenient than ever to stay in touch with relatives all over the world. Even if they are busy with their own lives or have little in common with their extended family, most people have a desire to stay in touch with relatives whether close or far away.

The birth or christening of a child is an appropriate time to pass on ancestral gifts such as christening gowns, engraved silver spoons, or even something the child might not use until adulthood. The importance of the past frequently becomes clear at this time of new beginnings.

Connecting Your Family from Childhood to Adulthood

Most children who grow up in America are descended from a patchwork of nationalities. It's not uncommon to find a mixture of Irish, French, Polish, and English in the background of a single family because of the blendings of families and traditions over the years.

Celebrate the many aspects of your unique heritage. Customs begun in childhood are treasured forever and assume greater importance as your children age. They are a permanent legacy. Family traditions give your child a sense of belonging.

Make a game out of your family history as your children hunt for clues to their grandparents' childhood among their left-behind belongings. Rekindle acquaintances with cousins and other relatives you haven't seen in some time. Socialize with cousins who have children the same ages as yours.

Expose your children to family members while they're young so they can create new memories that will last a lifetime. Develop strategies appropriate to your own family that will connect your children with their relatives. Remember, it is memories that connect families, not pedigree charts.

For those who feel they have few family members left, take heart from ancestors who anchor you to a past that is permanent and unchanging. For each successive generation you go back, the number of ancestors doubles. That also carries forward. Remember that you probably have cousins you've never met. To extend your family circle, cultivate relatives both at home and abroad who share your interest in family. Look into descendants of ancestors who did not emigrate with the rest of their family but instead chose to remain in the old country. Relatives are often receptive to hearing from family they've never met.

In his own historical pursuits David Lambert encountered a great deal of information on the Punkapoag Indians, an obscure tribe from Stoughton, Massachusetts. In the course of his research, he attended a powwow at which he had the good fortune to meet the tribal chief, who was impressed with his knowledge of the tribe's ancestry. As the Punkapoags

began to discover their identity and reclaim their past they became a more cohesive tribe, and Lambert eventually became their tribal historian.

Their long-standing relationship culminated in the chief's invitation to him to join the tribe. "You've lost enough family," the chief told him. "Now it's time to be part of ours." Lambert's name in the Punkapoag's tongue means "Finder of the Past."

You can assume the same role in the lives of your children. They will find their own future. It is up to you to help them find their past and bring them full circle.

Wordlessly, Janet Mallory walked up the steps of her mother's house with her daughter Megan. Beside them walked Megan's husband and their six-year-old daughter. It had been an adjustment for Janet to think of herself as an ancestor to little Isabelle Janet, and yet at the same time it was gratifying to have a granddaughter named after her and her own great-grandmother, Isabelle.

It was young Isabelle, after all, who would inherit the quilt made over a century ago now by Grandma Farnsworth. Even with its faded stitching and frayed edges, Isabelle might pass it on to her own daughter one day. Janet hoped Isabelle would cherish it as much as Megan had come to in recent years.

"The house has been closed up tight since the funeral," Janet said apologetically as she slipped the key into the lock, "although for the last couple of weeks the neighbor has been coming by to feed Grandma's kitty."

But Megan wasn't deterred by the mustiness of the house. Instead she was mesmerized by the old wallpaper, the columns that separated the parlor from the dining room, the old-fashioned kitchen cabinets she remembered from childhood, and the cat she hadn't seen since her last visit. Since she had been away for so many years, Megan admitted, the chance to buy her grandmother's house made her feel as if she were moving back home again.

"Just think how many times Grandma Farnsworth sat in this very room when she visited with her grandchildren," Janet said. "It probably hasn't changed all that much over the years."

Isabelle looked up at her, pulling her attention away from the cat she'd stooped to pet. "Who was Grandma Farnsworth?"

Janet smiled as she placed the key in Isabelle's hands. She had no doubt the past would matter to her granddaughter, who was to be raised in this house that held so much of her family's history.

When the miles make communication difficult, correspondence is the link that creates the family bond, makes it tighter, and holds it together.

CHAPTER EIGHT

Keeping in Touch
Your Family Correspondence

Grant Reeve and Lola Dawn Wright fell in love in the summer of 1939. After just a few months, their romance was put on hold while Grant flew around the world with the Civil Air Patrol in World War II. The young couple kept their relationship kindled with letters—handwritten promises for the future and remembrances of their shortened past. They talked about getting married, but the timing was never right.

After nearly four years of military service, Grant was given a four-day hiatus in early January, and he proposed to Lola Dawn on her porch on their first afternoon together again. They only had a few days to plan and host their wedding, and finding white material to make a dress was impossible during war time. Lola Dawn elected to make her wedding dress out of the only white fabric either of them owned—Grant's parachute.

Hours after the newlyweds said "I do," Grant was back in the air, and Lola Dawn was home alone. Again, letters kept the two in touch. When Grant was finally released from his war duties, the two settled down to raise their family. Over the years they retold the story of the parachute dress and their quick engagement many times to their children and grandchildren. The story wasn't complete without describing the feelings they had when each of them saw a hand-addressed envelope in the mailbox during their wartime courtship.

In truth, communication not only kept their relationship going, it also added a dimension and depth they hadn't experienced during their dating. Grant found that expressing his emotions about God, family, and country was easier with pen and paper than in person.

Lola Dawn, who became a high school English teacher, found joy in putting her thoughts on cards for Grant. The writing process helped her organize her thoughts during this unstable time in their relationship. She kept his letters in a metal box and reread them again and again—both before and after Grant's return.

Grant and Lola Dawn learned early in their relationship that in order to be a balanced family, there must be a connection. When the miles make getting together difficult, communication is the link that creates the family bond, makes it tighter, and holds it together during good times and bad. If family is a top priority, we must show consistent love to family members, even if they do not live close by. Communication in a variety of forms is the key to creating this closeness.

Essentially, we are writing so that we will not be forgotten by those who love us and whom we have loved. Write well; it may be your only chance to be remembered.

—Lawrence P. Gouldrup

The Reeves found what millions of other families around the world have discovered: making the effort to stay connected as a family leads to positive results in nearly every facet of life. Close-knit families experience joy, laughter, support, advice, and resources that simply cannot and do not come from the community, neighborhood, or even religious groups. But first, staying connected means staying in contact.

The Importance of Keeping in Touch

Staying in contact, even with advances in technology, is not as easy as it used to be. Changes in society have led to families who no longer live next door or across the farm field. Yet family closeness is a key element to having a fulfilling life. And staying connected is a must for closeness in families, whether they live in the same rural town or are spread throughout the country.

Grant and Lola Dawn Reeve stayed in touch during the war years with the help of the post office where Grant later worked as a postal carrier. But the family's communication methods grew over time as technology offered new opportunities. As long-distance calling became more reliable and affordable, Lola Dawn loved to call her grandchildren on the phone and send birthday cards along with homemade robes and dresses. Her death in 1984 was mourned by her entire family, but the silver lining was that each of her children and grandchildren had several cards and letters from her expressing her love for them.

Grant has kept the communication tradition alive with his twenty-eight grandchildren by sending e-mails, and with his five children scattered across the country from Rhode Island to Seattle, Grant has maintained a routine of e-mailing his children at least twice a week, along with letters in the mail to celebrate birthdays, holidays and "just because I thought this card was funny" days. He knows the method doesn't matter—it's the consistent contact between family members that keeps them connected. He also hosts yearly family reunions, with T-shirts and hats to commemorate the event.

Although needs and patterns differ from family to family, some of the basic communication options are letters, phone calls, newsletters, e-mail, Web sites, and family reunions. The goal remains: keeping the family connected.

Letters and Cards

It's hard to beat an old-fashioned, handwritten, personally sealed letter in the mailbox. Although technology has made e-mail and live chats a possibility, seeing a loved one's handwriting on a personalized envelope is a welcome relief among the usual stack of credit card applications and direct mail.

Rachelle Waite, an elementary education major, moved to Mexico for a semester to complete her student teaching. As a fluent Spanish speaker, she wasn't intimidated by the language or culture. Even the differences in food were not a barrier to her comfort and happiness. She did, however, eagerly await the arrival of the mail each day, hoping for something American, something familiar. Even a letter from her university adviser was a welcome sight—a bright white envelope with her university logo in the left-hand corner. The label would read "Rachelle Waite" rather than "Senora Waite," as her Mexican second-graders called her. Although formal correspondence from her educational institution was better than nothing, a letter from home was a true all-star mail day. A short letter from Mom explaining family news, insignificant happenings, and funny stories about neighbors and siblings was a fun read. And, if Rachelle was lucky, the letter would carry with it a smell from home—mom's perfume or the laundry soap fragrance that made the house smell clean.

Writing Good Letters

- Be yourself. Put your personality on paper. Talk out what you want to say, and then write it exactly the way you said it. Don't try to formulate a master's thesis in each letter.

- Share humorous experiences. If you thought it was funny, the reader will likely get a smile out of it, too.

- Talk about how you felt about an event, not just the facts. In the end, it's you the reader wants to hear about. Share a piece of your soul.

- Include photos, drawings, stickers. A letter doesn't just have to be words. In fact, an envelope with no letter but with a memento would be a fun change.

- For younger family members, try sending one piece of a puzzle in each of several letters. This will build excitement each day at the mailbox and give the child something to look forward to and work on. Perhaps the puzzle could be about an upcoming event—such as Christmas, a trip to the zoo, or a family camping trip. This will help the child count down the days.

- Send a familiar scent. Spray your perfume or air freshener on the letter itself or the envelope. A scent can bring back memories even more than a photograph.

- Consider taking pen to paper and writing at least part of the letter. Word processors are fast and easy, but a hand-written addition at the end personalizes the letter and lets the receiver know it wasn't simply a form letter sent to several family members.

- A form letter can be a useful way to write to several people at once, however. Try writing down the details of something important, such as a recent trip. Write a basic rundown of your travels to send to each person on your list. Then personalize each letter by adding details that would be pertinent to each specific reader.

- Include newspaper clippings, recipes, quotes or postcards. Not only do these "extras" brighten up the package, but they give the recipient a good idea of what the sender is thinking about and what is important to him or her.

Letters can also be an effective method of communicating with young family members. When Alice Knudsen's son was sent to England with the Air Force, he took his young daughter and wife with him. Communication was poor and expensive. Although Alice called once a month, the time difference made it so she often called while her granddaughter was sleeping. Alice often wrote letters, but she found that letters by themselves weren't creating a bond. "The only way our letters meant anything to this young child was for her parents to read the letter with her again and again, and then talk about grandparents and how they are a part of her life," Alice says. Long-distance grandparenting requires planning, desire, and creativity. Alice began sending pictures of herself with her letters, and then her granddaughter could put the picture on the fridge or in her room.

The grandchild-grandparent relationship is important for many reasons. For example, from grandparents, children can hear something of what their parents were like when they were young. This helps create the family chain that links generation to generation. Understanding where we've come from gives direction to the future.

For some, letters are an easier form of communication than conversation in person or on the phone. Letters can be written, edited, changed and shortened, or lengthened. A letter doesn't have to be sent until the writer is sure that it says only what is meant to be said. Letters have impact that a "by-the-way" phone conversation will never have.

Similarly, a greeting card may be the best $2.95 you spend this month. Cards send a message of caring even before the envelope is ripped open. Seeing the warm, decorative, hand-addressed envelope will bring a smile to most recipients.

Grandparents and parents often have a tradition of sending cards on birthdays, anniversaries, and holidays. But perhaps the most warmly-welcomed cards are those sent "just because." Showing that you care about the person even when it wasn't "scheduled" according to the calendar sends a clear message of love and caring for the individual or family.

For large families, buying gifts for siblings, in-laws, cousins, nieces, and nephews can be inconvenient at best and impossible at worst. Cards are a way to commemorate the occasion without spending great amounts of money or time finding the perfect gift. In fact, if forgetting occasions is an issue, cards could all be purchased in January. Take one day to write and address cards for all of the card-worthy occasions throughout the year. Then put them in order of when you want to mail them out, and keep the file near your phone or bill-paying station. Send the prewritten cards out three-to-five days before the important day.

Letters and cards are the oldest form of long-distance communication. As such, the advantages are clear. Letters require no training and no money (other than postage) to write. The writing can be done at the pace and convenience of the writer. Length can also be variable. A short, two-paragraph letter can convey the same "I'm thinking about you" notion as a six-page, single-spaced epistle. But a long letter is also an option when describing an in-depth situation or catching up on several months of events.

There are, however, some downsides to letter writing. Writing a personal, handwritten letter can be time-consuming, and, therefore, can easily be put off until tomorrow, and the next day, and on into the next month. Letters are also a relatively slow method of communication. Even across the city, a letter can take two days to arrive. International mail can take up to two weeks or more, depending on available services. Another downside to letter writing is the asynchronous quality brought on this delay. If there is conflict in the family, writing a letter may be the least effective way to solve the situation. Words can be misinterpreted, and with days going by between communication between the parties, emotions can change. The writer is also unable to sense how the receiver is interpreting the words.

Using the Phone Lines

Phone companies have prodded, promoted, and persuaded us to use our dialing fingers to open up the lines of communication. And we have done it in record numbers. Commercials focus on services that offer low rates for long distance, and gas stations and grocery stores offer calling cards with cheap minutes—some even include international calling. Americans want to talk, and they want to talk for cheap.

Phone communication is the quickest, easiest way to talk to family members we can't see face-to-face. Students studying abroad and business executives working overseas recognize the emotional lift involved with hearing a father's laugh or a mother's voice of concern.

The digital revolution has created clear phone lines. No longer are you able to detect a long-distance call the minute you pick up the phone and hear the static. You can talk to someone across the street or across the country and hear them equally well.

Phone calls allow for conversing in "real time." Parents can get a feel for their children's emotional state immediately. Grown siblings are able to talk through a serious matter and know right off what the feelings and reactions are on the other end. Also, if an event or issue needs to be coordinated or solved, phone calls are the easiest long-distance method. There's no waiting for a reply and a smaller chance for miscommunication. Talking on the phone is easy, too. It doesn't require typing skills, spell check, or finding a stamp. You can talk on the phone while you load the dishwasher or comb your daughter's hair.

And now there is an improvement on the telephone. New technology has made the videophone available, although the cost and know-how required currently make it prohibitive for the average family to own. Businesses, though, are using the device to save money on travel expenses. Video conferences can bring together executives from around the world for a real-time conversation.

In the near future, videophones will likely become part of the norm for families, just as computers, answering machines, and cell phones have become standard in the past few years.

Tips for Telephone Calls

- Ask the receiver if now is a good time to take a call. Although family members may be busy, some might not be good at telling others. They will simply feel frustrated.

- Consider bedtime, special family obligations, and meal times before dialing.

- Don't dominate the conversation. Ask questions and then truly listen to the answers.

- Be aware of the time differences. What might be after-dinner hours to you may be the dinner hour for another family member.

- When calling children, don't expect too much. If you ask a "yes or no" question, the child may simply nod his or her head without saying anything. Just let the child hear your voice and know you love him or her. As children grow, they will be more able to converse on the phone.

- If you are someone who feels unproductive while on the phone, invest in a cordless phone. This way you can change the laundry, check on the kids, turn on the sprinklers, and straighten the books all while chatting with your friends or family.

CELL PHONES

Like many new technologies, cell phones have become so commonplace that users wonder what they did before this convenient device came along. The cost to own a cell phone is generally reasonable depending on the range of service, long-distance capabilities, and number of minutes.

For busy parents, cell phones make it possible to reach each other while sitting at a baseball practice or driving home from the grocery store. During a critical time, such as when a daughter or sister is nine-months pregnant and counting, or when a family member is on his or her death bed, a cell phone can provide relief in knowing that communication is possible whenever and wherever the phone owner might be.

JUST THE FAX

Another technology enabling family communication is fax machines. Although only a small percentage of families have fax machines in their homes, most businesses have a fax machine. There are no envelopes to address or Web sites to create. You just have to know the fax number. One use might be for grandchildren to draw pictures and then fax them to Grandma or Grandpa. Faxes are also helpful when working on a survey. Family members can fax the form out, and then the people can write on the form and send it directly back.

Faxing long distance generally does cost based on the time it takes to transmit the document. However, the cost is minimal. And finding a personal greeting on a machine that generally has only cold business information is a welcome treat.

Creating a Family Newsletter

One of the great ironies in life is that we seem to have more to say to someone we talk to every day than someone we haven't spoken to in ten years. Logically, it seems like ten years would provide more fodder for discussion than one day, yet we can speak more easily with someone who knows what we did yesterday, and the day before that, and the year before that. Quality communication gives us more to talk about, not less.

Perhaps you have gone to a family reunion and had a hard time connecting with cousins, nieces, and even your grandparents. The problem is not the lack of love or care for one another. The problem is lack of communication, which has kept you from knowing the details of each other's lives. It becomes difficult to know where to start. We feel rude asking such elementary questions as, "So what do you do for a living?" We feel we should already know the basics, but often we don't unless an effort is made to keep the communication lines open.

A great way to keep those lines open is a family newsletter. It is through the sharing of life's details that family connectedness is built. In sharing with each other day-to-day activities, thoughts and aspirations, struggles and concerns, an intimacy is developed with each other that is otherwise missing. By sharing photos of children, vacations, and flower gardens in a newsletter, members of extended families are given a key to understanding each other. Through sharing stories and laughter, families create the unity that humor can provide.

You have heard and read about creating self-esteem in children. Everyone believes self-esteem is important. Experts also concur that there is something of a "family self-image" that needs to be created and nurtured in much the same way parents nurture their children. "People need to hear about the difficult times that their ancestors and relatives experienced and the ways those ancestors and relatives mastered those difficulties," writes Jeanne Nelson, author of *Absolutely Family!* "They need to hear about the accomplishments of present-day members of their family. They need to know what made it hard for some people in the family to achieve their dreams. By knowing the dramatic stories of ancestors and family members, and in comparing their own lives to those of their ancestors and family members, people come to see themselves as part of a long chain through history. They can take pride in their origins."

Family historians spend much of their time searching for basic facts—birthdates, number of children, and burial locations. A family newsletter creates a paper trail that solves many of these family history issues. But more than that, it creates a closeness within families. And there is no shortage of content ideas. Every birth that occurs in the family goes into the family newsletter. Every wedding, and every death. Honor roll announcements and high school football scores.

The ideal newsletter is an intimate publication that includes news and family stories of those who are closely related. If you all know each other on some level, it's easier to talk about yourselves and what you have been doing. A family newsletter is a perfect instru-

Items for a Newsletter

- Births
- Deaths
- Engagements, weddings
- Graduations
- Moves, including new addresses and e-mails
- Family history corner to share stories of ancestors
- Write about the origin of the family surname
- Quotes from children—or adults!
- Funny stories
- Photos from recent family reunions
- Surveys on favorite traditions, memories
- Plans for reunions
- Recipes

The Browning Bullet-in

Editor: Betseylee Browning
Jr. Editor: Devany Browning

Edition 3
November 1998

Charles Browning Book

The Descendants of Charles Henry Browning by Betseylee Browning will be available sometime in 1999.

Section One contains the history of Charles, including time line, autobiography, obituaries, funeral sketch and diaries.

Section Two will contain a scrapbook of about 90 pictures mostly black and white. Approximately thirty- eight of these pictures are of Charles and his farms and homes.

Section Three will contain the descendants of Charles formatted from Family Origins program complete with pictures. The pictures will be lazar printed and the printed pages photocopied. The book will be plastic bound with a card stock covers and a plastic sheet to protect the cover. The purchase price will be about $45 to cover costs including mailing.

If you would like to receive more issues. . .

1 Year subscription (4 issues) – **$10.00**

Money goes to support Genealogical Research
Send payments to: **Ken Browning**

Writing a book of this nature is proving to be a huge task, but with your patience and support it should be informative and interesting. And maybe with a little luck some fond memories will be stirred, a few precious moments revived and a grateful heart quickened as you reminisce about Charles Henry Browning and his descendants.

1998 Charles Browning Family Reunion Highlights
by Devany Browning

-- Big Cottonwood Canyon   July 24-25 –

The Browning reunion was a blast, even in the rain. I have to admit from the Pioneer Day Parade to the talent show, I think everyone would agree it was a great family reunion.

Newsletters give family members the chance to keep up-to-date on forthcoming events, and to learn about the extended family's past.

Get ready for Halloween!

October   2002

Printed by MyFamily.com™

Sunday	Monday	Tuesday	Wednesday	Thursday	Friday	Saturday
September 2002 S M T W T F S 1 2 3 4 5 6 7 8 9 10 11 12 13 14 15 16 17 18 19 20 21 22 23 24 25 26 27 28 29 30		1	2	3	4	5
6	7 Lucy's Birthday!	8	9	10 Tommy's Birthday! He'll be 34!	11	12
13	14	15	16	17	18 Lori's Birthday	19
20	21	22	23	24	25	26
27	28	29	30	31	November 2002 S M T W T F S 1 2 3 4 5 6 7 8 9 10 11 12 13 14 15 16 17 18 19 20 21 22 23 24 25 26 27 28 29 30	

A calendar that is personalized for your family will often list birthdays, anniversaries, even annual family reunions.

ment for gathering, sharing, and preserving a family's stories—its history, Nelson writes.

A family newsletter can be a major contributor to a family's cohesiveness—as a communication facilitator, a builder and reinforcer of a positive family image, an important paper trail for descendants, and a tool for gathering and sharing family history information.

GETTING STARTED

Nelson was hesitant about being the one to start the newsletter, but she was excited about the possibility of having one. With the help of family "reporters" and some family history and photos of her grandmother, she compiled her first family newsletter. It included an estimate of what a "subscription" would cost. "What I hadn't realized was how much my family had been craving such a publication," she writes.

"After I sent out our first issue, I received an overwhelming outpouring of gratitude from family members I hardly knew. Kudos came flying from all directions, along with checks to keep the newsletter coming." One family member said "When I read our family newsletter, I have a tremendously warm feeling of closeness for the entire family."

In the beginning, Nelson knew next to nothing about publishing a newsletter, and she didn't know how to go about organizing the information. "The result has been a tremendous growing experience for me and, I think also, for many of my family members," Nelson writes.

Many families enjoy sitting around the dining room table telling family stories. The stories seem to get funnier—and sometimes more sad—as the years go by. With distance moving family members around the globe, this roundtable discussion shouldn't be eliminated. It should be included in a family newsletter. Stories can be submitted from family members of all ages.

Some find Christmas newsletters sufficient for filling in former college roommates, neighbors, and coworkers about the happenings of the year. Larger families with resources at their fingertips may want to have a monthly newsletter. Quarterly publications may work for others. Newsletters don't need to fit any mold. Rather, they should reflect the personality and needs of the family. Don't promise more than you can or want to deliver. Newsletters don't have to be perfect. The idea is to convey information and have some fun. Don't worry, for example, if you have some unplanned white space or that the photo you were going to use turned out dark.

Newsletters offer the most concise way to convey a variety of family news. You can learn about which cousins had babies and who will graduate from high school this spring without having to write or call each person individually. Newsletters also give the family a sense of unity. Family members begin to feel, "This is what we are all about." Communication creates a family image that makes members proud of their heritage and gives them a desire to pass down a strong sense of family.

Burnham Review

It has been over a year since...

Grandma Burnham

Martin Family Newsletter

Vol. 6 No. 3

Your Cousin Joseph is No Ordinary Joe

BY JOY HARRIS

From the time he was just a boy, Joseph Martin (Judy Martin's second son) knew just what he wanted to do with his life: He wanted to sing.

His many hours of practice, starting with voice lessons at age four, have paid off. Last March, Joseph was named first tenor of the St. Louis Opera.

Having already starred in such productions as "Othello," "The Magic Flute," and "Aida," at the Duluth Community Repertory Theatre by the time he was 15, Joseph, now just 18, is prepared to star in the region's largest opera company. But it

see Joseph, p. 3

HAPPY TRAILS: Cousins Ja Nae and Marnie return to the cabin after blazing a trail through the sagebrush. Motorcycle riding was just one of the many activities at this year's reunion.

Family News

• The Annual Martin family reunion was a smash success. Thanks to all who participated with the food and different activities. Special thanks goes to Judy Martin who headed up this year's reunion committee. See you at next year's reunion!

• Ja Nae Matthews (grand-daughter of Constance Martin) has been awarded a cooking scholarship to the Betty Crocker University located in Minneapolis, MN.

• John Martin has gotten a job in New York City, and is in need of a place to stay in the city until he can find an apartment. Anyone with information can contact John directly at (555) 555-5566.

• Grandma Martin's surgery went great, and she is back home in time for her birthday celebration (August 15, at her home).

Don't forget Grandma Martin's birthday August 15. She would love to hear from you on her special day. Her phone number is (555) 555-5555.

A newsletter done well won't be entirely serious. Funny stories, quotes from three-year-olds and surveys such as "the funniest wedding present we received was ..." will lighten up the publication and keep readers of all ages looking forward to the next one.

Although fun to read, creating a newsletter can be a daunting task. Desktop publishing doesn't come easy to many, although software programs such as Microsoft Publisher, Adobe PageMaker, ClarisWorks and QuarkXPress have newsletter templates and good tutorials. Talk about this as a family. Is there someone with the computer skills and desire to be the publisher? If so, allow him or her to be the leader.

However, the responsibility to submit stories and facts is on everyone's shoulders. Have a firm deadline for submitting information. If possible, encourage family members to e-mail the information so it is already electronic; this will save the editor from retyping.

Consider rotating the responsibility among family members. However, make sure responsibilities are clear or your family newsletter may be out of print before its second issue.

E-mail and Family Web sites

While letters and phone calls have been communication staples for generations, e-mail and the Internet are quickly becoming an important source of family bonding. In fact, technology can even help create a family.

Laurie and Kevin both ended up in Idaho Falls, Idaho, for what they expected to be an uneventful summer. Because it's not a college town, the southeastern Idaho city isn't home to many twenty-somethings. Luckily, Laurie and Kevin—who had gone to high school together but hadn't known each other—ran into each other at a community event and began spending time together.

Kevin had recently returned from studying abroad in England for semester, and Laurie had spent the first part of the summer touring Europe with her dance company. Their time together was destined to be short; in early September Kevin would attend Idaho State University in Pocatello, and Laurie would move to Salt Lake City to study dance at the University of Utah. They spent much of the few remaining summer weeks together. Laurie helped Kevin and his family paint the exterior of their home. Kevin taught Laurie how to golf. As the end of August neared, the two exchanged e-mail addresses and began their interstate relationship.

E-mail allowed them a cheap and efficient way to share their daily thoughts and experiences. Occasionally they fought over e-mail. Making up over a modem connection wasn't as easy or as fun as in person, but putting thoughts onto a screen helped each of them realize what they hoped for the future and how they reacted to certain situations. When they both graduated, they logged off of their electronic relationship and got married. Now they e-mail each other at work, where they are only two blocks apart. E-mail is an important part of who they are as a couple.

Regarding E-mail Messages

- Don't forward Internet messages unless you are sure of its truth and feel that it is worthy to pass along.
- Keep your messages short and lively.
- Don't backbite other family members online. Having written proof of a conversation can be a potentially ugly situation.
- Send low-resolution photos so those family members with slow Internet connections don't have computer problems downloading the images.
- Create an e-mail list of all family members. Write an overall message to send to all the family members on your list. Then your family members can hit "reply all" and write back to the list of family members. This saves time repeating questions such as "Would the family reunion be better in June or July?" to each and every family member.

But it's not just young people who enjoy electronic communication.

The Waite family is spread from San Francisco to Baltimore and spans five generations. Great-grandma Waite lives in Denver, Colorado, and doesn't have a computer. Her son, Rod Waite, lives in Napa Valley, California. As a retired commercial airplane pilot, he has always fancied himself a technical guy. He tried Prodigy back when it was unheard of. He bought himself an Apple computer back in the early '80s. He does his own taxes online. For a seventy-year-old, he is, as they say, "with it." His three children are also well-educated and open to technology. So when Rod began talking about a family Web site, it

Items for Your Web Site

- **News** Family members can keep up on family events, easily share news items with all site members and reply to previous messages. Members can receive notification via e-mail when news items are posted.

- **Reviews** Become your very own movie critics. You can share opinions with other family members about movies, music and Web sites.

- **Calendar** Keep you family up to date. Birthdays and anniversaries can be automatically added to the calendar. Plan reunions, parties and other family get-togethers and receive e-mail reminders so you won't forget anything important.

- **History** Publish and archive those treasured stories of your family. Let others read your account and then respond with their own version of favorite family anecdotes, tell tales, and personal memories.

- **Photos** Share photos with site members.

- **File cabinet** Family members may upload any computer file to this area to share with other site members (such as legal documents, family records, shareware applications, and so on).

- **Chat/Who's Online** MyFamily.com sites show which family members are currently online and lets members instantly communicate with them.

- **Family communication** You don't have to keep track of everyone's e-mail addresses. A family Web site lets members easily send e-mail to all site members without requiring them to enter each member's e-mail address.

- **Recipes** Preserve traditional family recipes from fading away or getting lost. Share your most popular family favorites with others who enjoy good food.

was more than just banter. It was reality before the ink dried on the newest "It's great to be Waite" T-shirts.

A family Web site was set up so that members could economically remember birthdays and send appropriate greetings, post pictures of new babies, and share accomplishments as well as sorrows.

Great-grandma Waite cannot access the site herself, but family members who go to see her often print out the latest postings on the site. Although she doesn't understand the technology, she is comfortable with swapping stories about family members. After all, most of her ninety years have been spent living the family farm life, where closeness was the only option.

Creating a family Web site is the most difficult of the communication options discussed in this chapter. However, it can combine all of the advantages of the other options.

Having a family Web site is like having an online home. Relatives are always welcome, the door is always open, and you can easily communicate. You can hear the latest family news from across the world, being part of milestones like when your only nephew says his first word. You can also share pictures, video clips, and audio clips. An online scrapbook is easy to create, and you can find out for yourself if your cousin looks just like you do.

There are also commercial family Web sites such as MyFamily.com that will remind you of important events, such as birthdays or anniversaries. This saves family members from trying to keep track of the dates themselves. And if you like, rather than using regular ("snail") mail, you can simply send an e-mail when you realize that today is someone's special day. Families can also create message boards to discuss topics large and small: debate world issues or give ideas on how Mom should cut her hair.

A Web site is a central location to keep the important family stories, dates, and memories together. It's like a newsletter that can't get lost. Simply bookmark your Web site and visit it at your convenience.

Unfortunately, family Web sites can be overwhelming to some relatives. All parties may not have access to a computer. And even if everyone has a computer, there's no guarantee they'll be able to consistently find the site. Although creating a site is not as difficult as it sounds, taking the first step toward creating one can be intimidating, and one person often bears the burden of maintaining and adding information. While sharing photos and video online is an exciting opportunity, it can also be frustrating for those with slow computers or low-grade connection speeds. However, if the barriers to technology are removed, family Web sites are perhaps the most promising way of keeping loved ones connected.

Delilah "Mae" Robb had won another battle for her life, and she wanted a computer so she could log on and "talk" to her family. She wanted them to know she was all right. The 83-year-old hospital patient came to be known as "the computer lady" by the hospital staff. Mae had had many struggles during her life, and always knew how to get through them. "She tended to wage them remarkably well when she has her family gathered round her. This time was no exception," her daughter Marlene Cupit said.

While many people her age tend to avoid Internet technology, the computer allowed Mae to bring her family together. The night before her surgery, a special e-mail was sent out announcing an online chat session. Using the Internet, Mae "spoke" to the rest of the family.

The invitation to the chat session came unexpectedly. "It was an event I will always cherish," said Marlene, who lives in Texas. "We were chatting online when all of a sudden Mother's name appeared. It was like an angel had lit up my screen. We all hung on every word she had to say."

Mark, who participated in the chat from Northern California, said, "What a wonderful moment it was. Everyone typed in, old stories were recounted and there were lots of laughs all through the night as jokes and memories were shared. There

---

Emoticons in Your E-mail

When communicating online, you can use emoticons to represent the facial expressions and even the intonations that cannot be conveyed by plain text. Usually, emoticons are constructed by tilting your head to the left, so the right side of the emoticon is the bottom of the "picture."

The most common emoticons are:

:-) A smile, humor
:-(A frown, sadness, anger
;-) A wink, often for sarcasm
:-/ A wry look, wry humor

Some acronyms have also become common for expressing emotions online. These include:

BTW By the way   IMO In my opinion
JK Just kidding   TTYL Talk to you later
LOL Laugh out loud or Lots of love

was not a single dry eye as we enjoyed this special moment."

To facilitate her communication with the family, Mae used MyFamily.com. The site offers families free, private Web sites. Mae's grandson, Mark Wasden, set up the Web site for the entire family. The family response was positive and Mark quickly had forty family members participating. "With some instruction about the site, everyone overcame any hesitation about the technological side of it," Mark said.

The Robb family grew closer as family members communicated and shared their feelings about Mae's illness. Mark initiated the use of the MyFamily.com about the time Mae last health problems developed. With extended family scattered everywhere from California to Arkansas and Texas to Wyoming, immediate communication had been difficult. Mark pointed out that only a conference call would connect all concerned by telephone. Conference calls were too costly and difficult to arrange. The family Web site became the means to disseminate what Mark called the "health updates," and it quickly grew into a large communication net used to help untangle logistical problems related to Mae's illness. It was used to coordinate answers to questions about what help was needed at home, who would provide it, and what time it was needed.

In addition to serving as an alert line for health updates, the family site brought many other significant benefits to the Robb family. Chief among these was a feeling of unity. They were able to talk to each other, to get to know each other better, and to strengthen their relationships. It has erased the distances that separated them and brought them closer together. They were able to talk to cousins who we had previously only heard about second-hand.

The youngest generation loved the new Web site. In addition to keeping in touch *with their favorite cousins, they got to read family stories about all the pranks the aunts used to pull as children. The funny stories set the stage to tell the stories about serious moments and special family ties.*

Mae died in January of 2000. But because of the Web site her grandson created, she was able to express her feelings of love and gratitude for all her family members. "Our family Web site was such a blessing to my mother and to us all. I will treasure every chat, every message, and every moment," said Marlene.

FAMILY REUNIONS

Nothing beats face-to-face contact with family members as you enjoy great food, fun activities, and each other's company. Family reunions—whether formal or just a spontaneous get-together—are a great reason to have consistent communication. When you finally get together, you have a strong basis of friendship and understanding.

Families would do well not to always rely on Mom or oldest sister to plan family reunions. Each family member should take part in planning, coordinating, and enjoying reunions. (See chapter nine for an in-depth look at the reasons and methods for a great family reunion.)

The Wholeness of Family

Corresponding and connecting with family fits with the biological principle of systems, which are defined as "complexes of elements in interaction." John Bradshaw, author of *Bradshaw On: The Family* and host of four nationally broadcast public television series, says families would do well to understand the importance of acting as a system.

In biology and in family systems, "wholeness" and "relationship" are two defining characteristics. In a system, the whole is greater than the sum of its parts. In a family, the unit that the members create has more strength, power, creativity, and passion than the added quantities of each individual. A system is a result of interaction. Without interaction, there is no system. Without communication, there is no family.

While a neighborhood, community, religious, or social system may seem more important to us at times than the family structure we are a part of, when things are worth celebrating or crying over, it's family we turn to. At times of illness or cash-flow problems, we know we can count on family. When one of our children gets into the college of his or her dreams, it's usually Grandma who gets the first call and sends perhaps the only congratulatory letter. Our wedding day, which is often the most significant day of our lives, is one shared with family. We photograph our siblings and parents, and we often ask their help in planning the big event. The family system is at its best when seen as a whole.

How you choose to stay connected doesn't matter, whether through cards or letters, e-mails or Web sites, newsletters or phone calls. Pick the approach that fits your time schedule, budget, needs, and creativity.

Just as Grant Reeve and his young bride, Lola Dawn, kept their love alive through wartime letters and cards, so should we all put forth the effort to build and maintain strong family ties.

How you choose to stay connected doesn't matter, whether through cards or letters, e-mails or Web sites, newsletters or phone calls. Pick the approach that fits your time schedule, budget, needs, and creativity. If the funny story or deep sorrow can't wait another moment, pick up the phone. If you have a quick quote or idea to share with family members around the world, type up a quick e-mail. If you are planning the next family vacation, enlist the help of a Web site. If you can plan ahead, stop by the Hallmark section and pick out something that expresses your emotions. Your best efforts to stay connected will be met with happy hearts, and before long, your mailbox and "in" box will be full of replies and thank yous.

True, none of these methods can replace running next door or across town to Grandma's for a special treat or visit. Yet sometimes there are grandparents next door who are long-distance grandparents. Closeness as a family really has nothing to do with geographic boundaries. In this fast-paced and mobile world, remember that your only permanent role is your role in your family. You can never be replaced. And your position never ends.

A family reunion is the ultimate celebration of your family.

CHAPTER NINE

Getting Together
Your Family Reunion

Delores Williams radiated with a glow of satisfaction. The family reunion she and her sisters had worked so hard for almost a year to plan was an unqualified success. She, her mother, and her two sisters sat in the shade under the trees in the park overlooking Lake Michigan in Chicago. The weather was perfect, the temperature not too warm, the view of the lake and downtown was fabulous, and the smells wafting from the family's nearby barbecue grills promised a delicious feast.

The women looked around at the more than one hundred family members present. Some relatives had come from as far away as Mississippi, Florida, and California for this first-ever family reunion. The kids were tossing a football and shooting hoops at the nearby basketball court, while some of the men played softball. Others, led by Delores' husband, tended the grills filled with spareribs, sausages, hot dogs, and hamburgers. The women and older children helped set up the food tables. Almost everyone wore the reunion T-shirt created especially for the occasion.

"You all make me so proud," their mother said with a broad smile. "But, there's just one thing I want to know. How are you girls going to top this reunion next year?" The sisters grinned at each other and began to laugh.

This family's experience is not unique. Each year, thousands of family reunions are held in all sizes, in all kinds of places, and with all sorts of themes. Each family's reunion is a unique event, but they share a common goal: to bring together family members who may not have seen each other in months, years, or even decades. They introduce new family members, such as new spouses and babies, to the clan. They facilitate the sharing of stories and information and perpetuate family traditions and lore. Most of all, reunions serve to build and reinforce relationships that endure across the generations. A family reunion is, indeed, the ultimate celebration of your family.

The goal of any reunion, regardless of whether it involves ten people or two hundred, is to create a comfortable atmosphere in which family members can get together, renew old friendships, and build and strengthen new relationships.

When most people envision a family reunion, they picture a huge gathering with all their family members in one place at one time. However, a family reunion can be as simple an affair as a dinner or a cookout for immediate family members who haven't been able to get together for a while. The simple act of bringing family members together for some quality time spent communicating and socializing is sufficient to be classified as a reunion. The goal of any reunion, regardless of whether it involves ten people or two hundred, is to create a comfortable atmosphere in which family members can get together, renew old friendships, and build and strengthen new relationships.

Every family will have different incentives for holding a reunion. For most, the intent is merely to provide a place and time for people to meet. There may, however, be other motivations. You might consider hosting a family reunion in conjunction with a graduation, a birthday, a wedding, a confirmation, a bar or bat mitzvah, a landmark wedding anniversary, or some other event. Even a family funeral can provide the opportunity for an impromptu reunion if people can stay over for another day or two.

You also might want to use your family reunion as an event to raise money for a family project, such as replacing your great-grandfather's broken tombstone, providing funding for a scholarship for the children, helping a family member with medical bills, or providing seed money for next year's reunion. A family raffle, bake sale, talent show, or other activity can be devised to fit the occasion.

A Family Reunion to Fit Your Needs

Your own family reunion can be as simple or as elaborate as you like. A potluck dinner or barbecue at someone's home can be the basis for your reunion, even if it's a large one. One family in North Carolina hosts an annual family reunion each autumn at the farm of one of the cousins. The organizer, her husband, and her mother network with the extended family to invite every relative they can locate. This extends to second and third cousins, several times removed, from as far away as Pennsylvania, Florida, and other eastern states.

Cox family reunion, date unknown.

The result is an outdoor gathering under broad oak trees with between one hundred and one hundred and fifty family members. Everyone brings folding chairs for their group and a homemade dish to share. The celebration begins in the late morning when people begin to arrive. Older family members visit while the children play softball, volleyball, badminton, tag, and other games. A huge meal is served under the trees in the early afternoon, followed by storytelling, show-and-tell using family heirlooms, and a dessert of homemade ice cream and lemonade. People gradually depart about dusk with warm memories of yet another reunion. And throughout the year, family members continue to communicate and to anticipate the next family reunion.

You might consider other ideas, such as a group weekend trip to a campground, a resort, a dude ranch, or some other fun location. An extended get-together at a theme destination such as Disney World might be fun, providing different parks for people to visit and a variety of dining, shopping, and entertainment options. Or a three-night family cruise might provide a perfect upscale getaway event for a very special occasion.

You can organize any type of family reunion that suits the character and unique needs of your own family. The key to any successful reunion, however, is strong advance planning and organization, and paying proper attention to the details.

Getting Started

The first step to a memorable family reunion is, of course, getting family members to attend. In order to avoid lackluster attendance, start planning early and pique your family members' interest. You have to get people's attention, build their enthusiasm, and give them plenty of time to make plans to attend. It is not unusual to begin planning your next family reunion as much as eight months to a year in advance.

One woman made the mistake of deciding in May to invite family members from several states to a reunion in her city over the Independence Day holiday. She was devastated

---

Reunion Planning Summary

The following is a summary of the responses from our survey regarding our family reunion.

Preference for a place for the reunion:

Grandma Smith's house	8 responses
Aunt Elizabeth Weatherly's house	3 responses
Disney World in Orlando, FL	6 responses
Kansas City, MO (mid-point)	9 responses
No preference	1 response

Preference for time of year for the reunion:

June	11 responses
July	3 responses
August	9 responses
September	2 responses
No preference	2 responses

Estimated number of adults attending: 34

Estimated number of seniors attending: 13

Estimated number of children attending:

Ages 0-6	3
Ages 7-12	9
Ages 13-16	7
Total =	19

People expressing a willingness in participating on the planning committee:

John Swords - Mailing list and invitations
Ed Smith - Accounting and finance
Laura Wilson - Catering and food., menus, etc.
John Alexander, Jr. - Willing to work with hotel
Cathy Wilson and Beth Smith - Decorations
Marie McKnitt - Family history and genealogy
Walt Weatherly, Sam Morgan, Emma Dale Holder, Edith Morgan, Peter Frank, Murray West, and
Lydia Wilson - Willing to be assigned as needed

The following are some other ideas for the reunion:

Ideas regarding commemorative items:

T-shirt
Coffee mug
Sports water bottle
Group photograph

Suggested activities

Icebreaker games
Photo and heirloom display
Family history display
Pizza party for the younger set
Trip to see the old family home and the family cemetery
Softball, horseshoes, and badminton games
Banquet

Brady family reunion, 1971.

by the responses from her relatives who either had already made other plans or who could not afford on such short notice to pay for travel expenses to attend. Her good intentions were thwarted by her failure to do advance planning and to get the word out to her relatives in enough time for them to reserve time and finances to attend the event. Contact family members early on to determine their interest in attending. There are a number of factors that will influence their decision. Key among these are location, dates, cost of travel and accommodations, and activities offered for all members of the family. It is most important to offer a good, central location for the most people, as well as convenient dates for them to attend. Having something for everyone also provides the broad appeal that helps make the reunion an eagerly anticipated event.

Gauge the interest level of family members by contacting a good cross-section of the whole family. You can telephone or even develop a questionnaire to solicit input. You want to determine if the idea of a family reunion is appealing, which location is most convenient, what time of year is best, and the types of activities they might enjoy. Everyone's input is important and should be weighed in the decision-making process.

As you conduct your survey, make careful notes of the responses so you can tabulate and summarize them to provide a clearer picture of what your family members would prefer. Keep track of who you talk to, the numbers and ages of each family group, and their comments and suggestions. Based on this information, you can then decide whether you want to host a reunion for all of your relatives or for a smaller subset. Perhaps your first reunion will be a one-afternoon gathering tailored to local family members. Out-of-towners, although certainly welcome, may not be able to justify the trip for such a short event. You may want to measure the success of the first, smaller event before planning a larger, full-scale reunion with more extended family the next time. The input you receive from your relatives will help you determine what group is the right size.

The second consideration for the scope of your reunion is its duration. Should your reunion be a one-afternoon event, or do you want to host a full-day or multiple-day affair? Again, family members' responses will help you make the best decision.

SELECTING THE RIGHT LOCATION

The place you choose is critical to attendance at your reunion. You will usually want to hold it in a place that is convenient for the most people. For many, this is a hometown where family members still reside. For others who have moved to far corners of the country or the world, choosing another, more centrally located point may be preferable. Still others may not want to consider a visit to their hometown, but instead would prefer a group trip to some other destination.

You have a whole world from which to choose. A reunion held at a family member's home or farm may be ideal. A city or state park may be just the right place for a day-long outing. Some reunions are best held at a hotel or resort that has accommodations and amenities for persons of all ages and is located conveniently near a variety of attractions and activities. Family members with special interests such as skiing, camping, hiking, backpacking, golfing, and the like may prefer special environments. People preferring more sedentary pastimes such as museums, galleries, and cultural facilities might prefer a visit to a large city with these types of sites. A cruise may provide a unique combination of activities and amenities appealing to some.

Review the feedback from your family members to select the optimum locale for your reunion, one that will be most convenient and attractive to the most people. Based on this input, you can begin defining other requirements for your perfect reunion venue.

Reunion Resources

Reunions Magazine has a Web site (www.reunionsmag.com) that provides planning tips and advice to help you organize your family reunion. The site also includes a resource center, a collection of "successful reunion" stories, and a free reunion registry where you can announce your reunion online.

At www.family-reunion.com you can learn about Family Reunion Organizer, a software program for everyone who is planning a reunion. You can also subscribe to a family reunion newsletter and get advice from "Mr. Spiffy, the family reunion doctor."

Brady family reunion, 1940.

SELECTING THE DATE

The next most important factor in determining attendance will be when you schedule the reunion. Booking some accommodations, such as hotels and resorts, will require some substantial advance notice and flexibility in your schedule, especially if you are planning for a larger group. However, the convenience for your family members is most important. Family members with school-age children will find summer most convenient, as will people who are driving to the event. A reunion over a weekend will be best for a majority of people as well.

When soliciting input from family members, ask for times of year that would best suit their schedules. Suggest at least two dates, allowing them to pick a first and second choice. You can also ask for alternate date suggestions, and a better time than the dates you have proposed may emerge.

Once you have determined that your family's interest in a reunion is high, and have targeted a location and date for the event, it is time to start planning and organizing.

Getting Your Family Involved

You may be an expert organizer and a go-getter with plenty of energy, but organizing a family reunion can be an enormous job for one person. You will need help from other family members. Delores Williams learned how important this was when she and her sisters worked on their reunion in Chicago. They discovered that they were a great team.

CREATING YOUR TEAM

Every family has people with special talents. Some people can organize, some can make things happen, and some are creative or artistic. Others may have other aptitudes, such as being good with finances, or they may be computer experts, or gourmet cooks, or expert photographers. All of these skills can contribute to the success of your family reunion. Your job is to put together a core team to develop and manage the planning and organization process and then enlist family members to help with all the various tasks.

IDENTIFYING THE TASKS

The first item of business for your team is to develop a vision of the reunion, based on the input you obtained from other family members. Once you have decided the place, the date, and size of your reunion, make a list of everything you can think of that will have to be accomplished. Compile these tasks into logical groupings, such as communications, hotels and lodging, food, finances, registration, transportation, entertainment, and other areas. Next, organize each group's tasks according to your best estimate of the order in which they need to be accomplished. This sequence can always be adjusted later. Finally, examine all the groups' task lists side by side to determine which tasks from one list might be dependent on the completion of one or more tasks on other lists. For example, invitations can't be mailed out until a mailing list is created, and reunion T-shirts can't be ordered until you determine how many of each size family members will order.

It is most important to take the time to gather and enjoy each other's company, and to savor the joy of your family whenever and wherever you come together.

Once you have laid out a fair plan of what needs to be done in order to organize and stage your family reunion, you can begin to assess what resources you need to get the job done. George G. Morgan, author of the book *Your Family Reunion: How to Plan It, Organize It, and Enjoy It*, stresses the importance of developing the task list. "You really have to define all the pieces before you can start working on them. Once you've put together a list of what has to be done, you start the real work of figuring what family members can help and what help you may need from outside people." You won't always have the talent and expertise in all areas within your own family, but the tasks that family members can handle don't cost you money in professional fees. However, "don't make the mistake of assigning a task to someone if it's over their head, or you may be asking for failure," Morgan advises. "Asking your Aunt Mary to coordinate, prepare, and serve a sit-down banquet for fifty is probably a Herculean task best left to a professional caterer. Besides, you want her to be able to be a part of the banquet too."

Wilson Family Reunion

5619 S. Dorchester Avenue
Chicago, IL 60637

January 1, 2002

Greetings!

Happy New Year to you and your family! I hope you had a wonderful holiday season and that this letter finds everyone in good health.

You recently should have received your invitation to our Third Annual WILSON Family Reunion, scheduled for Saturday, June 23, 2002, at Promontory Point in Chicago. We're planning another exciting family get-together this year and want to make sure you're there to share the experience. It's not too early to begin making your plans now.

Enclosed is the registration form for your family and a self-addressed, stamped envelope. Please fill out the form and return it to me no later than **February 25th**. We will be ordering T-shirts to commemorate our reunion this year and ask that you get your registration form and payment in to us by that date so we can guarantee that everyone in your family gets one of these great shirts.

As in years past, we will have softball, soccer and frisbee competitions in the park for those so inclined and some special activities for the less athletically inclined in the pavilion. Our meal will be a family barbecue catered by Jimmy's Wonderful Barbecue. The meal prices are based on children, adult and senior citizen rates. In addition, you may bring a dessert to share with the family.

You don't want to miss our terrific family reunion. It has become a real tradition that everyone in the family looks forward to each year. If you have any questions, or if you would like to volunteer to help (and we always need volunteers to make the reunion a success!), please contact me by telephone at (312) 555-5555 or by e-mail at dwilson@email.net.

Mark your calendar and send in your registration form today! I can't wait to see you at the reunion!

Yours,

Della Wilson

Holder family reunion, ca. 1900.

DIVIDING THE WORK

Take a look at your task lists and attempt to match your needs to the talents and skills of family members. In some cases, it may make sense to assign one task to a number of people if it is too large or involved for one person to handle, and splitting the responsibility between two or more may make the job easier.

Based on how you decide to divide the workload, you need to develop a timetable of key dates of when tasks must be completed. You need not assign an exact date to every task; you may choose the milestone tasks—those that must be completed before other things can move forward—and assign dates to those. The milestone dates become targets against which you can measure your overall progress. Based on these dates, you can develop an overall reunion schedule that becomes a project management tool for you and your team. Add some dates for progress reports from the different areas of responsibility and schedule regular status meetings, perhaps as frequently as once a month. Progress reports and status meetings provide an excellent follow-up mechanism to assure that no balls are dropped.

Planning a Family Reunion on a Budget

Sometimes you don't have months of lead time to plan your family reunion or the financial resources to put together a luxury event. So what are you to do? There are ways to streamline the process and to keep expenses down. Here are some suggestions:

- Prepare a written announcement of potential dates and locations for a reunion, and divide names and telephone numbers of family members among a few relatives. Have them make calls, communicate the announcement information, and gather as much information as possible.

- Summarize responses from the calls, and select the best date and location for the most people. Figure out where to hold the gathering. A family buffet dinner, a cookout in a park, or a backyard barbecue can be ideal for almost any size group and costs little to stage.

- Determine what kind of food is appropriate for the location and time of year. Determine how the food might be prepared, or what foods and supplies can be brought by family members. Create a checklist of possible contributions people could make or bring.

- Once you have defined your date, location, and type of reunion, prepare another announcement script. Have the same people who made calls before make contact with the same list of family members again. This time, let them spread the definitive information and invite people to the reunion. Have them communicate a list of what is needed and ask them to call you back to let you know what family members are bringing.

- Decide on easy things to do that will get people communicating and interacting at the reunion. Nametags are inexpensive and can be handwritten by each attendee as they arrive. Develop a list of activities for people of all ages, and ask one or more family members to coordinate setting up the area required, and any equipment or supplies to be brought by others. A softball game might require only a softball, a bat, and something like paper plates to be used for bases.

- Ask someone to supply a portable stereo or boombox for musical entertainment, and ask family members to bring their favorite tapes or CDs.

- If you are planning an outing to a family home, a cemetery, or other place of family significance, ask for volunteers to drive carloads of attendees in a carpool-style trip. It will be fun and will save transportation money.

- Prepare your own simple decorations in advance. Colorful vinyl tablecloths are reusable, and color-coordinated paper napkins, plastic cups, and plastic dinnerware will look great and keep the expenses low. Craft stores often have small baskets and party favors on sale that can be assembled to make centerpieces.

- Make up a simple one-page announcement with all the details about the reunion: date; time; location; format; events to be held; suggested dress; and a contact name, telephone number and, if appropriate, an e-mail address. Suggest things that can be brought, including food items, folding chairs and tables, and supplies. Mail and/or e-mail the announcement to all family members, and ask them to RSVP so you know who will be coming. Also ask for volunteers to help with setup and cleanup.

- Make up signs to post on local roads to guide people who are unfamiliar with the area. Post welcome signs.

- Make the reunion a festive occasion in which family members will want to pitch in to make it a thoroughly enjoyable success. Most of all, make sure you have a good time, too!

With all of this preliminary work done, you can contact family members and determine if they can and will help. It is always helpful to have alternate names in mind in case someone's schedule, health, or other commitments prevent them from helping.

Developing a Budget

Another critical part of planning a successful reunion is developing a realistic budget. The costs of a banquet and/or other food, entertainment, souvenirs, photographs, and other components can add up fast. You need to identify and come up with realistic cost estimates from the beginning in order to set the right rate to charge family members. This may be less important when hosting a small reunion, but costs for a more involved affair can quickly get out of hand.

A good place to start is back at the task lists. For example, if the food involves a sit-down dinner for a large group, you will need to know what the cost will be for a choice of entrees, desserts, and beverages, so your food team will need to contact some caterers for sample menus and cost estimates. Remind them to be thorough, making certain that all the costs are included. Cocktails and appetizers, for instance, may be extra.

All cost estimates should be in writing, which makes it easier to compare products or services. "Written estimates are firm offers to provide something to you," advises Morgan. "Once you have a couple of estimates in hand, you can decide which one looks best. Always ask for references and always follow through and contact them." He urges that you always get a signed contract and read it carefully before you sign yourself. "A contract spells out expectations and pricing, and it provides both you and your vendor with legal protection. That way there are no surprises later on, and surprises can be very expensive."

Develop your budget from the cost estimates you obtain. A realistic budget will allow you to set finite spending limits up front for your task people, and prevent a shortage that someone will ultimately have to cover.

Locating and Inviting Family Members

One challenge of hosting a successful reunion lies in locating and inviting family members. This may not be a difficult task if you decide that your reunion will include only the local family. However, the larger the group, and the more dispersed they have become, the more difficult it may be to contact and invite them all to the reunion.

An important job early in the organization process is compiling a family address book. One or more relatives may be able to consolidate and compile contact information and then

Cousin Finder

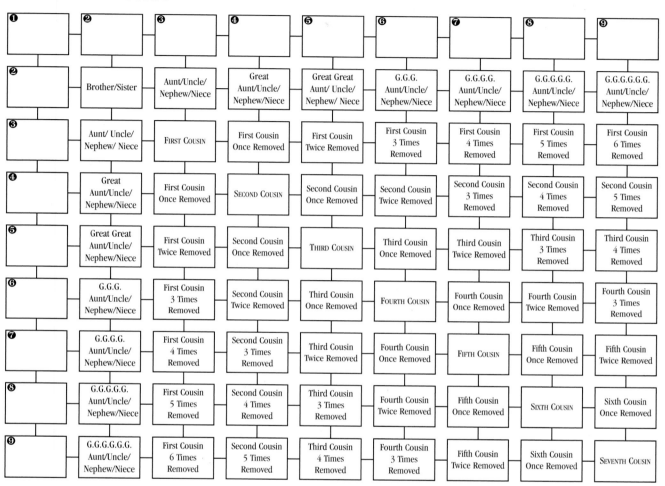

❶	❷	❸	❹	❺	❻	❼	❽	❾
❷	Brother/Sister	Aunt/Uncle/ Nephew/Niece	Great Aunt/Uncle/ Nephew/Niece	Great Great Aunt/ Uncle/ Nephew/ Niece	G.G.G. Aunt/Uncle/ Nephew/Niece	G.G.G.G. Aunt/Uncle/ Nephew/Niece	G.G.G.G.G. Aunt/Uncle/ Nephew/Niece	G.G.G.G.G.G. Aunt/Uncle/ Nephew/Niece
❸	Aunt/ Uncle/ Nephew/ Niece	FIRST COUSIN	First Cousin Once Removed	First Cousin Twice Removed	First Cousin 3 Times Removed	First Cousin 4 Times Removed	First Cousin 5 Times Removed	First Cousin 6 Times Removed
❹	Great Aunt/Uncle/ Nephew/Niece	First Cousin Once Removed	SECOND COUSIN	Second Cousin Once Removed	Second Cousin Twice Removed	Second Cousin 3 Times Removed	Second Cousin 4 Times Removed	Second Cousin 5 Times Removed
❺	Great Great Aunt/Uncle/ Nephew/Niece	First Cousin Twice Removed	Second Cousin Once Removed	THIRD COUSIN	Third Cousin Once Removed	Third Cousin Twice Removed	Third Cousin 3 Times Removed	Third Cousin 4 Times Removed
❻	G.G.G. Aunt/Uncle/ Nephew/Niece	First Cousin 3 Times Removed	Second Cousin Twice Removed	Third Cousin Once Removed	FOURTH COUSIN	Fourth Cousin Once Removed	Fourth Cousin Twice Removed	Fourth Cousin 3 Times Removed
❼	G.G.G.G. Aunt/Uncle/ Nephew/Niece	First Cousin 4 Times Removed	Second Cousin 3 Times Removed	Third Cousin Twice Removed	Fourth Cousin Once Removed	FIFTH COUSIN	Fifth Cousin Once Removed	Fifth Cousin Twice Removed
❽	G.G.G.G.G. Aunt/Uncle/ Nephew/Niece	First Cousin 5 Times Removed	Second Cousin 4 Times Removed	Third Cousin 3 Times Removed	Fourth Cousin Twice Removed	Fifth Cousin Once Removed	SIXTH COUSIN	Sixth Cousin Once Removed
❾	G.G.G.G.G.G. Aunt/Uncle/ Nephew/Niece	First Cousin 6 Times Removed	Second Cousin 5 Times Removed	Third Cousin 4 Times Removed	Fourth Cousin 3 Times Removed	Fifth Cousin Twice Removed	Sixth Cousin Once Removed	SEVENTH COUSIN

Cousin Finder instructions: To determine a relationship between two people, enter the common ancestor for both people in block ❶. Next, enter that common ancestor's descendants in the numbered blocks until you've entered the two people for whom you wish to determine a relationship (one family line along the top and the other down the side). Follow the column and row for the two people into the table. The intersecting block shows the relationship. (Hint: The people you enter in block ❷ are necessarily siblings; Those in block ❸ are grandchildren of the person in block ❶, and so on.)

network with others to fill in any blanks. The result should be a master list of names, addresses, telephone numbers, and perhaps e-mail addresses. This becomes your master contact file.

Your earliest mailing to some family members may be the interest survey discussed earlier. The first mass mailing to everyone will probably be the announcement of and invitation to the reunion. This mailing should go out some months in advance to ensure that people have enough time to make plans to attend. The invitation should provide enough information about the date, place, and events planned to generate excitement and anticipation.

The excitement can be sustained with additional mailings later on, particularly with a second mailing containing full details and a registration form. Another mailing a month or so before the reunion can help keep the level of anticipation high.

A FAMILY REUNION WEB PAGE

Donna Johnson took a class in Web page design and has created several Web pages for herself, as well as one for her husband's plumbing contractor business. She also has been working on her family genealogy for several years. In the course of her research, she came across the MyFamily.com Web site (www.myfamily.com). There, she was able to build a Web site for her family. Only the family members she invites and to whom she provides access can visit the site. When her family decided to host a family reunion two years ago, she volunteered to set up a MyFamily.com Web site to help provide reunion information to family members.

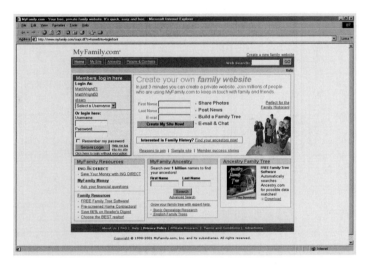

Donna started by posting an announcement of the family reunion in the News area of her site and placing the date on the Calendar. Then she e-mailed family members and invited them to visit the site. The response was tremendous. Soon there were photographs uploaded, birthdays added, messages posted, and online chats going on. The initial family members invited sent Donna e-mail addresses of other family members to be added and invited. Not only was her Web site successful in promoting the family reunion, but in the last two years more than seventy family members have visited it on a regular basis, and the site has become an effective year-round family communication vehicle. In addition, their family reunion is now a well-attended, much-anticipated annual event.

The Internet is a fantastic tool for promoting family reunions and maintaining communications. Like Donna, someone in your family—perhaps your son or daughter, niece or nephew—may be a budding Webmaster, able to create a Web page for your family and to help hype your reunion. While the MyFamily.com site offers a free, private, and pre-structured family Web site facility, there are also other places on the Internet that will provide a limited amount of Web page space. In addition, many people use the Internet and e-mail today and have found it to be a great cost-effective way of staying in touch.

At the Reunion

Jim and Beth Alexander left the interstate at the exit shown on the map provided in the mailing from Jim's cousin Larry. On the right at the foot of the ramp was the Marriott where the Alexander family reunion was to be held this weekend. The hotel's sign read, "Welcome Alexander Family Reunion!" Jim and Beth smiled at the sight and pulled into the parking lot.

As they entered the hotel lobby, Beth spotted a sign on an easel near the front desk. The sign announced, "Alexander Reunion—Welcome and Registration—Royal Palm Meeting Room." After checking in and freshening up, Jim and Beth went downstairs to find the Royal Palm room. Another sign, posted beside the meeting room's open doors, read, "Welcome Alexander Family!"

As the couple entered the room, they were greeted by Cousin Larry Alexander, his wife Ellen, and Aunt Betsy Alexander sitting behind a registration table distributing welcome packets and name tags. On another table at the opposite side of the room were soft drinks and ice, and several people were already visiting. Several children were busy creating and coloring their own nametags for the event.

"Well, hello there," chimed Larry. "I see you got here okay."

"Yes," replied Jim. "Your map and directions were just great. No trouble at all. Thank you."

"Step right up and get your nametags and information packet," Aunt Betsy beckoned. "You'll find the whole schedule for the weekend, a map of the hotel complex, a map of the area, and some brochures on some local attractions inside. There are also two tickets for the family raffle in there, so be sure not to lose them. We've got some great prizes this year!"

"Jim and Beth, I want you to meet some new cousins," said Ellen, standing with the people at the other side of the room. "Put on your nametags and come on over here. We have a bunch of new folks this year, and the nametags are really going to help." They all were introduced and began to get to know one another.

Jim and Beth were certainly made welcome right away, and the "new cousins" were already being made a part of the family. This family is an old hand at reunions and knows how to get started on the right note.

As the date of your reunion approaches, you'll be preparing for your on-site family celebration. Envision your family members arriving at the hotel, park, or campground where your weekend reunion is being held. As they arrive, they will be looking around for the familiar faces of family members. What do you want them to discover?

Taking a tip from the Alexanders, you can see the importance of having something highly visible to welcome your family to the reunion site. A welcome sign and signage that

Fun Activities for Your Family Reunion

General Activities

Plant a tree to commemorate the reunion. You may want to make this an annual event at your family reunion.

Hire a caricature artist to come to the reunion for an hour or two to draw portraits of family members. The caricatures are sure to become treasured keepsakes as well as provide great entertainment.

Rent a karaoke machine or hire a disc jockey or square dancing caller and open up the activities to include dancing and singing.

Put on a family talent show. Family members may want to perform skits, sing songs, play musical instruments, perform magic tricks, tell jokes, or demonstrate other talents or hobbies.

Make homemade ice cream with fresh fruits of the season. The ice cream is sure to be a welcome refreshment on hot summer afternoons.

Hold a best-dessert contest. Ask family members of different ages to act as judges who sample each of the desserts and choose the first, second, and third place winners. You may also want to collect the recipes for a family recipe book.

Hold a family raffle or auction. Ask attendees to contribute knickknacks, costume jewelry, baked goods, even specific services to raffle or auction off. This activity can be an entertaining event, and the proceeds can be used for the next family reunion.

Play card games. Bring several decks of cards, score pads, and pencils to the reunion so everyone can get involved in a card game. Many families play a traditional card game when they get together, such as rummy, canasta, bridge, pinochle, rook, or hearts.

Family History–Related Activities

Ask family members to bring funny pictures of ancestors. They may be dressed in strange clothing, may be making silly faces or standing in strange poses, or may have unusual hairstyles. Set up a display of the photos and label each picture. For more fun, omit the label and let people guess who the individuals in the pictures are.

Create a family mural. Buy a roll of heavy-duty white banner paper and post it on a wall. Provide crayons and nontoxic markers and ask everyone to contribute to the project. Family members may draw a picture, write a poem, contribute a favorite saying, etc. Ask each person to sign his or her name on the mural.

Organize a "family" scavenger hunt. Prepare a form with random family-related questions such as: Who is the youngest/oldest family member at the reunion? What was Great-Grandfather Jones' first name? How many babies at the reunion are under the age of two? Distribute the form and set a deadline for its completion, then gather the family together to review the results. You may choose to award prizes to the people who get the most answers correct.

Bring old records and tapes of the music you enjoyed when you were growing up. The music will spark memories of the past and will encourage reminiscing among family members.

Collect baby pictures of as many relatives as possible and set up a display. Have attendees guess who the babies are, and award a prize to the person who gets the most answers correct.

Post a large family tree on a wall that illustrates as many generations of the family as possible. Ask family members to find themselves, highlight their names, and correct any inaccurate information. The family tree then becomes a record of the event and is a good source of genealogical information. Family members will have a visual representation of the family structure, its history, and their place in it.

Organize an ancestral "fashion show" in which family members model or display old-time clothing and explain what they know about it—who owned it, when it was fashionable, etc. Someone in the family can act as the disc jockey and play music for the parade of family costumes.

Activities Just for Kids

Host an evening pizza party for the kids. You can order pizzas, supply soft drinks, and organize activities for the kids to get to know each other. You might even rent a couple of movies and serve popcorn and snacks later.

Organize a family show-and-tell for the younger children. Ask them to learn a story about one of their ancestors and to prepare a short speech or story about that person. Then let the children dress up in old clothes or costumes they have created so they can get into the character of the ancestor they are representing.

Provide a supply of sidewalk chalk and encourage the kids to exercise their creativity. Ask them to draw pictures of their families or a favorite activity they have taken part in during the family reunion.

Organize a story hour. Set aside a quiet place for the younger children to gather with one or more grandparents. Ask the adults to tell stories about their childhoods. This is a great way for the children and the older generations to connect.

Outdoor Activities

Play outdoor group games. Form teams and organize games of "Tug-of-war," "Pass the Orange," "Toss the Egg," "Telephone," and others. These group games can include a large or small number of people.

Build a sand castle. If your reunion is being held at a beach or in a park where there is a lot of sand, organize a competition to build the biggest or best sand castle. People of all ages will enjoy participating in this activity, and it will lend itself to individual and/or team competition.

Organize a family softball game. Bring a bat and softball. Teams can be formed based on any criteria you choose, such as a members of a single family, people with the same surname, people with the same hair or eye color, or people wearing the same color T-shirts.

Organize a sack race. Ask each family to bring an old pillowcase or a gunnysack to the reunion for a sack race. You can make this an individual competition or organize teams to compete in a relay-style race.

Organize a volleyball game. If you don't have a net, don't worry. All you really need is the ball. However, if you want something to act as a net, use a rope or cord of some kind stretched between two posts or tree trunks.

Burgon family reunion, 1920.

directs people to the events is extremely helpful. A reunion held in a park, in a forest preserve, or at a hotel or resort is made friendlier and less confusing through the use of well-placed signs.

Nametags are absolutely essential for a larger reunion or in situations where there are likely to be a number of people who don't know one another. Remember, too, that people's appearances change over time, and nametags can help overcome the "Gee, you look familiar but …" syndrome. Some families use preprinted nametags while others opt for the create-them-yourself sort. You might consider using nametags that also list the wearer's parents and/or grandparents—anything you can do to help people recognize and place one another in the larger family context.

Depending on the size and scope of your reunion, you may find it necessary to provide a registration or welcome package to family members. The contents of your package may include preprinted nametags, a schedule of events, tickets to events, brochures and maps, a list of all attendees who preregistered, and information concerning ordering or pickup of commemorative clothing, photos, or other items.

Another consideration as you are planning your welcome is how to handle communications. Some families set up a cork board for messages, while others publish a list in the welcome package of family members and their hotel room numbers. In the event of an emergency or if someone is particularly eager to make contact with another person, be prepared with a plan for how to locate people. And be sure you know how to keep track of children's whereabouts, as they have a tendency to wander off or get lost.

GET PEOPLE TALKING

Facilitating communication and interaction at a family reunion can sometimes be a challenge. With smaller groups, introducing people and getting them talking is not so much of a problem. With a larger group, however, sheer numbers can be daunting, if not downright overwhelming, especially for someone who is new to or unfamiliar with the group. Sometimes there are problems finding common ground to help the different generations connect with one another. Your job is to help things along so that people communicate and build relationships.

The value of nametags cannot be stressed enough. A legible nametag with just one additional fact on it can be the catalyst for a personal connection. The name of the person's parents can help people connect one person to another. The name of the city or town where a person lives can start a conversation. Common ground and common experiences can also be the sparks of relationships.

GROUP ACTIVITIES

Group activities such as mixers and games help people connect with one another. Icebreaker games can help spur personal interaction. You can use a piece of supplemental information placed on a nametag, such as favorite color, to get people to gather into groups. Then you can introduce a team-building or get-acquainted activity.

Team sports provide great opportunities for the more athletically inclined to get to know one another. Encourage people who don't know each other well to team up for the games. Softball, volleyball, badminton, three-legged races, tug-of-war, and other games can be easily organized and will get people talking.

Celebrating Family History at the Reunion

Mario Rossi sat with his nieces, Anna and Carmen, at the side of the table in the hotel dining room. There were photographs of his Grandpa Bruno Rossi in his U.S. Army uniform during World War II, along with his Purple Heart, his Bible, and some letters written to Grandma Rossi. Mario had brought these family treasures to the family reunion for a purpose: to tell the younger generation about his grandfather, how he lived, and how he died.

Mario was born in 1952, eight years after his grandfather was killed in France during World War II. Although he had never known his grandfather, he had been an avid listener when his grandmother and his father told stories about Grandpa Rossi. Those stories brought the man in the photographs to life in his mind, and he knew more about his grandfather than anyone else left alive did. "It's important to pass this knowledge on to the kids. I've told my boys stories about my Grandpa Bruno, and it's important for the girls to know that their great-grandpa was a hero. I want them to understand that they are descended from a hero."

Telling family stories, illustrated by photographs and family heirlooms, can help bring your ancestors and history to life at your family reunion. You can arrange to have people share stories in a quiet setting, or you might consider a group presentation.

Other families choose to set up displays of family photographs, clothing, jewelry, and other heirlooms at their reunions. It is good to let others see for themselves the substantive materials that belonged to their forebears rather than shutting these treasures away from view. These artifacts reflect the real lives of real people, rather than just names and dates on tombstones and in Bibles. Displaying these items provides family members with tangible evidence of their ancestors' existence.

Another important way to use your reunion to celebrate your family's history is to gather and help preserve the facts. Take photographs of every attendee and create an album with each picture labeled. You or your family genealogist, if you have one, can compile a family tree listing each person's name, birth date, birth location, and other information. Compiling and building this history for posterity is a way of preserving the family's heritage.

Other Ways to Ensure Success

Your want you reunion to be a gala celebration that everyone enjoys. And while it may not be possible to please everyone, there are some other things you can do to help ensure success. Most important, you should consciously begin your planning with a goal of providing something enjoyable for everyone. Once you know the general makeup of those attending, prepare a list like the one shown at right. Define age groups and breakdowns of males and females, and then list some possible activities appropriate for each group. Your list, of course, will be different based on your family's composition, but this exercise will help you focus on planning activities for every group.

As you can see from this example, you want to develop activities that get people helping with the reunion while also providing enjoyable pastimes. Keep in mind that men and women may like different activities, but don't pigeonhole or stereotype anyone. Give people options; they will be happy they are able to do exactly what they like.

Making sure people feel included is a key to a successful family reunion. Have everyone sign in on a family reunion register. Placing their names on the family sign-in sheet immediately makes people feel a part of the group. Make sure that lots of photo-

Ages	Male	Female	Possible Activities
2–5	4	6	Playground games Coloring Sidewalk art with chalk
6–12	3	4	Sidewalk art with chalk Playground games Badminton Ancestor dress-up and biography Help with cleanup
13–18	9	4	Help with tables and chairs Take family photographs Badminton Softball
19–24	6	5	Meal table setup Take family photographs Badminton Softball
25–54	17	24	Meal preparation Barbecue grills Badminton Softball Family album photo identification Family heirloom display Meal cleanup
55 & Up	8	10	Storytelling for children Meal preparation Barbecue grills Family album photo identification Family heirloom display
TOTALS	**47**	**53**	**Grand Total = 100**

graphs are taken, especially group photos where people must stand close together. Even this small shared experience can help draw people closer together. Encourage family members to help with setup and cleanup. By working together, they will experience a sense of involvement, purpose, and accomplishment in the reunion's success. They will also build a certain "family team" rapport while chatting together and accomplishing the various tasks they perform.

Encourage communication and interaction any way you can. A shy relative may have a terrible time at a reunion if he or she has no one to talk to, yet most people can find some area of common ground if given the opportunity. So try the icebreaker activities and games mentioned in this chapter or others that you know. And don't forget to take advantage of turning nametags into conversation starters.

Another key to success is maintaining a positive atmosphere. There may be one or two people who are less than satisfied with the location, some of the food choices, or with some other detail of the reunion. You often can win these people over by doing your best to provide activities in which they can participate and interact with other family members. Once everyone feels included, they will feel like family.

Planning the Next Reunion

It's important to assess your reunion while it is still fresh in your mind and to get feedback from attendees. During the reunion, you probably saw things you would have liked to have changed or improved. Perhaps you saw ways to improve how, when, and where different family members or age groups interacted. Make notes on these things for yourself and others who may work on the next reunion.

Most professional party planners seek feedback on the successes and/or failures of their events, and your relatives can provide valuable opinions about the success of the reunion. Their perspective may be different from yours and other members of your planning team. They also may not have noticed the little things that you thought were obviously not as smooth as you would have liked. To them, the entire event may have appeared beautifully organized.

You might take some time shortly after the reunion to telephone a few relatives to discuss the event. Ask for their comments and suggestions on how to improve the next reunion. Keep the conversation positive, and be alert and receptive to valid input. You may even find volunteers to help with the next one. In any case, make careful notes for yourself while events are fresh in your mind.

Continuing the Celebration Throughout the Year

Beth Loeb and her second cousin, George, had gotten to know each other as children when their families visited one another in the 1950s and 1960s. The families lived more than eighty miles apart, though, and these visits were infrequent. Still, Beth and George were close in age and in their interests. Unfortunately, as the years passed and they grew older, their interests changed and contact between them dwindled to the exchange of a family holiday card.

More than thirty years later, in 1998, Beth was working with another cousin to organize a family reunion for their branch of the family. Beth mentioned how nice it would be to invite Cousin George and members from the other branch of the family. It sounded like a good idea, so Beth made a telephone call. George was ecstatic to renew contact. Although he now lived three states away, he immediately promised that he would come to the reunion. In addition, he contacted his own brother and arranged to get him there, too.

On the day of the reunion, more than one hundred family members gathered to share food, games, company, and reminiscences. Beth and George had not seen one another for more than three decades but immediately recognized one another. Their brothers, it turned out, now lived in the same city only a few miles apart. Beth and George have since renewed their friendship, growing closer than ever before, and they share e-mail and telephone calls on a regular basis. They also try to visit with one another in person at least once a year. Their brothers, who because of an age difference never really knew one another before, have discovered they share a similar wry sense of humor. They, too, are working to establish a relationship. Most important, Beth's invitation to the reunion has helped both George and his brother find another significant set of family with whom they can communicate and share.

For Beth and George, the celebration of family that began with that family reunion has become the basis of continued communication and interaction. The reconnection of family ties and the establishment of new relationships between heretofore unacquainted family members has proved a wonderful dividend.

It is important to nurture the seeds of communication that were planted at the reunion. Year-round interaction between family members can happen with some promotion. Here are some things that can help. (See chapter 8 for more detailed information on family communication.)

A FAMILY DIRECTORY, NEWSLETTER, AND WEB PAGE

During the reunion-planning process, you probably developed a master address list that includes names, addresses, telephone numbers, and, in many cases, e-mail addresses. The address list can be typed, printed, and distributed to help family members stay in touch. The contents of your directory can be as simple or detailed as you like. In addition to the names and basic contact information for each family member, you might also include their birthdays, wedding anniversaries, personal Web page addresses, and any other information you think might be of interest.

You may have discovered at the reunion that people had a real thirst to reconnect and stay in touch with one another. One way to perpetuate that sense of family is to start a

Weatherly Reunion News

Day 3 ~ Saturday, June 2, 2001

GOOD MORNING!

It's going to be a GREAT day at the reunion today! What better place to enjoy yourself than here in the cradle of our family tree -- Rome, GA. There are lots of wonderful events planned for the day that will give us a chance to get to know one another and renew our relationships. Here is today's schedule:

8:00-10:00 AM - Breakfast at Emma Dale Holder's home at 104 East Sixth Avenue

10:30 AM - Relaxation by the hotel pool

Noon-1:30 PM - Pizza party for the younger set (to age 18) in the Roman Room at the Forrest Hotel

Noon - Everyone else is on their own for lunch

2:00-5:00 PM - Softball, badminton and croquet at Heritage Park (see map in your packet)

2:00-4:00 PM - Walking tour of Myrtle Hill Cemetery

5:00-6:30 PM - Our Family Pictures and Heirlooms Exhibition and Family Genealogy Display - Roman Room at the Forrest Hotel

6:30-8:30 PM - Reunion Banquet in the Grand Ballroom at the Forrest Hotel The kids will stage their "I'm My Own Grandpa/Grandma" show

8:30-11:00 PM - Dancing in the Grand Ballroom with entertainment provided by DJ "Cool Eddie" Masterson

10:00-Midnight - Late night snacks available in the Bell Tower Cafe

Pick Up Your Reunion T-shirts

If you ordered a T-shirt for this reunion, they are available from 9:00 AM to 5:00 PM at our registration/information desk in the Forrest Hotel lobby. Pick yours up and wear it with pride today!

OUR FAMILY FOUNDERS

Walton & Elizabeth Holder Weatherly's Wedding Day - September 16, 1908 - Rome, Georgia
(Copies of picture can be ordered from Cousin George.)

Reunion Banquet

Your presence is requested at the Weatherly Family Banquet at 6:30 o'clock this evening in the Grand Ballroom of the Forrest Hotel.

Pizza Party!

Kids of all ages! Join us in the hotel's Roman Room for a pizza party from Noon to 1:30 today! Great food! Prizes! Special entertainment just for you!

---

family newsletter. It doesn't have to be fancy, and family members can certainly provide content and reimburse you for the photocopying and postage costs. However, a newsletter can provide a communication vehicle which family members will anticipate receiving. In her book *Absolutely Family! A Guide to Publishing a Family Newsletter*, Jeanne Rundquist Nelson says, "I have established relationships with family members I hardly knew and have reestablished friendships with family members I had drifted away from over the years. Phone calls about newsletter business give way to conversations about family relationships."

We've already mentioned Donna Johnson and the family Web page she used to promote and share information about her family reunion. The site she created at

MyFamily.com has almost taken on a life of its own. In the two years since she set the Web site up, it has become an informational hub for the family members who are online. People post messages, upload photographs, exchange files, celebrate birthdays, and chat in their own private chat room. The youngsters have taught their parents and grandparents how to use the computer to get the most of the site too, and this has helped bridge the generational and technological gaps.

All of these are excellent tools for establishing and maintaining contact with one another. You and your family will come up with other great ideas for keeping the communications lines open. The point is to sustain and increase the family's excitement and enthusiasm level.

Just being a family and wanting to get together is reason enough to converge and share some quality time. There is no need to wait for a formal occasion such as a graduation, a marriage, or a funeral. Nor does your reunion have to be an extended or extravagant affair. What is most important is to take the time to gather and enjoy each other's company, and to savor the joy of your family whenever and wherever you come together.

Appendices

Ancestral Chart

Chart No. _____

No. 1 on this chart is
the same person as No. _____
          On Chart No. _____

1
BORN
PLACE
MARRIED
PLACE
DIED
PLACE

NAME OF SPOUSE

2
BORN
PLACE
MARRIED
PLACE
DIED
PLACE

3
BORN
PLACE
DIED
PLACE

4
BORN
PLACE
MARRIED
PLACE
DIED
PLACE

5
BORN
PLACE
DIED
PLACE

6
BORN
PLACE
MARRIED
PLACE
DIED
PLACE

7
BORN
PLACE
DIED
PLACE

8
CONT. ON CHART _____

9
CONT. ON CHART _____

10
CONT. ON CHART _____

11
CONT. ON CHART _____

12
CONT. ON CHART _____

13
CONT. ON CHART _____

14
CONT. ON CHART _____

15
CONT. ON CHART _____

© MyFamily.com, Inc. 2002

www.ancestry.com/save/charts/ancchart.htm

Form # F120

Family Group Record

Prepared By _____ Relationship to Preparer _____

Address _____ Date _____ Ancestral Chart # _____ Family Unit # _____

Husband

Occupation(s) _____ Religion

	Date —Day, Month, Year	City	County	State or Country	
Born					
Christened					Name of Church
Married					Name of Church
Died					Cause of Death
Buried					
		Cem/Place			Date Will Written/Proved
Father		Other Wives			
Mother					

Wife maiden name

Occupation(s) _____ Religion

Born					
Christened					Name of Church
Died					Cause of Death
Buried					
		Cem/Place			Date Will Written/Proved
Father		Other Husbands			
Mother					

Date of first marriage/Place _____

Name of Spouse _____

✗	Sex M/F	Children Given Names	Birth Day	Month	Year	Birthplace City	County	St./Ctry.	Date of Death/Cause City	County	State/Country	Computer I.D. #
		1										
		2										
		3										
		4										
		5										
		6										
		7										
		8										
		9										
		10										
		11										
		12										

NOTE: ✗ =Direct Ancestor   Form # F106

©MyFamily.com, Inc. 2002

http://www.ancestry.com/save/charts/ancchart.htm

Research Calendar

Family _____   Researcher _____

Date	Repository Call #/Microfilm #	Description of Source	Time Period/ Names Searched	Results

Correspondence Record

Family _____   Researcher _____

Date Sent	Addressee/address	Purpose	Date Replied	Results

Form # F105

http://www.ancestry.com/save/charts/ancchart.htm

©MyFamily.com, Inc 2002

Reaching Out: Associations, Foundations, and Support

Hundreds of associations and foundations disseminate information about diseases, treatment, and research; provide community; and support continuing research. The following list will give you an idea of what's available:

Alzheimer's Association
919 N. Michigan Avenue
Suite 1100
Chicago, IL 60611-1676
(800) 272-3900
www.alz.org

American Cancer Society, Inc.
P.O. Box 102454
Atlanta, GA 30368-2454
(800) ACS-2345
www.cancer.org

American Cleft Palate-Craniofacial
    Association
1218 Grandview Avenue
Pittsburgh, PA 15211
(412) 481-1376
www.cleftline.org

American Diabetes Association
1701 North Beauregard Street
Alexandria, VA 22311
(800) DIABETES
www.diabetes.org

American Heart Association
7272 Greenville Avenue
Dallas, TX 75231
(800) AHA-USA1
www.americanheart.org

American Lung Association
1740 Broadway
New York, NY 10019
(212) 315-8700
www.lungusa.org

Arthritis Foundation
P.O. Box 7669
Atlanta, GA 30357-0669
(800) 283-7800
www.arthritis.org

Association for Children with Down's
    Syndrome
4 Fern Place
Plainview, NY 11803
(866) LUV-ACDS
www.acds.org

Children and Adults with Attention
    Deficit Disorder
8181 Professional Place
Suite 201
Landover, MD 20765
(800) 233-4050
www.chadd.org

Colon Cancer Alliance
175 Ninth Avenue
New York, NY 10011
(877) 422-2030
www.ccalliance.org

Cooley's Anemia Foundation, Inc.
129-09 26th Avenue, #203
Flushing, NY 11354
(800) 522-7222
www.cooleysanemia.org

Cystic Fibrosis Foundation
6931 Arlington Road
Bethesda, MD 20814
(800) FIGHT-CF
www.cff.org

Fanconi Anemia Research Fund, Inc.
1801 Willamette Street, Suite 200
Eugene, OR 97401
(541) 687-4658
www.fanconi.org

Glaucoma Research Foundation
200 Pine Street
Suite 200
San Francisco, CA 94104
(800) 826-6693
www.glaucoma.org

Guardians of Hydrocephalus
Research Foundation
2618 Avenue Z
Brooklyn, NY 11235-2023
(800) 458-8655

The Hemochromatosis Research
    Foundation, Inc.
P.O. Box 8569
Albany, NY 12208
(518) 489-0972

Hereditary Disease Foundation
11400 West Olympic Boulevard
Suite 855
Los Angeles, CA 90064-1560
(310) 575-9656
www.hdfoundation.org

The Huntington's Disease Society of
    America, Inc.
158 West 29th Street, 7th floor
New York, NY 10001-5300
(800) 345-4372
www.hdsa.org

Hydrocephalus Parent Support Group
610 Verdant Place
Vista, CA 92084-5560
(619) 282-1070

Juvenile Diabetes Research Foundation
    International
120 Wall Street, 19th floor
New York, NY 10005-4001
(800) 533-CURE
www.jdf.org

Susan G. Komen Breast Cancer
    Foundation
5005 LBJ Freeway
Suite 250
Dallas, TX 75244
(800) IM-AWARE
www.komen.org

The Leukemia and Lymphoma Society
1311 Mamaroneck Avenue
White Plains, NY 10605
(914) 949-5213
www.leukemia.org

Malignant Hyperthermia Association of
    the United States
39 East State Street
P.O. Box 1069
Sherburne, NY 13460-1069
(800) 98-MHAUS
www.mhaus.org

March of Dimes Birth Defects
  Foundation
1275 Mamaroneck Avenue
White Plains, NY 10605
(888) MODIMES
www.modimes.org

Melanoma Research Foundation
23704-5 El Toro Road, # 206
Lake Forest, CA 92630
(800) MRF-1290
www.melanoma.org

Multiple Sclerosis Foundation
6350 N. Andrews Avenue
Ft. Lauderdale, FL 33309-2130
(888) MS-FOCUS
www.msfacts.org

Muscular Dystrophy Association
3300 E. Sunrise Drive
Tucson, AZ 85718
(800) 572-1717
www.mdausa.org

National Association for Sickle Cell
  Disease, Inc.
3345 Wilshire Boulevard
Suite 1106
Los Angeles, CA 90010-3503
(800) 421-8453

National Depressive and Manic-
  Depressive Association
730 North Franklin Street
Suite 501
Chicago, IL 60610-7204
(800) 826-3632
www.ndmda.org

National Down Syndrome Society
666 Broadway
New York, NY 10012
(800) 221-4602
www.ndss.org

The National Foundation for Jewish
  Genetic Diseases
250 Park Avenue
Suite 1000
New York, NY 10177
(212) 371-1030
www.nfjgd.org

National Fragile X Foundation
P.O. Box 190488
San Francisco, CA 94119
(800) 688-8765
www.nfxf.org

National Gaucher Foundation
11140 Rockville Pike, Suite 101
Rockville, MD 20852-3106
(800) 925-8885
www.gaucherdisease.org

The National Hemophilia Foundation
116 West 32nd Street, 11th floor
New York, NY 10001
(800) 42-HANDI
www.hemophilia.org

The National Hydrocephalus Foundation
12413 Centralia Road
Lakewood, CA 90715-1623
(562) 402-3523
www.nfonline.org

National Kidney Cancer Association
1234 Sherman Avenue
Suite 203
Evanston, IL 60202-1375
(800) 850-9132
www.nkca.org

National Kidney Foundation, Inc.
30 East 33rd Street
Suite 1100
New York, NY 10016
(800) 622-9010
www.kidney.org

National Marfan Foundation
32 Main Street
Port Washington, NY 11050
(800) 8MARFAN
www.marfan.org

National Multiple Sclerosis Society
733 Third Avenue, 6th floor
New York, NY 10017
(800) FIGHT-MS
www.nmss.org

The National Neurofibromatosis
  Foundation, Inc.
95 Pine Street, 16th floor
New York, NY 10005
(800) 323-7938
www.nf.org

National Organization for Rare
  Disorders, Inc.
P.O. Box 8923
New Fairfield, CT 08612-8923
(800) 999-NORD
www.rarediseases.org

National Ovarian Cancer Coalition, Inc.
500 NE Spanish River Boulevard, Ste 14
Boca Raton, FL 33431
(888) OVARIAN
www.ovarian.org

The National Tay-Sachs and Allied
  Diseases Association, Inc.
2001 Beacon Street
Suite 204
Brighton, MA 02135
(800) 906-8723
www.ntsad.org

Pancreatic Cancer Action Network
P.O. Box 1010
Torrance, CA 90505
(877) 2-PANCAN
www.pancan.org

Parkinson's Disease Foundation
710 West 168th Street
New York, NY 10032-9982
(800) 457-6676
www.pdf.org

Sickle Cell Disease Association of
  America
200 Corporate Pointe
Suite 495
Culver City, CA 90230-8727
(800) 421-8453
www.sicklecelldisease.org

Spina Bifida Association of America
4590 MacArthur Boulevard, NW
Suite 250
Washington, DC 20007-4226
(800) 621-3141
www.sbaa.org

Tourette Syndrome Association, Inc.
42-40 Bell Boulevard
Bayside, NY 11361
(718) 224-2999
www.tsa-usa.org

United Parkinson's Foundation
833 W. Washington Boulevard
Chicago, IL 60607
(312) 733-1893

Web Resources for Genetic Information

General Education:

National Genealogical Society Family Health and Heredity Committee

www.ngsgenealogy.org/comfamhealth.htm

This newly redesigned site answers questions about how to begin researching your family's health history, the type of information you can learn, and where to find more information.

Human Genome Project

www.ornl.gov/hgmis/

Get the latest news on the project and link to educational sites and publications. The site also presents some case studies and addresses ethical issues surrounding the project.

Genetic Disorders and Diseases:

Genetic and Rare Conditions Site

www.kumc.edu/gec/support/

What's particularly useful from this site are links to lists of support groups, genetic counselors and geneticists, and medical information.

Office of Rare Diseases

rarediseasesinfo.nih.gov

Find information on more than 6,000 rare diseases, including patient support groups and the latest on research.

The Online Mendelian Inheritance in Man

www.ncbi.nlm.nih.gov/Omim

This database catalogs all known human genes and genetic disorders, providing links to relevant literature.

Glossary of Ancient Diseases

olivetreegenealogy.com/misc/disease.shtml

Old Diseases and Their Modern Definitions

www.geocities.com/Heartland/Hills/2840/diseases.html

Suppose your ancestor's cause of death was listed as dropsy. Access one of these two sites and you'll find out what dropsy actually entailed. The second site will tell you dropsy would be known as congestive heart failure in today's parlance. Descriptions range from abscess to yellow fever.

History of Epidemics

www.geocities.com:0080/Heartland/Prairie/9166/epidemics.htm

www.genealogy-quest.com/glossaries/epidemics.html

A review of these sites can provide you with historical background on family diseases.

National Library of Medicine—PubMed

www.ncbi.nlm.nih.gov/entrez/query.fcgi?db=PubMed

This site can help you find genetic research articles about a particular condition. They are not intended for the lay person and may be difficult to absorb. However, if you're looking for the latest research on something that afflicts your family, this is the place to go—and it's free (vs. fee-based download services).

National Society of Genetic Counselors

www.nsgc.org

More than 1,500 counselors are members of this society. Download pamphlets about genetic counseling and certain disorders, and link to a listing of genetic counselors.

Online Discussion Groups:

www.adata.org/text-other-lists.html

Instructions for signing up for a variety of groups dealing with specific illnesses and disabilities, including Gen-Disease-J, a discussion list for individuals concerned with the various genetically-transmitted diseases affecting Jewish populations, though discussions are not limited to Jews.

Google Beta Groups

groups.google.com

Google offers seven health-related discussion groups, including one on AIDS, one on arthritis, and one on diabetes. Just click on "miscellaneous" and then "health."

Ancestry Message Boards

boards.ancestry.com

Choose from hundreds of locality and surname-based groups to find others interested in genetic heritage.

Ethnic Sites:

Stanley Diamond's Beta-Thalassemia Research Web Site

www.geocities.com/heartland/pointe/1439

A part of his outreach program, Diamond presents a summary of his research, links to other family names carrying the beta-thalassemia trait, and links to genetic research articles and sites.

Jewish Records Indexing—Poland Project

www.jewishgen.org/jri-pl

While not a health-related site per se, the JRI-Poland site allows visitors to query its database by surname or geographic location. Results of your search will lead you to specific LDS microfilms or to repositories in Poland, such as the Polish State Archives and the Jewish Historical Institute.

Henry Strongin-Goldberg

www.hsg.org

Read from Henry's mother's journal, and learn more about Fanconi anemia and about this young hero.

Joslin Diabetes Center—Amish Community

www.joslin.org/news/shuldiner_amish.html

An article describing the work of Dr. Alan Shuldiner in diabetes among the Amish.

Compiling a Health History for Your Italian Ancestors

www.daddezio.com/genealogy/research/grs-il1c.html

Presents a how-to article by Laura Heidekrueger with links to other sites.

DNA Services:

GeneSaver

www.genesaver.com

Create your private family DNA bank to link the past with the future.

DNA Identification Systems

www.dnaidsys.com

Family Tree DNA

www.familytreedna.com

Oxford Ancestors

www.oxfordancestors.com

Common Genetic Diseases

Heart disease:

Coronary atherosclerosis The most common cause of angina in which blockages prevent blood from reaching the heart muscle. Risk factors include a family history of coronary heart disease before the age of fifty-five.

High blood pressure Increased or elevated blood pressure above 140/90 mmHG. About one in every five adult Americans suffer from it, though it occurs more frequently among men than women and twice as often in African-Americans than Caucasians.

Hyperlipidemia Elevation of lipids (fats) in the bloodstream including high levels of cholesterol and high levels of triglycerides.

Diabetes A common disorder caused by the pancreas's inability to produce enough insulin to support the body's needs. The low absorption of glucose creates a buildup. In Type 1 (also called juvenile diabetes or insulin-dependent), the defect is caused by damaged insulin-producing cells. In Type 2 (also called maturity onset or insulin-independent), which usually affects people over the age of 40, the pancreas does not produce enough insulin. Obesity and heredity play a significant role. Most individuals with Type 2 have a relative with it. Compared to Caucasians, African-Americans have a 60 percent higher rate of Type 2 while Hispanics have a 90 percent higher rate.

Cancer:

Retinoblastomas A malignant tumor of the retina that occurs in one or both eyes, usually in children under the age of five. If genetic in nature, it is passed on through the autosomal dominant pattern.

Colon Individuals with a history of colon cancer in the family should have screening on a regular basis, especially after age thirty-five. Recent studies indicate that a new genetic mutation doubles the risk of this form of cancer among Ashkenazic Jews.

Stomach May first begin to express itself with a peptic ulcer and is twice as common in men than in women. Risk increases with age and has strong genetic and dietary links.

Endometrium Also known as uterine cancer, this affects the tissue that lines your uterus.

Lung Cancer of the lungs is the number one cancer-causing death among both men and women. The major risk factor is smoking and the risk increases with volume and frequency of smoking.

Bladder Either benign or malignant, tumors of the urinary bladder come from cells that line the bladder, tending to produce a growth that projects inward into the space containing urine. The main symptom is blood in the urine.

Breast If you've inherited one of the mutated genes BRCA1 and BRCA2, research indicates you've got about a 55-85 percent risk of inheriting the disease.

Ovarian Less common than breast cancer, this "silent killer" has genetic links that can be important health indicators. Breast cancer can also be an important predictor.

Skin (melanoma) The most severe form of skin cancer resulting from the cancerous growth of pigment (melanin) producing cells. It can develop on your trunk, legs, and feet as well as other skin areas and can infiltrate the deep layers of your skin, spreading to other parts of your body. It can begin with an existing mole or birthmark or a new skin lesion.

Prostate The most common form of cancer among men after skin cancer. About 9 percent of cases show a familial pattern. If you have such a pattern in your family, make sure you get screened regularly beginning at age 40. Check with your medical professional about your specific risk based on your family's history.

Neurological illnesses and disorders:

Alzheimer's disease A progressive degenerative disease with continual mental deterioration that cannot be halted. It can begin as early as age twenty-five or as late as age eighty. Those with symptoms showing at an earlier age are more likely to have familial Alzheimer's, inherited through an autosomal dominant pattern. It involves short-term memory loss, personality changes, decreasing ability to perform daily care and hygiene. Confusion, speech difficulty, loss of muscle control and emotional outbursts that ensue necessitates constant supervision.

Amyotrophic lateral sclerosis (Lou Gehrig's disease) Another progressive degenerative disease resulting in continuous destruction of muscles within the spinal cord and lower brain stem. About 10 percent of the cases are inherited and the gene responsible has been identified. It can affect those between the ages of forty and seventy, beginning with muscle weakness and cramping in the arms and legs. Survival after onset is estimated at ten years.

Gaucher disease The most common genetic disorder among the Ashkenazic population with carrier frequency of about one in eighteen, this disease involves spleen and liver enlargement and blood abnormalities and orthopedic problems. Enzyme replacement therapy has shown to be useful in treating it.

Huntington's disease Transmitted through an autosomal dominant pattern, this disease appears later in life, usually between the ages of thirty-five to forty-five. It involves the progressive destruction of nerve cells within certain areas of the brain. It primarily affects Caucasians.

Multiple sclerosis A degenerative disease that affects the brain and spinal cord, interfering with muscle strength and movement. It occurs more often in some families than the general population. Symptoms usually begin between the ages of twenty and forty.

Neurofibromatosis Transmitted through an autosomal dominant pattern, it can affect both males and females regardless of ethnic background. About half of the cases result from new gene mutation in the egg or sperm. It's also known as von Recklinghausen disease. Its first symptoms take the form of nodular skin lesions.

Parkinson's disease A progressive neurological disorder resulting from degeneration of nerve cells in a region of the brain that controls movement. The first symptom of the disease is usually the tremor of a limb, especially when the body is resting. Communication between the brain and muscles weakens. It typically affects people aged fifty and older.

Tay-Sachs disease A fatal disorder of infancy that progressively destroys the central nervous system. It can be traced to the lack of a single enzyme. Approximately one in every twenty-five Ashkenazic Jew carries the gene versus one in every 250 in the general population.

Tourette's syndrome Inherited as an autosomal dominant trait, this disorder is generally classified as a tic, which when mild, may wear off. Thought to be fairly common, it affects more males than females. Its onset usually begins between the ages of two and fifteen. It can also accompany attention deficit disorder, obsessive-compulsive disorder, and some anxiety and depressive disorders.

Mental illnesses and behavioral conditions:

Alcoholism A pattern of addiction that tends to repeat itself in families. No specific gene has been identified to cause it nor have studies shown it to be purely genetic. It appears to be a very complex inheritance, if inherited at all.

Anxiety disorders Includes Obsessive-Compulsive Disorder, Panic Disorder, Phobic Disorder, and Post-traumatic Stress Disorder; usually affects more females than males. Family history can increase risk as well as thyroid gland abnormalities, chemical substance abuse, exposure to physical or psychological danger, and long-term exposure to criticism or disapproval.

Common Genetic Diseases

Attention deficit disorder Current thinking suggests a biochemical imbalance or a lower-than-normal glucose metabolism in the brain causes this condition. More than one-third of the parents of ADD children have or have had the disorder themselves. It is characterized by impulsivity, lack of focus, and hyperactivity (in its Attention Deficit Hyperactive Disorder form). It affects on average about one child in every classroom.

Eating disorders Includes bulimia, a cycle of binge-and-purge eating behavior, and anorexia nervosa, self-imposed starvation. Both have genetic risk factors, including chemical imbalances in the brain and a history of depression.

Manic depression Also known as bipolar disorder, this condition involves mood swings from euphoria to severe depression.

Schizophrenia A group of emotional disorders in which an individual has difficulty distinguishing fact from fiction. Some doctors believe it is inherited and symptoms may first appear in late adolescence or early adulthood.

Other genetic diseases:

Cleft lip and cleft palate A cleft lip has a vertical split in the upper lip, either partial or all the way up to the nose. Children can have more than one split. The cleft palate is the gap that runs along the middle of the palate from behind the teeth to the nasal cavity. These disorders can run in families and can be corrected with surgery.

Clubfoot A condition in which one of both feet bend either downward and inward or upward and outward. It may run in families and can be detected at birth and treated.

Cystic fibrosis No cure is available for this progressive, lifelong condition in which the glands that produce mucus, sweat, and intestinal secretions do not function the way they should. It is not restricted to any ethnic group, but it is most common among Caucasians, with carrier frequency of about one in twenty-five.

Duchenne muscular dystrophy A progressive degeneration of the muscles. It affects only males, usually beginning in early childhood and begins with the muscles in the shoulders, hips, thighs, and calves. It then leads to immobility and weakens the respiratory system. It is usually inherited through female carriers, though about 30 to 50 percent of the cases occur in families with no history of the condition.

Galactosemia An enzyme deficiency inherited through an automsomal recessive pattern. It results in an inability to break down the simple sugar galactose or the milk sugar lactose into glucose, the blood sugar the body uses for energy.

Hemophilia A sex-linked bleeding disorder that typically only affects males. Hemophilia A is caused by deficiency of a protein known as Factor VIII that is a necessary ingredient to normal blood clotting. More rare is Hemophilia B, caused by deficiency of clotting Factor IX. Queen Victoria's family and its constant inbreeding are among the most well-known cases.

Hurler's syndrome Caused by an enzyme deficiency, this disorder is characterized by vision problems, skeletal defects, enlargement of the liver and spleen, and mental retardation.

Marfan's syndrome Transmitted through autosomal dominant inheritance, this disorder causes weakness of the heart valves and the aorta. Children with this disorder grow tall and thin, with unusually long arms, legs, fingers, and toes. The lenses in their eyes may also be displaced.

Phenylketonuria (PKU) You may have noticed warnings on foods with aspartame about the risks if you are phenylketonuric because it contains the amino acid phenylalanine. PKU is an inherited defect that inhibits a person's ability to break down this acid. As a result, the acid builds up and causes brain damage. A test for PKU is performed on all babies shortly after birth.

Sickle-cell disease A blood condition caused by a single base pair change in one of the genes that codes for hemoglobin, the blood protein that carries oxygen. The mutation causes the red blood cells to take on a sickle shape rather than a typical donut shape. Those of African ancestry have a higher risk of the disorder than the general population. The disease can cause serious damage to the heart, lungs, and kidneys.

Thalassemia There are two main types of thalassemia, alpha and beta. Beta-thalassemia, the gene which doctors believe is carried by two million Americans, is found in three forms: thalassemia major, the most severe for, often called Cooley's anemia after the doctor who first described it; thalassemia intermedia, a mild Cooley's anemia; and thalassemia minor, also known as thalassemia trait. Children with the disease cannot make enough hemoglobin, requiring frequent blood transfusions and medical attention. It is inherited through an autosomal recessive pattern. It affects people of Mediterranean, Middle Eastern, Southeast Asian, and African descent, but a new mutation has been found among Ashkenazic Jews.

Medical conditions with genetic links:

Rheumatoid arthritis An autoimmune condition that tends to run in families. Though genes associated with it have been identified, many who possess them are unaffected.

Asthma May be inherited as an autosomal dominant trait and is considered to be multifactorial.

Baldness Recent research has identified the gene that causes balding, passed from generation to generation in an autosomal dominant pattern. It's usually expressed in males because of the presence of male hormones. Females can pass on the gene.

Migraine headaches These often debilitating headaches can run in families. For instance, in one family of four girls, three suffer from them and usually on the same days.

Obesity Genetics may play a part in your predisposition to gain weight easily. Studies show that if both your parents are obese, you have an 80 percent likelihood of being obese yourself versus a 15 percent likelihood if your parents are of normal weight.

Periodontal disease Inflammation, ulceration, and infection of the gums, ligaments, and bones that support your teeth. If you have a family history of periodontal disease, you may see symptoms as early as age twenty-five. Risk is also increased by diabetes or thyroid disease, certain medications, and tobacco use. Symptoms can include bleeding gums with toothbrushing, tender and/or swollen gums, separation between gum and teeth, and loosening or shifting teeth.

Speech disorders Recent research has identified that a defect on Chromosome 7 causes speech disorders, bearing out that it can run in families.

Bibliography

Bradshaw, John. *Bradshaw On: The Family: A Revolutionary Way of Self-Discovery.* Pompano Beach, FL: Health Communications, 1987.

Cox, Meg. *The Heart of a Family: Searching American for New Traditions That Fulfill Us.* New York: Random House, 1998.

Goldrup, Lawrence P., Ph.D. *Writing the Family Narrative.* Salt Lake City: Ancestry Publishing, 1987.

Goldrup, Lawrence P., Ph.D. *Writing the Family Narrative Workbook.* Salt Lake City: Ancestry Publishing, 1993.

Hallman, Anita. *Self-Preservation: A Complete Guide to Keeping Your Memories Alive.* Salt Lake City: Deseret Book Company, 1997.

LeBey, Barbara. *Family Estrangements.* Atlanta: Longstreet Press, 2001.

Morgan, George G. *Your Family Reunion: How to Plan It, Organize It, and Enjoy It.* Orem, Utah: Ancestry, 2001.

Nelson, Jeanne Rundquist. *Absolutely Family! A Guide to Publishing a Family Newsletter.* Kansas City, MO: Family Times Publishing, 1999.

Stephenson, Lynda Rutledge. *The Complete Idiot's Guide to Writing Your Family History.* Indianapolis, IN: Alpha Books, 2000.

Szucs, Loretto Dennis and Sandra Hargreaves Luebking. *The Source: A Guidebook of American Genealogy* rev. ed. Provo, UT: Ancestry, 1996.

Zallen, Dr. Doris Teichler. *Does It Run in the Family: A Consumer's Guide to DNA Testing for Genetic Disorders.* Piscataway, NJ: Rutgers University Press, 1997.

Notes

Notes

Notes

Notes

Index

All of the photographs in this volume originate from the collection of MyFamily.com, with the following exceptions:

Mark Andersen/RubberBall Productions: 179
Joe Atlas: 199
Christopher Bain collection: 2, 31, 53, 85, 159, 225
Digital Vision: 133
Steve Mason/PhotoDisc: 113